"PICKLE IT!"

Minor League Baseball
of Carrollton, Georgia

Best wishes,

[signature]

08-12-03

Other books by John Bell:

Shoeless Summer:
The summer of 1923 when Shoeless Joe Jackson
played baseball in Americus, Georgia
(published 2001)

"PICKLE IT!"

Minor League Baseball of Carrollton, Georgia

by John Bell

Vabella Publishing

Vabella Publishing
P.O. Box 1052
Carrollton, Georgia 30112

A portion of the proceeds from the sale of this book will be donated to a children's recreation organization.

This book is a factual account based on sources considered to be accurate, reliable, and taken in good faith. Any information that is inaccurate or mistaken is completely unintentional. This book is sold with the understanding that the publisher and author are not responsible or liable for inaccuracies from sources considered to be reliable. The publisher and author will not be held responsible or liable for any repercussions or actions stemming from information, accurate or not, made known in this book.

Cover design by Vabella Publishing.

Manufactured in the United States of America

Library of Congress Control Number: 2002111201

ISBN 0-9712204-1-7

For my sons, Jacob and Andrew

Table of Contents

Title Explanation

Legend has it that the commonly heard baseball expression "Pickle It!" originated in Carrollton, Georgia. In 1920, the first year an organized minor league baseball team played in Carrollton, the South Street Ballpark was constructed to serve as the club's home field. The local diamond quickly gained the moniker "The Pickle Factory" because of the two large cucumber-pickling vats that were located beyond the deep center field fence. During the games in the inaugural year, when fans wanted to see player hit a home run, they would yell "Pickle It!" literally meaning to hit the ball to the pickling vats. The phrase took root and spread like kudzu throughout the baseball world. So, the next time somebody yells "Pickle It!" at a baseball game, remember that Carrollton, Georgia is where the expression began.

Author's Notes

Shortly after the publication of my first book, *Shoeless Summer*, last year, I was sitting at a table at Horton's Book and Gifts on the square in Carrollton signing copies of it for local patrons. A young man came up to me and asked if I knew anything about the minor league teams that played in Carrollton during the "Golden Years" of baseball. At the time, I knew the years that teams had played here as I had done a limited amount of research to meet my own interests. During our brief discussion, he mentioned that it would really be great if somebody would do a book on Carrollton minor league baseball. Since that day, I've had numerous such conversations with Carrollton natives, long-time residents, and fairly newcomers, like myself. Each time I would talk about it with somebody else, the thoughts of putting together a project took a deeper root. So now I've decided to try and meet the desire of Carrollton history buffs and baseball fans.

I'm probably going out on a limb here since I only moved to Carrollton in 1996. But I have enjoyed these past few years here so much and have experienced such a great feeling of acceptance that it truly feels like home. It is my intention to lay down this record of the baseball history of this great city with integrity and accuracy. If you should have any questions or comments about any portion of this book or the book as a whole, please feel free to let me know through e-mail at *belljg@aol.com* or by letter addressed to the publisher.

I hope that you all will find this book pleasurable to read and satisfying to your hunger for local history. It has been both a privilege and an honor to write it.

Foreword

by Hiram Bray

The war was over. Men were returning home from the war, victorious over the evil engineer of Pearl Harbor and the invasion of Europe. Many of the veterans resumed their education at West Georgia College, which had a record enrollment of about four hundred.

Cotton was king in Carroll County. In fact, the county was third in Georgia in the production of cotton. Life in Carrollton was centered around the square with its beautiful, tall trees and a statue of a Confederate soldier facing north, I suppose on guard for another Yankee invasion.

Industrialization had not yet arrived in Carrollton. Mandeville Mills was the major employer. Southwire, Douglas & Lomason, and Printed Fabrics were a few years away.

It was in this setting that professional baseball returned to Carrollton in the late 1940's in the form of the Carrollton Hornets who became a powerhouse in the Georgia-Alabama League.

In this publication, author John Bell turns back the clock to the days of Shorty Marshall, Charlie Roberts, Jim Morelli, and others whose names you will recognize. There are complete rosters, pictures, and Bell's superbly-written narrative.

But there was baseball in Carroll County before the Hornets of the late 1940's and early 1950's. The author takes us back to 1914, through the 20's and 30's, and to the end of professional baseball in these red clay hills of west Georgia.

The final Hornets teams flourished until something called "television" came along. Fans deserted the old city ballpark as well as parks throughout the league. It was over.

In summation, John Bell has given us years of baseball drama and cherished memories. He hasn't missed a ball or strike. With this history, he truly has "Pickled It."

Introduction

There is not a specific date when baseball was invented. The sport evolved over time with numerous versions and rule changes through the years. Following the Civil War, American cities began to grow at a rapid rate through industrialization, and many of the larger cities began to form baseball teams by the 1870's. Leagues were loose and the rules still varied from club to club, but a game against a neighboring city was quite an appealing form of entertainment for a massive number of people at one time.

At first, there was no indication of major or minor league teams. There were simply baseball teams representing cities or some other sort of organization. As the popularity of baseball grew, so did the number of teams around the country. Most of the larger cities could afford to pay players much more for their services, thus the better players went to these clubs. The smaller towns' ball clubs were usually comprised of local men who had limited baseball skills and a few players of higher caliber recruited from elsewhere.

In 1901, the National Association of minor leagues was formed that would officially signify the difference between major and minor leagues. While there were fifteen leagues that belonged to the National Association as official minor leagues, there remained to be multiples of independent leagues of all calibers all over the country.

Generally referred to as semi-pro, industrial, or outlaw leagues, these independent leagues typically only lasted for a season or two before folding. But another league of the same genre was usually right behind in the next few seasons. As time went on, more leagues would gain charters from the National Association. Having a governing body over a league gave much more stability to most circuits, and longevity improved.

The first few teams that represented the city of Carrollton were of the semi-pro or outlaw variety. While these teams and leagues served the purposes of entertaining large groups of people at once and fanned the flames of local pride, they were almost destined to be one-season shows. In 1920, Carrollton formed its first National Association sanctioned baseball club as part of the Georgia State League. Carrollton played in this league again in 1921, but the circuit went defunct shortly after the end of the season. Carrollton organized a team to play in the Georgia-Alabama League from 1928 through 1930 and then again from 1946 through 1950. The city also had several teams that played in independent, semi-pro leagues between the two Georgia-Alabama League eras, and another team known as the Carrollton Lakers played semi-pro ball in the West Georgia Association from 1961 through 1965 to round out the minor league and semi-pro baseball history of Carrollton, Georgia.

Season Reviews

Pre-1920

The city of Carrollton had its first ever full time baseball team in the year 1914. The team was independent of any league and completely separate from the ranks of organized baseball. Nonetheless, the brand of ball played by Carrollton's first team was exciting and productive.

CARROLLTON'S NEW BASE BALL TEAM

On June 11, 1914, the very first game was played at a newly constructed ballpark on Depot Street against East Point. The following is Carrollton's starting lineup for the first game:

Millican	C
Raburn	P
New, Mose	1B
Moncrief, Frank	2B
Cheeves	SS
Carmichael, N.	3B
Brock	LF
Burns, Bob	CF
Hamrick	RF

Mayor W.H. Shaw declared a half-holiday in the city on the day of the first game so that patrons could go out and support the new team. The ceremonial first pitch was thrown out by the mayor christening Carrollton as a "baseball town." Carrollton easily won the first game by a score of 15 to 3 over East Point.

As the season progressed, new faces joined the team such as Jess Craven, Tommie Craven, Gene Knott, Whitney, and Kimbrell. Chief opponents of the team included East Point, Griffin, LaGrange, Cedartown, and College Park. Several games were also played against barnstorming teams such as the Agogos of Atlanta, the Indians of Nebraska, and the Atlanta All-Stars. Most of the teams that the Carrollton nine played were served a loss, and the nickname "Champs" was soon tagged onto the local ball club.

Following the win of both games of a double header against Cedartown on August 21, the Champs were declared by area baseball aficionados as the "best baseball team in the state." Pitcher Raburn, also known as "Big Indian," pitched and won both sides of the twin bill against Cedartown. Raburn had the unique ability to pitch with right-handed and left-handed with equal effectiveness.

In 1915, the Champs came together again with many of the same faces as the previous summer. Although most of the opponents were the same as well, the team did not enjoy the same level of success as before. By the summer of 1916, support of baseball began to wane mainly due to the growing unrest in Europe. The champs did not play this season, but a pickup team called the Carrollton Yannigans Baseball Club played an abbreviated season of only five games in the month of August against other nearby teams. The Yannigans won all five of the games they played.

Baseball was put on the back burner in Carrollton as it became evident that the United States would get involved in the Great War, later called World War I. Many players were called from all ranks of the diamond to serve their country as the United States declared war on Germany on April 6, 1917. The war lasted until an Armistice was signed by the United States and Germany on November 11, 1918 ending the Great War. Clean up efforts put baseball on hold through the 1919 season, and it was not until 1920 that Carrollton would have another baseball team to represent the city.

1920

Georgia State League President: J.P. Nichols, Jr.
Team Operated by Carroll County Baseball Association
Team Owner: Mann Long
Team President: Jess Travis
Manager(s): Charlie Bell
Games played at South Street Baseball Field

Carrollton Team Roster

Player	AB	R	H	AVG	POS
Allen, Harry	93	5	10	.108	P, OF
Ardis, ---	3	0	0	.000	
Bales, ---	60	3	16	.267	
Beck, ---	43	9	5	.116	P, OF
Bell, Charlie	343	68	109	.318	M, IF, P
Bonifay, Albert	71	6	15	.211	P
Brandon, Goat	284	52	87	.306	OF
Brinson, ---					SS
Carter, Russ					OF
Chaplin, Ed	281	73	87	.310	OF, C
Chatham, Happy	109	12	28	.257	3B, SS, 2B
Craven, Jess	325	52	87	.268	OF, 1B
Dugan, ---					P
Fuller, Bertram	45	6	9	.200	SS
Henderson, Hap	40	7	8	.200	P, OF
Holtz, Red	13	3	4	.308	1B
Ingram, Jimmy	7	1	1	.143	P
Lassetter, Roy	8	1	2	.250	
Long, H.L.	29	6	0	.000	
McKinnon, Bill	25	4	7	.280	P
Pratt, Frank	205	29	60	.293	OF, SS
Pressley, Babe	112	20	35	.313	UT
Pulliam, J.C	33	6	4	.121	SS
Reese, Red	144	21	32	.222	C, 2B
Register, ---	85	16	31	.365	1B, OF, P
Robertson, ---					P, OF
Shaw, Pop	111	17	30	.270	OF
Summerlin, Fritz					OF
Sutton, Lefty	7	1	2	.286	P
Swann, P.P.	26	1	0	.000	P
Watson, Jules	224	22	62	.277	2B, OF
Williams, Luke	42	3	7	.167	SS
Wilson, Jack	85	8	18	.212	OF, IF

Georgia State League Final Standings

Team	W	L	Pct	GB	Affiliate
Carrollton	53	39	.276	----	Unaffiliated
Rome	50	40	.555	2.0	Unaffiliated
Lindale Pepperels	47	43	.522	5.0	Unaffiliated
Cedartown Cedars	44	48	.478	9.0	Unaffiliated
Griffin	42	52	.447	12.0	Unaffiliated
LaGrange	39	53	.424	14.0	Unaffiliated

1920 Georgia State League Map

On May 20, 1920, the baseball team representing the city of Carrollton, Georgia played its first official game as an established minor league team in the newly formed, class-D minor league Georgia State League. The Griffin, Georgia team played host to Carrollton in a marathon, twelve-inning contest that ended with Carrollton on top, 7 to 6. Rome defeated Lindale by a score of 8 to 7, and Cedartown shut out LaGrange, 7 to 0 to round out the first-day action in the six-team circuit.

CARROLLTON TAKES FIRST GAME FROM GRIFFIN--7 TO 6

In a new stadium on South Street that was just finished days before the season started, Carrollton hosted its first home game on May 24 when LaGrange came to town. Every store in town closed at 2:30 that afternoon, and a large parade led by the Carrollton band stretched from the square to the ball park. Mayor Flournoy threw out the ceremonial first pitch that sailed over the catcher's head to the back stop. The LaGrange pitching was wild as

well, and their fielding was sloppy as Carrollton won the home opener 4 to 0 with several errors, walks, key base hits, and strong pitching from Babe Pressley. Carrollton also won one more game of the three-game set with LaGrange behind the knowledgeable leadership of player-manager Charlie Bell.

This map shows the location of the South Street Ball Park, the home field of the Carrollton baseball teams of 1920 and 1921. South Park Street stopped at Maple Street from the north at the time and is depicted here in gray indicating this section had not yet been built. South Aycock Street was known as Oscoda Place at the time.

CEDARTOWN'S STEAM ROLLER WRECKED BY CARROLLTON

One week into the season, the Cedartown "Cedars" were leading the league with a seemingly unstoppable winning streak. But in the second game of three against Carrollton, it was Carrollton "wrecking the steam-roller" with an embarrassing 22 to 1 trouncing. The one Cedartown run came in the bottom of the ninth inning and was considered to be nothing more than charity. Rome, Griffin, and Carrollton all followed closely behind first place Cedartown in the league standings in the young season.

Carrollton first baseman/outfielder Jess Craven had a thirteen consecutive game hitting streak up until it ended on June 22 in a game against Griffin. There were a total of five Carrollton players batting over .300 at this point of the season. Utility Babe Pressley was hitting .313, Craven had a .315 average, outfielder/catcher Ed Chaplin was at .330, infielder/manager Charlie Bell was batting .339, and outfielder/first baseman Register was leading the team with .422, although he had about half as many at bats as the other four players on the list.

ROME'S FANS MAKE AN ATTEMPT TO MOB CARROLLTON PLAYERS

By the end June, the Rome ball club had gained the reputation of being a "dirty, yellow bunch." Numerous fights had broken out on the field in Rome, and the umpires were calling plays in favor of Rome when it clearly should have gone the other way just to prevent a ruckus from the players and the fans. The other teams didn't like it, but they were all good enough sports to realize the reason and go along with it for the most part. One incident occurred immediately following a game of Carrollton at Rome in which a group of fans attacked Carrollton's player/manager Charlie Bell and outfielder/catcher Ed Chaplin. The fans claimed that Bell and Chaplin insulted them by calling them names and would not recant their remarks when asked. Both players received minor bumps and bruises before they were able to escape the Roman mob.

SHAKE-UP NEEDED ON OUR TEAM

The Carrollton team stood at the top of the league with 23 wins and 18 losses as of July 8, one-half game ahead of second place Rome. This margin should have been greater, many fans believed, but was not because of sloppy play during the past few weeks. The Carroll County Times newspaper offered suggestions to improve the team's play and keep first place firm. Infielder Chatham and Utility man Babe Pressley had left the team in previous weeks on terms that were not conducive to an easy return. Nevertheless, the paper wanted to see them back in the lineup instead of Jule "Old Folks" Watson and Luke Williams. The criticism was meant to be positive and not of the "knocking" nature.

In a game on Monday, July 5 between Carrollton and Cedartown, the final score was a record high 20 to 15 in favor of Cedartown. The game was described as resembling more of a track meet than a ball game, and the errors were many with Carrollton booting five and Cedartown two. Pitching was all but present in the game, as both team's offerings to the plate were ineffective.

GEORGIA STATE LEAGUE PASSES HALF MILE POST

By the half way point of the season on July 13, Carrollton had slipped into third place in the Georgia State League standings. Rome sat at the top of the heap with Cedartown holding a close second. Fourth place was held by the Lindale Pepperels, fifth place was occupied by Griffin, and LaGrange brought up the distant rear. Carrollton had what was believed to be the strongest ball team, and hopes were high that she would reach her full potential in the second half of the ninety-six game season.

The Carrollton bunch was leading the league in team batting average with .294, and Pratt, Beck, and Allen were all in the top seven ranking among pitchers in the league. Bell was leading the league in hits with 63 and was also first in doubles with 13. Chaplin led the circuit in the total runs category with 43, and Bell followed him with 41. Chaplin also had the most triples with 7 and was third in the league in stolen bases with 11.

Carrollton Wins Two Out of Three From League Leaders

Out of the gate the Carrollton team went to start the second half taking two out of three games from the league leading Rome. The fans were credited for doing their part in the games by coming out and rooting the team on. The undying, never-quitting spirit by the fans spread to the team and was praised by the newspapers of the other cities in the circuit.

CARROLLTON TAKES THREE STRAIGHTS FROM GRIFFIN

The first place spot for Carrollton was regained by a half game over Rome during the second week of the second half as Carrollton swept Griffin in a three-game set. Pitcher Harry Allen threw shut-out baseball and allowed only three hits in the first game, and Pop Shaw went four for five in game two and stole three bases, including home, in game three. The team batting average was now .304 with eight

players all hitting above this mark. Charlie Bell's gang now had a 33 and 25 record, and the momentum was gaining as a pennant race was now in sight. Third place Lindale was still in it trailing first by only a three-game margin, and Cedartown was only another half game behind the Pepperels.

"Crucial Series" Between Rome and Carrollton Begins Today

Carrollton and Rome both continued their respective winning ways through the first three weeks in August. They swapped places several times between first and second in the league standings, and it was becoming clear that the pennant would be claimed by one of these two teams at the end of the 1920 season. Clearly, the deciding factor on the winner would be the upcoming eight-game set between the two leaders, three games at the Carrollton pickle factory and five at Rome starting August 19. As clear as it might have looked, a split down the middle was the last thing that was expected. Now, the league standings were about the same as before these games, and the other teams were in position to play upset as the finish line came near.

Georgia State League Closes Monday

The final games of the 1920 Georgia State League season were scheduled to be played on Monday, September 6, and Rome held a half game lead over Charlie Bell's wrecking crew going into the weekend. With last-place LaGrange coming to town, it looked like it would be a four-game cakewalk for the Carrollton bunch. Rome was up against Griffin in the final set of the season. In order for Carrollton to come out on top at the end of the season, Griffin needed to win only one of the last four against Rome, as Carrollton was confidently counting on a sweep of LaGrange. Lindale and Cedartown would play each other in games that would have no effect on the final outcome of the pennant race to finish their seasons honorably.

CARROLLTON COPS GEORGIA STATE LEAGUE PENNANT

Griffin was defeated by Carrollton on Friday and Saturday as planned, and Griffin did their part by winning one game from Rome but losing the other. The most unexpected part of the final equation occurred on Monday when double-headers were scheduled for both pairings. Griffin upset Rome in both games giving Carrollton the pennant. The rest of Carrollton's plan was perfectly executed by winning the last two against LaGrange, even though these wins were not needed to claim the pennant. Carrollton took the first game behind the strong pitching of Albert Bonifay who was perfect through seven and one-third innings. With the final score of 4 to 1, LaGrange only garnered two hits off Bonifay. In the second game, Charlie Bell sent Lefty Sutton to the mound. LaGrange batters were only able to get three scratch hits and scored no runs in the 11 to 0 contest. Goat Brandon and Pop Shaw were credited with several great catches each in the outfield in both games of the

doubleheader, and the entire Carrollton team put on a batting demonstration starting in the fifth inning of game two that showed why five of them hit over .300 for the season. Pitcher Sutton even helped his own cause by hitting safely three times in four trips to the plate.

With no post-season championship planned for the end of the 1920 season, the inaugural Georgia State League baseball season was now over. The coveted pennant for the best team of the league would forever fly high over Carrollton in the city's first shot at established minor league baseball.

7

1921

League President: H.P. Meikleham
League Secretary: William O. Wells
Team Operated by Carroll County Baseball Association
Team Owner: Mann Long
Team President: Jess Travis
Manager(s): Cy Hawkins, Jules Watson
Games played at South Street Baseball Field

Carrollton Team Roster

Player	AB	R	H	AVG	POS
Allen, Harry	28	2	1	.036	P
Barber, ---	319	62	108	.339	OF
Barnes, ---					P
Bruner, B.E.	104	7	14	.135	SS
Cannon, Shorty	195	37	59	.303	OF, SS
Carmichael, ---	14	1	8	.571	
Coombs, ---					P
Cornelius, Rusty					P
Davenport, ---	103	10	24	.233	2B
Gallagher, ---					OF
Garvey, ---					P
Hasty, Bob					P
Hathaway, R.H.	110	20	18	.164	P
Hawkins, Cy	108	7	23	.213	M, OF
Hicks, R.E.	56	7	14	.250	1B, P
Jesmer, W.H.	142	17	40	.282	1B
Kitts, Claude	56	9	9	.161	P
Lehman, Otto	20	1	2	.100	P
Little, ---					SS
Long, H.L.	6	0	1	.167	P
Martin, S.R.	101	11	25	.248	
Moore, Clem	95	21	38	.400	OF
Powers, ---					SS
Reis, ---	52	7	9	.173	P
Richards, Babe	166	23	60	.361	OF, P
Schulte, J.	108	12	24	.222	OF
Sessions, Pete					3B
Smith, J.	174	15	36	.207	C
Suratt, Clyde					P
Taylor, Bill	285	37	77	.270	3B
Walton, Battleaxe	139	14	39	.281	C, OF, 3B
Watson, Jules	199	19	39	.196	M, 2B

Georgia State League Final Standings

Team	W	L	Pct	GB	Affiliate
Lindale Pepperells	69	29	.704	----	Unaffiliated
Griffin	53	48	.525	17.5	Unaffiliated
LaGrange	52	49	.515	18.5	Unaffiliated
Cedartown Cedars	52	49	.525	18.5	Unaffiliated
Rome	50	49	.505	19.5	Unaffiliated
Carrollton	24	76	.240	46.0	Unaffiliated

May 9 marked the beginning of the 1921 Georgia State League season. The same six teams made up the loop as did in 1920, but numerous off-season roster changes throughout the league made previously weak teams strong and vice versa.   The Lindale Pepperels, who finished third in 1920, came out of their corner swinging and won the first three games they played. At the end of the first week, Lindale sat on top undefeated with five wins. Cedartown was in second with a three and two record, and Rome was only a half a game behind them in third with three wins and three losses. Griffin was fourth in the standings with two in the win column and three in the loss, and LaGrange was fifth with a two and four record. Carrollton had won only one of their games in the first week and was sitting at the bottom of the pile. As the teams felt each other out and got to know one another, the league standings would most likely change numerous times.

CARROLLTON CAN'T WIN FOR LOSING

Carrollton manager/outfielder Cy Hawkins watched his team fall deeper and deeper into a losing streak through the second week of the season. The Cedars of Cedartown came calling and beat the home team in two consecutive games. Pitcher Coombs had great stuff in the first game for manager Hawkins, but Cedartown displayed above average hitting and won by an 8 to 5 margin. The same thing happened to Kitts on the mound for Carrollton in the second game. The local bunch had good hitting from Babe Richards and Cy Hawkins as well as a host of others, and Shorty Cannon showed off his quick feet around the bases. But Carrollton was nudged out in the tenth inning by Cedartown and stayed on the losing path. At the end of week two, Carrollton remained in last place with only two wins in eleven games.

Play continued to be sub-par from the Carrollton team as most players had the attitude that they were going to lose before the game even started. Morale was low in the grand-stands as well with fans only half-heartedly supporting the players when they needed support the most. The Carroll County times ran the following poem that Morgan Blake had previously run in the Atlanta newspaper to try to boost the down-trodden home team players and fans.

If you think you are beaten—you are,
If you think you don't dare—you don't.
If you'd like to win but think you can't
It's almost a cinch you won't.
If you think you'll lose—you've lost,
For, out in the world you find
Success begins with a fellow's will—
It's all in the state of mind.

Full many a race is lost
Ere even a step to run,
And many a coward falls
Ere even his work's begun.
Think big and your deeds will grow,
Think small and you'll fall behind,
Think that you can and you will,
It's all in the state of mind.

If you think you're outclassed—you are,
You've got to think high to rise,
You've got to be sure of yourself before
You can ever win a prize.
Life's battles don't always go
To the stronger or faster man,
But soon or late, the man who wins,
Is the fellow who thinks he can.

Errors plagued Cy Hawkins' squad in game after game. Carrollton's losing was caused mainly by the boots on the field and were most present in a three-game series against Griffin in which a total of twenty-three balls were mishandled. For about a week mid-way through the first half of the Georgia State League season, Carrollton climbed out of the cellar and was not the last place team. This was only a slight glimmer of hope for the struggling club, as LaGrange took the sixth position with a three and twenty record. The fifth place Carrollton had four wins and eighteen losses at the end of the fourth week; eight games behind fourth place Cedartown and thirteen and a half games behind the league-leading Lindale team. The Rome and Griffin clubs held second and third places respectively at this juncture of the relatively young season.

With three weeks to go before the mid-season mark, rumor stirred quickly around the Georgia State League about the possibility of the struggling Carrollton team disbanding. The talk of Columbus buying the club and continuing play in the league was also part of the scuttlebutt.

League secretary William O. Wells of Griffin said in an interview on June 15 that the rumors were "all a horrible mistake." Wells admitted, "There was a time when Carrollton looked a bit shaky. At that time, we were looking around for a city to take over the franchise, but the situation is changed now. Carrollton is not even threatened with leaving the league." He continued to explain that the new players were being looked at to send to play at Carrollton to pick things up.

The presentation of the 1920 pennant was scheduled for the upcoming July 4 afternoon game against Cedartown. Wells agreed that it would be quite shameful for the winning city to go defunct only half-way into the next season and not be present to collect and fly the flag. "The attendance hasn't been bad in Carrollton. The guarantee to maintain the club in our organization has already been subscribed and is in the bank ready to be used in any emergency," the secretary reassured.

BASEBALL MEETING

First National Bank Bldg.
(Fourth Floor)

FRIDAY NIGHT

8:00 o'Clock

_____

At this meeting we are to decide whether to quit or not. If you want to stay in, be there; if not, stay away.

Carrollton Baseball Association

The overwhelming positive response and support at the meeting on whether or not to continue play coupled with William Wells remarks etched in stone Carrollton's decision not to disband. Hopes were high that a turnaround would come for the Carrollton ball-tossers in the second half of the Georgia State League season.

Carrollton Drops Four Straights to Lindale

It appeared that the news of staying in the league did not suit the current roster of Carrollton players well. They immediately dropped four straight games to Lindale setting the mark for the longest sweep from an opponent of the season. The team looked good on the field and lost all the games but one by narrow margins. One of the games was credited to the umpire who made numerous bad calls against Carrollton. Last place was reclaimed once again by Carrollton by a one-half game margin between them and LaGrange.

The 1920 Georgia State League Pennant that was garnered by Charlie Bell's squad in the previous season was presented in full ceremony on the July 4th, Independence Day afternoon game. League President H.P. Meikleham was on hand to present the flag before the game against Cedartown with several of the 1920 Carrollton players there to receive the trophy. Seeing the championship honors flying above the diamond restored pride and renewed the team's determination to play a better brand of baseball.

Carrollton Will Present Strong Line-up Second Half

New players were being secured for the second half of the season by the Carrollton club. The pitching staff was believed to be the weakest link of the chain by the club management. Bob Hasty, a new pitcher, came highly recommended by a Philadelphia Athletics scout, and another pitcher, Garvey, would report from the Spartanburg team of the South Atlantic League. Harry Allen of the 1920 pennant winning team would also report to once again hurl for Carrollton rounding out the new strength on the mound.

Manager Cy Hawkins was released from the club, and Jules "Old Folks" Watson was appointed as the new skipper. Watson, who was strong down the stretch for Carrollton in the 1920 pennant race, was one of the most experienced members of the team and the natural choice for the job.

Georgia State League.

CLUBS.	Won.	Lost.	Pct.
Lindale	36	13	.735
Griffin	32	18	.647
Rome	29	20	.592
Cedartown	27	23	.540
LaGrange	16	34	.320
Carrollton	8	41	.163

Lindale took the mid-season title with an impressive record of thirty-six wins and thirteen losses. This assured them a spot in the league championship to be held at the end of the second half against the pennant winner of that portion of the season. In second place was Griffin by a four game margin followed by Rome at seven games out of first. Cedartown occupied the fourth position nine and a half games behind Lindale, and LaGrange took fifth by an eleven game gap between them and Cedartown. Finally, Carrollton was in last place in the Georgia State League; eight games behind LaGrange and twenty-eight games out of first.

CARROLLTON CLUB PLAYING GOOD BALL

By all indications, things appeared to be turning around for the Carrollton club at the beginning of the second half of the season. After a week and a half of play, Carrollton was in second place with five wins and only three losses. First half winner Lindale even fell victim to Jules Watson's bunch in two of these games; the first time Carrollton had defeated Lindale all season. The newly acquired talent was providing the necessary support to win games, and the rest of the squad was finally playing up to their potential.

By the end of the second week of act two of the season, Carrollton had dropped to the fourth spot in the standings. And at the end of July, the home team had sunken all the way back to the bottom once again. The Cedars were on fire at the top of the heap followed in order by LaGrange, Lindale, Rome, Griffin, and finally Carrollton.

Booster Day" For Carrollton Ball Club

Booster day was held on August 15 at the pickle factory for the Carrollton club with stores closing early so fans could go out and support the home team. In the following week, Carrollton went from a nine and twenty record to a twelve and twenty-one mark. Although the quality of play had improved, the team remained in the last place position one game behind fifth place Rome.

When the "boost" from Booster day wore off, Watson's squad lost five games straight, and going into the end of August was fourteen games out of first place. It looked like it would be LaGrange taking the second half title to face Lindale in the post-season championship series.

At the close of the regular season, Lindale's combined first and second half record put them on top of the standings by seventeen and a half games. Griffin, LaGrange, Cedartown, and Rome were second, third, fourth and fifth respectively all bunched together. Carrollton brought up the distant rear by a breath-taking forty-six game margin between them and first place. The post-season saw LaGrange upset Lindale four games to one in a fast-paced best of seven championship series.

Carrollton's drop from first to worst from one season to the next was said to be a record for the most dramatic fall ever in organized baseball at the time. Due to financial difficulties, the Georgia State League disbanded after the 1921 season.

1922-1927

In the years following the 1921 season, Carrollton did not have a baseball team to represent the city. From 1922 to 1927, the minor league and semi-pro baseball diamond lay dormant in the city.

1928

League President: C.I. Scarborough
League Secretary: Walter M. Booz
Team Operated by the Carrollton Baseball Club
Team President: A.W. "Andy" Ford
Manager(s): Paul Fittery
Games played at City Athletic Field; seating capacity 3,250

Carrollton Frogs Roster

Player	G	HR	AVG	POS	W	L	ERA
Atchley, Loy	61	4	.319	P, OF	3	6	3.52
(includes Anniston and Cedartown stats)							
Avery, ---			.190				
Bailey, ---	5			P, OF	0	0	12.00
Boswell, Brant	88	12	.272	2B			
Butts, ---			.467	1B			
Carter, Homer	28	1	.253	P, OF	9	8	4.00
(includes Gadsden stats)							
Cosby, ---	15	0	.293				
(includes Lindale stats)							
Dumas, Otto	20	1	.298	OF			
Fittery, Paul	33		.227	M, P, OF	21	2	1.60
Frakes, Ben	20	0	.082	P	5	9	2.62
(includes Gadsden stats)							
Garrett, Tige	30	1	.193	3B			
Goggans, G.E.	87	14	.309	C			
Grimes, ---	10	0	.380	SS			
(includes Lindale stats)							
Howell, Red	93		.392	OF			
Huggins, Miller	79	1	.250	3B			
(includes Gadsden stats)							
James, Fob	73	1	.292	1B			
Lacey, ---	6			P	4	2	3.68
Laird, Red	32	1	.237	P, OF	9	4	4.80
Mathewson, ---			.250				
McKinney, ---	41	2	.284	C			
(includes Lindale stats)							
Moore, J.	8		.150	P	1	2	5.85
Rowe, Bob	68	6	.316	OF			
Taliaferro, Dick	70	9	.392	SS			
White, Abe	29	1	.171	P	13	10	3.36
White, Jo Jo	96	27	.330	OF			
Wicker, Kemp			.500	P			

Georgia-Alabama League Final Standings

Team	W	L	Pct	GB	Affiliate
Cedartown Sea Cows	55	34	.618	----	Unaffiliated
Carrollton Frogs	54	34	.614	0.5	Unaffiliated
Anniston Nobles	47	42	.528	8.0	Unaffiliated
Talladega Indians	45	43	.511	9.5	Unaffiliated
Gadsden Eagles	37	49	.430	16.5	Unaffiliated
Lindale Dragons	26	62	.295	28.5	Unaffiliated

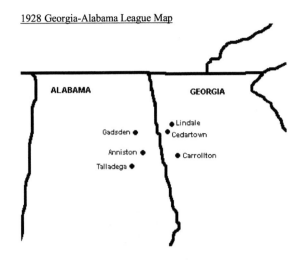

1928 Georgia-Alabama League Map

Cows won that game over the yet-to-be-named Carrollton team. But Carrollton reciprocated the very next day in the home opener at the new City Athletic Field on West Avenue behind the high school.

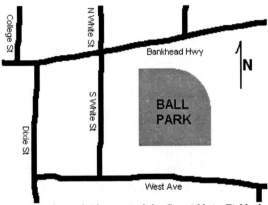

This map shows the location of the City Athletic Field, the home field of the Carrollton baseball teams of 1928-30 and 1946-50. A small section of the grand stand still remains in the side of the embankment behind the old high school.

In 1928, the Georgia-Alabama League returned to the Class-D echelon of professional baseball after an eleven year sabbatical, and Carrollton was back in organized baseball for the first time since 1921. The new league with an old, familiar name was organized by Major Trammell Scott of Atlanta, R.J. Spiller, president of the Atlanta Crackers, and the Brooklyn Dodgers major league baseball club. Teams from the cities of Anniston, Talladega, and Gadsden made up the Alabama side of the circuit, and Carrollton, Cedartown, and Lindale were the clubs from Georgia in the first year.

New Class 'D' League Opens Season Today

Carrollton played their first game under the field management of former major league pitcher Paul Fittery on the Cedartown diamond on May 24. The Sea

With teams getting to know each other through the first couple of weeks, it appeared that the Georgia teams were stronger that the ones from Alabama. Cedartown sat at the top of the standings two weeks in with a record of twelve wins and five losses. Lindale was second with an eleven and six record, and Carrollton took third with ten wins and seven losses. Talladega held the fourth position with six wins and ten losses, and Anniston was in the fifth slot with a six and ten mark. Gadsden brought up the rear having won only five and losing the other twelve games they had played.

CARROLLTON TAKES SIX STRAIGHT GAMES—TEAM PLAYING GOOD BALL

Paul Fittery's bunch had just won six games in a row when the previously mentioned standings were reported boosting their position in the league. The strong pitching of Fittery, Homer Carter, Abe White, and J. Moore combined with the outstanding hitting of Red Howell and G.E. "Cheese" Goggans, among others, could not be outdone by Anniston and Gadsden as each lost three games to Carrollton. Fittery's Dick Taliaferro and Brant Boswell plugged up the middle infield allowing very few ground balls to pass through. It was apparent early on that the Carrollton team was to be taken seriously.

In week three of the first half of the Georgia-Alabama League season, Carrollton's already best-in-the-league pitching staff was enhanced even more. Green Flake "Red" Laird, who gained fame playing on Shoeless Joe Jackson's championship Americus, Georgia team in 1923, was signed on to replace J. Moore in the rotation. June 17 was Red's debut for Carrollton, and he held the Indians of Talladega to one run on eight hits and also lined a triple of the center field fence.

CARROLLTON WINS FOUR GAMES OUT OF SIX DURING THE PAST WEEK

Carrollton had moved up to second place in the circuit standings by the end of the third week of play. In a clean three-game sweep of Talladega, Carrollton scored a total of thirty runs and allowed their opponents only two. The victory in the first game against Lindale gave Carrollton a ten game win streak, but Lindale took the next two games from Fittery's gang.

Second place became a home for the Carrollton team as the season progressed. Week four of the season saw the home bunch win another four out of six

contests. Lindale and Talladega each lost two of three games against Carrollton. In a 19-6 win in game one against Lindale, Carrollton's "Murderer's Row" put on a hitting exhibition that was said to be equivalent to Independence Day fireworks. Joyner "Jo-Jo" White, and Dick Taliaferro led the batting going four for six each, and Jo-Jo and Red Howell each had a home run.

HOWELL LEADS LEAGUE IN HITTING

J. White Leads In Home Runs Knocked

Red Howell was leading the league in batting with an average of .486, a full .089 points ahead of second place Shipley of Cedartown. He was also in a four-way tie for second in home runs with five round-trips trailing Jo-Jo White who held that lead with six. With a team batting average of over .300, it was easy to see why Paul Fittery's bunch was on the winning track.

Carrollton and Cedartown continued to beat the eyes out of the rest of the league with the exception of Cedartown. In the middle of July, Cedartown was still in the lead of the league with thirty-two wins and fourteen losses. Carrollton trailed by two and a half games with a twenty-nine and sixteen record. Anniston and Lindale were tied for third with eighteen in the win column and twenty-five in the loss. Talladega and Gadsden were also tied in the back of the pack with records of seventeen and twenty-five, only a half game behind Anniston and Lindale.

Pushing the Sea Cows hard for the league lead, Carrollton players continued to dominate the league in numerous categories of performance. Jo-Jo White showed fans time and time again why he was called the "Ten-Thousand Dollar Baby as he increased his home run number to fourteen. Red Howell was still hitting over .400 and was joined there by a new man on the Carrollton squad, Miller Huggins. Dick Taliaferro, Jo-Jo White, Cheese Goggans, and Fob James all were contributing well by batting over .300. Paul Fittery was leading the league pitching with eleven wins and only one loss, while Red Laird and Abe White had records of five and one and five and two respectively.

Can You Suggest a Name

The Carrollton team had played the 1928 season so far as the only team in the circuit without a nickname. Team president, A.W. Ford, appealed to the fans to come up with a suitable name for his club, and the winning suggestion was the Carrollton "Frogs." So, from mid-July to the end of the 1928 season, the baseball club from Carrollton would be affectionately known as the "Frogs."

Carrollton Club Is Fighting Hard For League Leadership

Only One and One-Half Games Between Carrollton and Cedartown

With one week to go before the close of the first half of the season on July 28,

Carrollton trailed Cedartown by only a game and a half. The defining moment was coming in the last three games of act one of the season with the Frogs squaring off against the Sea Cows. The rest of the league was out of the hunt for the first slot of the post-season championship that would be determined by who was on top at the close of the first half.

On Friday, July 20, the Carrollton Baseball Club sponsored a production of the play *Here Comes Arabella*. Red Laird and Dick Taliaferro showed that baseball was not their only talent as each had a starring role. Laird played the part of "Bill," and Taliaferro played "Abraham Luvinski." The show was deemed an astounding success, and both players received rave reviews as actors.

TAKING THREE FROM CEDARTOWN CARROLLTON WINS FIRST HALF

The Carrollton Frogs took their brooms up to Cedartown and used them well to sweep the three-game set from the Sea Cows and capture the first half flag. With strong pitching from Fittery, Abe White, and Red Laird, and amazing hitting from Boswell, Goggans, James, Taliaferro, Jo-Jo White, and most of the rest of the team, the frogs assured a post-season championship berth no matter what happened in the second half. After winning game one of the set, Carrollton was only one half game behind Cedartown. The second game was a nail-biter with the lead changing six times before Fittery's gang finally ended up on top and now holding a half game lead in the league. Game three was Cedartown's last chance to take back their long-standing first position and the first half-pennant they had had their eyes on for weeks now. Apparently, the Sea Cows were either not interested in post-season play, or they thought they could just as easily win the second half as they seemed to lay down and give Carrollton the victory in game three. Cedartown used three pitchers as Carrollton put on an astounding hitting display complete with Jo-Jo White's daily dinger.

Carrollton won twenty-one of the last twenty-five games the team played storming their way to the first half title with a record of thirty-nine wins and eighteen losses. Cedartown won thirty eight games and lost twenty in the first half finishing one and a half games behind Carrollton. Third place was garnered by Anniston thirteen games behind first with a twenty-six and thirty-one final record, and Gadsden took fourth with twenty-two in the win column and thirty-one in the loss fifteen games behind Carrollton. Talladega wound up sixteen and a half games out of first in fifth place with twenty-one wins and thirty-three losses, and Lindale brought up the rear one game behind Talladega with twenty wins and thirty-four losses at the end of the first half.

CARROLLTON AGAIN LEADING LEAGUE AS SECOND HALF OPENS

At the end of the first week of the second half of the Georgia-Alabama League season, Carrollton was leading the league but had company in the form of Cedartown and Anniston. All three teams had records of four wins and two losses through their first six games. Talladega, with a three and three record, was next,

and Gadsden followed with two wins and four losses. Lindale, in last place, had been taking most of the blows during the week winning only one of the six games they had played.

By the end of week two of the second half, the Frogs had dropped to third place behind Cedartown in first and Talladega in second. And at the end of the third week, Talladega had moved into the top spot and had become the favorite to face Carrollton in the league championship series at the end of the season.

PLAY-OFF FOR PENNANT STARTS NEXT WEEK—TWO GAMES HERE

TALLEDEGA IS ALMOST SURE TO WIN THE SECOND HALF

With only a week to go in the regular season, now more than ever, it looked like Talladega would be Carrollton's opponent in the league championship. The Indians had a seventeen and seven record and a two and a half game advantage over second place Anniston and Cedartown who were tied with fourteen wins and nine losses. Carrollton was now in fourth place followed by Gadsden and Lindale.

OFFICIAL LEAGUE STANDING

At end of Second Half)

	Won	Lost	Pct.
Anniston	19	10	.655
Talladega	19	10	.655
Cedartown	16	12	.571
Carrollton	14	14	.500
Gadsden	13	16	.446
Lindale	5	24	.172

The heir-apparent for the second half crown, Talladega, met a hard challenge in the final stretch. Anniston decided that they were not giving up without a fight and pressed hard in their final six games winning five of them. These victories coupled with Talladega losing four of the final six games of their schedule created a tie of nineteen wins and ten losses between the two teams. A best two of three games series would now be played to determine the rightful winner of the season's second stanza. This tie-breaking series started on September 6, the original scheduled date of the beginning of the league championship series. The delay was feared to be a disadvantage for Fittery's Frogs in that it could make them over-confident and lackadaisical.

Only two of the three games were needed by the Indians to take care of the Nobles and to win the championship berth to face Carrollton. Now the post-season series to determine who the best team was in the Georgia-Alabama League would finally begin on Monday, September 10 with Carrollton hosting Talladega. The series was nicknamed "Georgia's Little World's Series."

Indians Lose Opening Tilt To Carrollton

It was the Paul Fittery show in game one as Carrollton defeated Talladega by a 4 to 3 final at the City Athletic Field. Fittery struck out eighteen Indian batters and allowed only seven hits. Carrollton booted five balls in the game that gave Talladega two of their three runs. Bob Rowe had the big stick for the Frogs

driving in two runs and scoring another with a home run in the game.

In game two, Lacey took the mound on the Carrollton diamond for the Frogs and was slaughtered by the Indians, 10 to 1. Allowing the first seven Talladega tallies through the first two innings, Lacey was relieved by Abe White who gave up the other three. The series, now tied at one game apiece, would go to Talladega for games three and four.

Indians Win 3rd Tilt, 3-2, To Go 1 Up

Game three was a pitcher's duel between Kemp Wicker for Carrollton and Jack Waller for Talladega that ended up 3 to 2 with Talladega on top. The Indians crossed all three of their runs in the third inning and took the lead in the championship series two games to one.

Carrollton evened the series at two games each in game four on the Talladega home field in a 7 to 5 contest. Fittery manned the mound for the Frogs and allowed two runs in the first inning. But the Carrollton bats were hot in the top of the second as the visitors scored all seven of their runs. Red Howell led the hitting with two doubles and a single in five times at bat.

On Friday, September 15, game five was played on the Carrollton field with the home team winning 5 to 0. Abe White surrendered only five hits to the Indians in the shut-out game, and Jo-Jo White slammed his twenty-eighth home run of the season. Carrollton now led "Georgia's Little World's Series" three games to two with game six scheduled in Talladega for Saturday.

CARROLLTON DEFEATS TALLEDEGA FOR PENNANT IN GA.-ALA. LEAGUE

Takes Four Out of Six, Outclassing Opponents In Every Department.

The Carrollton Frogs became the winner of the 1928 Georgia-Alabama League pennant by winning game six of the series 5 to 1 on the Indians home field. Lacey started the game for the Frogs and pitched shut out ball into the seventh inning. Fittery pulled Lacey and put Wicker in to hurl at that point, and then replaced Wicker with himself in the eighth inning when Talladega threatened to score. The lone Talladega run was given up by Fittery as a result of the eighth inning threat, but the bleeding was then stopped cold by the Frog skipper. Fittery finished the game and the series by striking out the last three Indian batters in the bottom of the ninth. Carrollton scored two runs in the third inning on a long home run by Cheese Goggans with a man on base. The other three Carrollton runs came in the eighth inning on consecutive singles by Red Howell, Jo-Jo White, Bob Rowe, and Miller Huggins, and a sacrifice fly by Kemp Wicker.

Local newspapers bragged highly on the Carrollton team for copping the flag of the league champion now twice in three times playing in an organized baseball league. One reporter wrote, "Not even the New York Yankees can boast such an impressive feat."

1929

League President: C.I. Scarborough
League Secretary: B.A. Lancaster
Team Operated by the Carrollton Baseball Club
Team President: A.W. "Andy" Ford
Manager(s): Paul Fittery
Games played at City Athletic Field; seating capacity 3,250

Carrollton Champs Roster

Player	G	HR	AVG	POS	W	L
Anderson, Marion	74	0	.350	2B		
Buford, Red	10-		.077	OF		
Christiansen, ---			.324			
Crowe, Hoyt	21	0	.188	P	8	7
Davis, Carl	10-		.105	P		
Ezzell, Bob	95	13	.369	1B		
Fittery, Paul	39	2	.213	M, P	16	2
Freedman, Benny	88	15	.312	OF, C		
Goggans, G.E.	92	6	.287	C		
Harrison, ---	16	1	.309	OF		
Holsomback, Squirt	98	8	.269	3B		
Justiss, Red	29	0	.225	P	10	12
Lacey, ---	10-		.222	P		
Lopez, ---	19	1	.243	OF		
Marks, Max	10-			P		
McGhee, Bill	61	0	.311	OF, 1B		
Nettles, Hoke	6		.556	OF		
Patton, Henry	99	12	.285	OF, SS		
Reese, Eddie	37	4	.278	SS		
Sappenfield, Colon	54	4	.323	SS		
Stanfield, Ralph	26	1	.167	P	8	8
Strickland, ---	10-		.182	OF		
Tate, J.R.			.248	2B		
White, Abe	31	0	.259	P	10	11
Winn, Breezy	10-		.250	OF, P		

Georgia-Alabama League Final Standings

Team	W	L	Pct	GB	Affiliate
Lindale Collegians	60	39	.606	----	Unaffiliated
Carrollton Champs	56	44	.560	4.5	Unaffiliated
Talladega Indians	49	49	.500	10.5	Unaffiliated
Gadsden Eagles	49	50	.495	11.0	Unaffiliated
Anniston Nobles	44	56	.440	16.5	Unaffiliated
Cedartown Sea Cows	40	60	.400	20.5	Unaffiliated

1929 Georgia-Alabama League Map

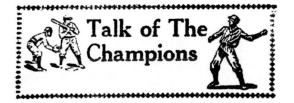

With the 1928 Georgia-Alabama League championship pennant on the wall, the Carrollton team returned for the 1929 season bearing a new, more appropriate nickname than previously. Instead of being the "Frogs," the team was now going by the moniker "Champs."

Manager Paul Fittery returned for the new season to give direction to the team and was joined by team veteran catcher Cheese Goggans and pitchers Abe White and Lacey. Preseason action saw Carrollton defeat a team from Cartersville 17 to 5 and the Grinnell Fire Extinguisher team of Atlanta by a 7 to 4 final score. The regular games were scheduled to start on Friday, May 10 with Carrollton hosting Lindale at the City Athletic Field.

Anniston manager Bud Ammons sent a friendly, in-good-sportsmanship letter to Carrollton's Paul Fittery just prior to the opening of the season. The letter read as follows:

"Dear Paul:

The Grand Opening is right here on us. Hope it finds you with a good club and me with a better one, but – you have something to look forward to other than defeat on your next visit here.

You remember Mr. Leo Pruett, the 'Big Noise' of every ball game. He is one of our best baseball fans and a cracking good sport with it. Always in for anything concerning his favorite sport.

Mr. Pruett requests that each visiting club, their first game with us, have their first supper, a STEAK supper, at his place, 'Pruett's – The Place To Eat' at the expense of himself.

As to his steaks, I have failed to lose twenty unnecessary pounds during training because I couldn't lay off those Big Steaks.

Trusting you beat everybody but me, I am

Sincerely,
Bud Ammons
Manager Anniston Ball Club"

GEORGIA-ALABAMA LEAGUE OPENS TODAY

The Champs opened the 1929 season in winning style on Friday, May 10 by taking the game from the Lindale Collegians in a 6 to 3 score. Skipper Fittery manned the mound for the home team in the opener, and old-reliable Cheese Goggans completed the battery behind the plate. Carrollton also won the second game of the season from Lindale and proceeded to win season games three and four from Cedartown and game five from Gadsden.

After only six games with the Carrollton Club, outfielder Hoke Nettles was released from the club even though he was leading the team in batting with an astounding .556 average. He was suspected of being a "class-man" with more playing experience than previously believed making him ineligible to play for the team under the leaugue rules of the time. The possibility of forfeiture of games that Nettles played in was a matter that would be decided by the league directorate. Team President A.W. "Andy" Ford thought it best to cut Nettles and hope that the league would let the games stand as victories and not be stripped away for the rule violation.

With no other team in the league yet able to defeat Carrollton, the Indians of Talladega came to town on Wednesday, May 22 to see the 1928 Georgia-Alabama League championship pennant raised over the City Athletic Field. This was only fitting as Talladega was the team the Champs, then the Frogs, beat out to win the flag. After appropriate ceremonies were carried out, Carrollton won number nine in a row. The game was the toughest win yet for Fittery's bunch as Henry Patton scored the tie-breaking, winning run in the bottom of the ninth.

The winning streak continued for the Champs all the way through the first two weeks of the season. With ten straight victories, the first loss was finally suffered at the hand of the Cedartown Sea Cows. In a barn-burner on the Cedartown

diamond, Carrollton lost by a narrow 9 to 8 margin on Friday, May 24.

LEAGUE STANDING
(Thru Wed. May 29th)

	Won	Lost	Pct.
Carrollton	13	2	.867
Cedartown	10	6	.625
Gadsden	8	7	.533
Anniston	8	9	.471
Lindale	4	11	.267
Talladega	4	12	.250

By the end of the third week of the first half of the season, Carrollton looked to be the early favorite to win the initial play-off position at the end of the season. The club with the best record at the end of each half of the season would have the privilege of facing each other for the pennant championship series at the end of regular season play. Carrollton's thirteen wins and two losses led the league by three and a half games over second place Cedartown. The formula Paul Fittery was using seemed to be the correct one with pitchers Davis, White, Marks, Lacey, and himself throwing well and keeping opponent hitters at bay. On the offense side of the equation, Bob Ezzell, Henry Patton, and Colon Sappenfield were all batting over .400, and Benny Freedman and Cheese Goggans were both over the .300 mark.

Georgia-Alabama League.

TEAMS.	Won	Lost	Pct.
Cedartown	12	9	.571
Lindale	11	9	.550
Gadsden	11	9	.550
Carrollton	10	10	.500
Anniston	10	11	.476
Talladega	8	13	.381

Over the course of the next week, Carrollton won three of the five games played, but the team's record dropped to an even ten wins and ten losses. The league came down with the decision to take the first six games of the season away from the Champs due to the fact that Hoke Nettles was, in fact, a class man and ineligible to play. The teams on the losing end of these games were given wins to replace the losses suffered at the hand of the unknowingly rule-breaking Carrollton club. Now, the Carrollton team was resting in fourth place instead of first in the league standings, and Cedartown stood tall at the top spot and took credit for bringing the truth of Hoke Nettles to the surface.

Carrollton Defeats Cedartown 21 to 11

In first class fashion, the Carrollton squad regained first place in the league in the matter of only one week. Winning seven out of eight games, the Champs were once again on top. These victories were ever sweeter as three of the wins came from a sweep of the league tattle-tail Cedartown. The first game of the set resembled a track meet as the Champs won 21 to 11. Cedartown dropped to the fourth slot losing three of the other four games they played during the second week of June.

Pitcher Ralph Stanfield, having just been acquired from Lindale, made a good first impression on the mound for Carrollton defeating Anniston and allowing only four hits. Another strong acquisition by the Champs was second baseman Marion Anderson, son of Oglethorpe University coach Frank Anderson. In the junior Anderson's first professional game, he handled the ball

well for the Champs, and scored a run to help secure the win.

Through the next two weeks, Carrollton stayed at the top of the heap, joined there on one occasion by Lindale who was in second place the rest of the time. Toward the end of June, initial sacker Bob Ezzell went down with a back injury. A new man by the name of Bill McGhee, who could also play outfield, was hired to fill the vacancy. The Champs were nearing their opportunity to take the first slot for the end of the season pennant championship with the season's first half set to wind down on July 4.

With Carrollton one and a half games ahead of second place Lindale and three games for each team left in the first half, it looked like the first post-season playoff spot would easily belong to the Champs. Carrollton was scheduled to play Gadsden for three games, and Lindale was up against Cedartown for three.

Georgia-Alabama League.
STANDING.

TEAMS	Won.	Lost.	Pct.
Carrollton	29	20	....
Lindale	28	20	.583
Gadsden	23	24	.480
Anniston	23	25	.479
Talladega	22	25	.468
Cedartown	21	28	.429

Following a loss by Fittery's bunch and a win by the Collegians in the July 3 contests, there was but a half-game margin between Carrollton and Lindale. The Champs decided that the best strategy would be to win both sides of the Independence Day double bill and claim the first, assured berth for the post-season. This strategy worked as Carrollton won the first game 6 to 3 behind the mound work of Hoyt Crowe and Abe White. Bill McGhee was a perfect three for three with the bat, and Cheese Goggans got two key hits in three trips.

In game two of the day, Red Justiss pitched masterful ball in a duel of the moundsmen that ended with Carrollton on top 2 to 1. Little offense was had by either team with only twelve scratch hits throughout the game. This win was enough to give Carrollton the much sought after first half pennant and the guaranteed spot in the post-season championship. Both wins were needed as Lindale won both ends of their holiday double-header from Cedartown. Rumor was that Cedartown laid down purposefully in an attempt to stop rival Carrollton from winning the first half of the season.

The second half of the season started right after the end of the first, and Carrollton darted out of the shoot once again. Pledging to fans to do everything in their power to win every game possible, the Champs let everybody know that no game would be less than exciting. Just because they had already secured a role in the championship series, the Carrollton team promised not to relax at all and to always give the fans a good game to watch.

All the way through July, the Champs continued to win more than they lost, but Talladega was winning more than anybody else in the circuit. On August 1, the Indians were in the front of the pack with thirteen wins and seven losses. The second place Champs held a twelve and nine record followed by the eleven and nine Lindale Collegians. Fourth place was occupied by the Gadsden Eagles with ten wins and eleven losses along side the Anniston Nobles with the same record.

Last place in the second half of the season was being taken by the Sea Cows of Cedartown with only six victories and fifteen defeats.

Ten Homers Hit In One Ball Game

On Monday, August 12, in a game between Cedartown and Anniston, a record ten home runs were hit. Anniston started off the long-ball display in the first inning, and it continued into the eighth frame. Cedartown batters had six of the round-trips, and Anniston swatted the other four. Both teams tried to get the bleeding under control as Anniston used three different pitchers and Cedartown two. This was a new Georgia-Alabama League record for the most combined home runs in one game.

LEAGUE STANDING
(Through Tuesday, August 13)

	Won	Lost	Games from Top
Lindale	18	13	0
Carrollton	17	15	1½
Gadsden	17	15	1½
Talladega	16	15	2
Anniston	16	16	2½
Cedartown	11	21	7½

With less than three weeks to go in the season, Lindale still had the lead in the race for the second slot in the post-season championship. The lead was only a half game over second place Talladega, and Carrollton, Gadsden, and Anniston were all knotted within a game's margin of Talladega. Bringing up the rear was Cedartown five games out of first place certainly not completely out of the running.

A surprising, three-game sweep was handed to Carrollton by the last-place Cedartown Sea Cows during the third week of August. Umpires Floyd and Rowe were given credit for their efforts in helping Cedartown win at least one of the games. So bad were the calls by both officials that the Carrollton fans showered them with gifts of Coke bottles and miniature replicas of Stone Mountain. The officiating was bad throughout the game, but the dam burst in the seventh when Squirt Holsomback was called out at first even after the Sea Cows first baseman dropped the ball. Amidst the chaos, Floyd and Rowe fled the ball park in an awaiting car.

SCHEDULE OF LITTLE WORLD'S SERIES

Playoff Between Carrollton and Lindale For Championship.

Wednesday, Sept. 4th, in Lindale.
Thursday, Sept. 5th, in Carrollton.
Friday, Sept. 6th, in Carrollton.
Saturday, Sept. 7th, in Lindale.

Then until one team has won four games as follows:

Monday, Sept 9th, in Carrollton.
Tuesday, Sept 10th, in Lindale.
Wednesday, Sept. 11th, decided by draw.

Champ Manager Paul Fittery began making preparations to face Lindale in the post-season league championship series as the regular season wound down. With five games left for each team, it was apparent that Lindale would be the second half winner and Carrollton's opponent in the "Little World's Series." Lindale would have to lose three of their last five games, and second place Talladega would have to win all five games left in their

schedule for the Collegians to not make the bonus baseball festivities.

LEAGUE STANDING
(At end of regular season)

	won	lost	pct.
Lindale	31	19	.620
Talladega	27	23	.540
Carrollton	26	24	.520
Gadsden	26	24	.520
Anniston	22	28	.440
Cedartown	18	32	.360

Lindale took the second half flag leaving Talladega in the first runner-up position and now would face Carrollton in the first game of the post-season on Wednesday, September 4. On the Lindale diamond, Carrollton proceeded to take game one by a final score of 7 to 4. Paul Fittery pitched his usual outstanding game and got great run support from the bats of Bob Ezzell, Benny Freedman, and Squirt Holsomback, each hitting a home run. It was Freedman's dinger in the top of the eighth with Marion Anderson on first and Ezzell on second that gave the Champs the lead. Cheese Goggans hit a long triple to dead center and was driven in by Fittery batting next for one more run in the big inning. The best of seven games series now moved to the City Athletic Field in Carrollton for games two and three.

On Thursday, September 5, game two was played on the Carrollton home field with Carrollton winning 8 to 4. At least that was the score at the end of the game before the league directors ruled on a protest by Lindale manager Jack "Slick" Moulton. In the top of the seventh inning, Lindale had the bases loaded when pitcher Wood hit a lazy fly ball that looked like it would fall in shallow right field. All three base runners started running thinking the ball would drop, but right fielder Benny Freedman got on his horse and made a diving catch. Slick Moulton was the runner on third who, upon seeing the catch, made a dash back toward the bag. Freedman threw home instead of to third, and the ball sailed past catcher Goggans and hit a row of bats in front of the Carrollton dugout. Goggans retrieved the ball and threw it to Squirt Holsomback covering third in time to get Moulton out. This is when the tidal wave of protest came from Moulton who said that the base runners should get a free pass back to their bases they held before the play since the ball was overthrown. Umpire Vick agreed with Moulton, but the next batter made the third out of the inning.

Before Carrollton came to bat in the bottom of the inning, Moulton declared to Umpire Vick that he wanted to protest the game because of the confusion. A meeting was held of the anti-Carrollton league directorate, and they voted five to one to throw the game out as if it were never played. The one vote of the debacle being Carrollton, and the other five were the rest of the league.

Although the game didn't count in the end, Red Justiss pitched perfect ball until the fifth inning when he eased up. Bob Ezzell hit another home run this time with the bases juiced.

In game three, which was now actually game two, Carrollton won in exciting fashion in the bottom of the ninth inning by a 3 to 2 final. The Friday, September 6 game was a duel of the pitchers between Carrollton's Abe White and Lindale's Stoutenboro. Lindale struck first on the Carrollton diamond in the top of the

fourth with one manufactured run. The champs got two tallies in the bottom of the sixth when Bob Ezzell hit his third home run of the series with Henry Patton on first. The Collegians tied it in the top of the seventh, and it stayed that way until the bottom of the ninth. Patton and Ezzell again combined to score with the former leading off garnering a double to right and the latter driving him in on a line drive to center. Lindale should have scored previously in the top of the ninth but was robbed by third baseman Squirt Holsomback. With a man on second and one out, Lindale's Shorty Smith looped one over third, but Holsy sprinted out and made the catch preventing the sure run.

With a two games to none lead, the series went to Lindale for game three. It took three pitchers for each team in the ten-inning contest that was finally called for darkness with the score tied at six. Hoyt Crowe, Ralph Stanfield, and Paul Fittery each hurled for the Champs, and Colon Sappenfield came off the bench to save the game for Carrollton offensively in the top of the ninth frame. In what would be his only at bat of the series, Sap lined one to the wall in left for a double driving in Bill McGhee and Cheese Goggans giving Carrollton a 6 to 5 lead. Lindale answered in the bottom of the ninth pushing the game into free baseball for the fans. Neither team scored in the tenth, and, upon the last out in the bottom of the inning, the umpires called the game due to darkness.

Now that four games had been played but only two counted toward the final series score, the series moved to Lindale for the Saturday game before the Sunday break. Paul Fittery took the mound and pitched his way to an easy 6 to 1 victory. He even added to his own run support by smashing one out for the round trip. Bob Ezzell hit his fourth long ball of the "Little World's Series," and Eddie Reese and Squirt Holsomback were the defensive stars with perfect fielding at short and third respectively.

Game six was played in Lindale on Monday, September 9, and the Champs demonstrated to all why they were the Champs. Red Justiss manned the mound for Carrollton and gave up nine scattered hits. Henry Patton drew three walks and hit a home run and two singles in six trips to the plate. Benny Freedman hit safely four times in five at bats, and Bob Ezzell made it five home runs for the series with a three runs shot in the third inning. The Champs won the game by a 10 to 2 final score.

Entire Team Played Sensational Ball in Play-off Ezzell Gets 5 Homers

While the whole Carrollton team played exceptionally well throughout the series not allowing a single defeat, Bob Ezzell was easily the Champs' most valuable player of the series. He batted .500 throughout and had a total of 33 bases in 26 at bats for a slugging percentage of 1.269.

CARROLLTON WINS PENNANT IN GA.-ALA. LEAGUE BY TAKING FOUR STRAIGHTS FROM LINDALE

The Georgia-Alabama League championship series took six games to play before Carrollton won it by a four games to none score. Undaunted throughout the series by the many anti-Carrollton forces, Paul Fittery led his outfit to their second consecutive league championship.

1930

League President: L.H. Carre
League Secretary: L.M. Carre
Team Operated by the Carrollton Baseball Club
Team President: A.W. "Andy" Ford
Secretary: Wiley Creel
Manager(s): Carl East, Erskine Thompson
Games played at City Athletic Field; seating capacity 3,250

Carrollton Champs Roster

Player	G	HR	AVG	POS	W	L	ERA
Alexander, Bill	85	5	.343	2B, SS, OF			
Bettison, ---	10	-		C			
Cain, Sugar	35	0	.283	P	8	10	4.80
Caldara, ---	1			P	0	1	18.00
Carter, Homer			.150	P			
Coker, E.R.			.265	SS			
Davenport, ---	10	-	.100				
Davis, Carl	10	-		P			
East, Carl			.453	M, OF			
Ezzell, Bob	84	20	.312	1B			
Finney, Lou	55	7	.388	OF			
Fisher, ---	19	1	.283	2B			
Gallivan, Phil	7			P	1	2	4.05
Goggans, G.E.	10	-		C			
Goode, ---	19	0	.184	SS			
Griffith, ---	19	1	.229	P	5	5	7.07
Hardwick, George	12	0	.333	P	3	5	6.46
Holcomb, Hot	2			P	1	1	7.71
Holsomback, Squirt	84	7	.301	3B			
Humphries, ---	10	-		P			
Justiss, Red			.288	P			
Lacey, ---	10	-		P			
Manning, ---	2			P	0	1	6.75
Martin, Amos	27	5	.333	2B, SS			
McGhee, Bill	19	2	.180	SS			
Milner, Holt	10	-					
Reese, Eddie			.255	SS			
Smith, Reuben	10	-		C			
Soward, Jim			.273	P			
Stanfield, Ralph			.324	P, OF			
Taylor, Zachery	55	4	.352	C			
Thompson, Erskine	28	0	.271	M, C			
Turk, ---	10	-	.118	C			
Turner, ---	10	-		P			
Wesley, ---	10	-					
White, Abe	10	-	.125	P			
White, H.	23	0	.261	2B, SS			

Georgia-Alabama League Final Standings

Team	W	L	Pct	GB	Affiliate
Lindale Pepperells	63	38	.624	----	Unaffiliated
Cedartown Braves	60	41	.594	3.0	Unaffiliated
Anniston Nobles	57	44	.564	6.0	Unaffiliated
Huntsville Springers	35	66	.347	28.0	Atlanta
Carrollton Champs	38	46	.452	N/A*	Unaffiliated
Talladega Indians	33	51	.393	N/A*	Unaffiliated

*Carrollton and Talladega both disbanded on August 14.

1930 Georgia-Alabama League Map

ROUNDING UP A NEW CHAMPIONSHIP CLUB

With two Georgia-Alabama League pennants flying in Carrollton, the fans were optimistic that a third was just a matter of time. Manager Paul Fittery, who led both of the championship teams to their many victories, was now the competition as he had taken a job as the manager of Anniston Nobles team. Former major leaguer Carl East was hired to manage the Champs in their quest for a third straight championship.

Manager East set out to build a winning team with many of the previous year's players returning. Pitchers Red Justiss and Abe White, outfielder Ralph Stanfield, infielders Squirt Holsomback and Bill Alexander, and the stalwart catcher Cheese Goggans formed a good foundation for East to build a new team upon. Numerous other players were vying for positions on the fourteen-player roster. Carrollton looked promising in pre-season exhibition games played against teams such as Oglethorpe College of Atlanta, the Meritas Mill team of Columbus, Tubby Walton's Firecrackers of Atlanta, the Woco-Pep team of Atlanta, and Bud Harris' Bowdon College team of Bowdon. These games were often used as auditions for new talent since the outcomes were not pertinent to league standings.

Georgia-Alabama League Opens Friday, May 9th

Good news came to Carrollton baseball fans with a week left before the opening game of the season. First baseman Bob Ezzell, who hit five home runs in the 1929 league championship series for Carrollton, had been acquired to play for the Champs once again. Ezzell, who was playing pre-season games with Macon of the class-B South Atlantic League, injured his arm and wasn't going to see much action in that league. So Carrollton seized the opportunity and outright purchased Ezzell's contract for the 1930 season.

Mayor Luck's Proclamation

Desiring to contribute in every way to the development of our city and as an evidence of our civic pride, I as Mayor, bmy virtue of authority vested in me, hereby declare Friday afternoon, May 9th, a public holiday and urge all business men and others to close their places of business in order that they themselves and their employes may attend and witness the opening game of the baseball season in our town.

Witness my hand and official seal this the 8th day of May, 1930, and the 101st year of our city.

T. R. LUCK
Mayor of Carrollton.

The opening day attendance trophy was held in high regard among cities in the circuit, and Carrollton had narrowly missed winning it every year. In great efforts to have the largest crowd in the league for the home opener, Carrollton Mayor T.R. Luck proclaimed a half-holiday for Friday, May 9, so that more fans could attend the game. Stores were ordered closed at 2:00 p.m. so that fans could attend the 3:00 game at the City Athletic Field.

Carrollton Wins Georgia-Alabama Attendance Cup

Fans packed the stands enough to give Carrollton the honor of the largest opening day attendance. The Champs, much obliged by this gesture, gave the fans their money's worth by defeating Lindale 6 to 3. Red Justiss pitched for Carrollton and allowed only nine scattered hits, while manager Carl East had the big bat with a solo home run in the seventh. The Pepperells felt even more charitable in the bottom of the eighth inning when they gave Carrollton a run on three errors without a hit.

By the end of the first week of the season, Cedartown was in first place with five wins and two losses, Carrollton held second with a three and two record, Lindale was next with an even mark of two and two, Anniston and Talladega were tied in the fourth spot with two victories and three defeats each, and Huntsville, the new team in the league replacing Gadsden, brought up the rear with a two and four record.

On May 15, G.E. "Cheese" Goggans was sold to Anniston, and rookie Zachery Taylor was made the new catcher for the Champs. Goggans served Carrollton well in 1928 and 1929 as the cornerstone of the team, but his salary demands were out of reach for Carrollton, and he was let go.

In a great pitchers' dual, Anniston's Paul Fittery came back to his old stomping ground to face Carrollton's Abe White. Fittery, the ex-major leaguer, schooled White, the young up and comer, and won the game 3 to 1. While Carrollton garnered nine hits and Anniston only got seven, it was the timing of the hits that scored the runs. White struck out eleven Nobles batters in the game but was not a cool as Fittery when base runners were aboard.

The rumor mill was hard at work with word that the class-A Atlanta Crackers of the Southern Association would soon be taking over the Huntsville Springers club. This was a violation of the Georgia-Alabama League rules as all teams were not to have "official" ties to any higher-class baseball clubs. On Tuesday, May 27, the Springers showed up in Carrollton with Tubby Walton acting as the business manager of the new Huntsville "Junior Crackers" signifying that the acquisition had taken place. Huntsville now had on their roster several players who had previously been in the Atlanta lineup which violated the class-man limitation rule. Completely undaunted, the Champs proceeded to hand Huntsville their hats with a 16 to 1 routing placed inside. Merritt "Sugar" Cain pitched mercilessly for Carrollton and allowed the lone Huntsville tally in the eighth as a humanitarian act. The Carrollton bats were hot with seventeen total hits including nine doubles and a three-run homer by skipper Carl East.

MONDAY WILL BE BIG DAY IN CARROLLTON— PENNANT RAISED—ATTENDANCE TROPHY AWARDED

June 2 was the day of trophy presentation at the Carrollton ball yard. Georgia-Alabama League president L.H. Carre was on hand to present Carrollton with the attendance trophy for having the largest number of fans in the stands for the opening day game. Carre continued the ceremonies with the presentation of the 1929 championship pennant that the Champs won in the previous season. It was only fitting that Lindale was the visiting team for this game as they were the ones on the losing end of the 1929 championship series.

After the presentation of the awards to the Carrollton club, the game was presented back and forth to one another by each team. Lindale took the lead with two runs scored in the top of the first. Carrollton tied it in the bottom of the second, and went ahead by one in the bottom of the third. Lindale scored one in the top of the fourth tying it at three runs each and went ahead by two in the top of the fifth. The Pepperells scored one more in the top of the sixth to make it 6 to 3, but the Champs broke out with seven tallies in the bottom of the same inning. Not to be outdone, the visitors scored one more in the eighth and three more in their half of the ninth to tie the game. Carrollton finally took the game in the bottom of the tenth frame as Jim Soward doubled to center field with two outs driving Squirt Holsomback home from second.

At the end of four weeks of play, Cedartown was in first place in the standings with fifteen wins and six losses. Carrollton, eleven and nine, was in second by three and a half games. Huntsville took third with ten victories and eleven defeats, and Lindale was a half game behind them with nine wins and eleven losses. Fifth place was held by Anniston with a nine and twelve record, and Talladega was riding in the caboose with eight in the win column and thirteen in the loss.

Manager Carl East sustained a side-lining injury on June 23 in a game at Lindale. He was hit in the head with the ball during a double play by Lindale short stop Frank Costa. East was taken to a medical clinic in Carrollton and would have to sit out at least until the end of the season's first half.

By the last week of June with only one more week to go in the first half, it looked like the Champs would make another run at the first half pennant. The Sea Cows of

Cedartown still led the league, but Carrollton was hot on their heals only one game back. Anniston was only a game and a half behind Carrollton while Lindale, Talladega, and Huntsville came in order to round out the standings. Without East's big bat in the lineup, the Champs really had their work cut out if the first half title was to be claimed.

CEDARS VICTORS IN FIRST HALF

After four games with Anniston, the Champs slipped to third place. And following the July 4th Independence Day double headers to end the first half of the season, Carrollton found themselves in a tie for third with Lindale. It was Cedartown coming out on top to claim the first half flag and the assured spot in the post-season, league championship series. The Sea Cows sported a record of thirty-one wins and seventeen losses for act one followed by Anniston by five games with twenty-seven victories and twenty-three defeats. Lindale and Carrollton both had twenty-five and twenty-three records for third place, and Talladega came next with nineteen wins and thirty losses. Huntsville brought up the rear only a half game behind Talladega and thirteen games behind first place Cedartown with a eighteen in the win column and thirty in the loss. Rosters now had to be trimmed from fourteen players to twelve for the second half of the Georgia-Alabama League season.

TALLEDEGA OPENS SECOND HALF HERE

The second half of the season got under way on the Cedartown diamond as the Champs dropped three straight to the first half winners. The first game on Monday, July 7 was a barn-burner ending in a final of 19 to 16. Only one run won each of the other two games of the set, and now Carrollton would go home to host Talladega in the second half home opener.

From the cellar, the Champs took two out of three from the Indians. And by the middle of the second week, Carrollton had moved up to fourth place in the standings.

Numerous roster changes came early on in the second half of the split season. Young catcher, Zach Taylor was sold to the Birmingham Barons club of the class-A Southern Association. Taylor was replaced by Reuben Smith of LaGrange, but Smith lasted less than ten games with the Champs. Erskine Thompson, formerly of Oglethorpe College and the Atlanta Crackers was acquired to be on the receiving end of the Carrollton battery and to serve as manager of the club. Carl East tendered his resignation when he realized that he would not be able to recover from his head injury as quickly as previously believed. East, a Carrollton resident at the time, pledged to do all he could to help the club. Amos Martin, another Oglethorpe alumnus, was hired to play infield for the Champs. Squirt Holsomback, who was playing well above the standard of class-D baseball at third, was purchased by the Atlanta Crackers

but would not report until the end of the season. The pitching rotation was now comprised of Jim Soward, Abe White, Red Justiss, and Sugar Cain.

In the last week of July, outfielder Lou Finney and pitcher Sugar Cain were purchased by Connie Mack and the Philadelphia Athletics of the American League. Both players, like Holsomback, would stay with the Champs until the end of the season, then report to a higher classification of ball.

LEAGUE STANDING
(Thru Aug. 4th)

	Won	Lost	Pct.
Lindale	20	5	.800
Anniston	14	8	.636
Cedartown	14	11	.650
Carrollton	10	15	.400
Talledega	9	15	.375
Huntsville	5	18	.217

By the end of the first week of August, the Lindale team had taken a commanding lead of the league for the second half. Anniston was second by a four and a half game margin, and Cedartown was third by a margin of six games from first place. Carrollton held fourth place four games behind Cedartown, and Talladega was only a half game behind Carrollton. Huntsville had the final position in the standings three and a half games in back of Carrollton and fourteen games out of first place.

Carrollton May Withdraw From Ga-Ala. League

On August 14, a storm that had been mildly brewing gathered strength quickly and finally came to a head. Earlier in the season, Lindale was found to have been playing and ineligible class man by the name of Red Sanders. Upon learning this, league president Carre ruled that the four games Sanders had played in would be forfeited by Lindale and awarded to the opponent of each game. Now it was learned that Huntsville was playing a class man named Watson, and Anniston had a class man called Sidwell. Furthermore, Lindale was again breaking the rule by playing an outfielder by the name of Doc Land. Lindale contended that Land was not a class man and that everyone had him confused with his brother who also had the nickname "Doc." In the 1929 season, Carrollton had to give up six games won because Hoke Nettles, a class man, was found to be in the lineup. It was suggested that the same punishment be handed down in these most recent infractions to Huntsville, Anniston, and Lindale. At a meeting of the league directorate and president Carre, the phrase "that would break up the league!" was heard multiple times from the mouths the rule violators of late. Bowing to these strong words, president Carre ruled as follows: "No games will be forfeited (the previous forfeits against Lindale being rescinded), but the teams will have to rid themselves of these class men, and it is distinctly understood in the future that should any team in the league be found to be using an ineligible class man, the games will be forfeited without any question and without any equivocation."

Carre's decision was made to try to keep the league together, but Carrollton and Talladega would not stand for such injustice. Upon hearing the statement at the meeting, both teams immediately withdrew from the league and declared all players on their rosters free agents with the exception of those who were previously purchased by other clubs. Carrollton and Talladega both went on record stating financial difficulties as the reason for their withdrawal.

Talladega held fourth place upon their resignation with twelve wins and nineteen losses. Carrollton was a half game behind them in fifth with a twelve and twenty record. The remaining four teams rearranged the league schedule for the final weeks of the season, and many players from the defunct teams were picked up to play for one of the four teams left.

Lindale went on to win the second half of the season and faced Cedartown in the league championship series. Cedartown, the lone club not using ineligible class players, took the series four games to three. It took eight games to determine a winner as game one was called at a tie for darkness.

President Carre solicited LaGrange and Gadsden to be in the league in the 1931 season to replace Carrollton and Talladega. Neither city accepted, and the Georgia-Alabama League in turn disbanded before the 1931 season materialized. Carre was caught between a rock and a hard place with the class man accusations. If he had ruled against the teams using the ineligible players, they would have possibly withdrawn from the league. Instead, he ruled in favor of the ineligible player using teams causing two honest teams to quit. It was inevitable that the Georgia-Alabama League would break apart no matter how Carre ruled on the ineligible class man scandal.

1931-1945

With the hardships of the Great Depression came the lack of resources to support a baseball team in Carrollton. Most of the area cities that had teams in prior years decided not to play baseball in 1931, and Carrollton was no exception. Many began to realize that baseball might be an oasis in the quagmire of America's sunken morale, and the sport slowly began to make its way back to life.

An upstart team by the name of the Sharp's Lake Bulldogs came into being in 1932 to represent Carrollton on the diamond. "Memphis Bill" Sharp was the star pitcher for the team that played in a loose circuit consisting of eight teams. The other teams in the industrial/semi-pro baseball loop were Villa Rica Mills, the Athletics, Roopville, Buck Creek, Burwell, the Carrot Tops, and the Pineknots. Phil Astin also starred on the mound for the Bulldogs who virtually dominated the other teams of the aggregation.

The Sharp's Lake Bulldogs organized again in 1933 and played in an independent circuit called the Tri-County League. Now resembling more of the industrial league genre, common of the day, than in the previous year, the Tri-County League consisted of six clubs which included Sharp's Lake of Carrollton, Villa Rica Mills, Douglasville, Bremen, Tallapoosa, and Mandeville Mills, also of Carrollton. Tallapoosa dropped out, and Roopville came in to fill the vacancy very early in the summer. Douglasville also dropped out of the league half way through the season but

was not replaced. All games played against them were awarded to their opponents as victories causing Roopville to take first place over Sharp's Lake in the final league standings.

Carrollton, having had two teams represent the city in 1933 with Sharp's Lake and Mandeville Mills, joined the independent West Georgia League in 1934. The league, in its second year of operation, was a six-team loop with teams from Villa Rica, Douglasville, Clarksdale, Buford, Bowdon, and Carrollton. For the first time, the city's team went by the nickname "Hornets" that would later become quite familiar to local baseball fans. The Hornets finished the season in third place behind Villa Rica and Douglasville. Villa Rica won the league championship series over Douglasville. Carrollton was led by manager Ed Copeland, who also played outfield, and pitcher Theron "Tommie" Tomasello of Oglethorpe University won eighteen games and lost none during the season for the Hornets.

Another independent league with commonly known name was organized in 1935. The Georgia-Alabama League, no relation to the league of 1928-30, came into being when Carrollton, Bowdon, Villa Rica, Buchanan, Tallapoosa, Bremen, Mandeville Mills (another Carrollton team) and Heflin got together to form their own semi-pro circuit. Heflin, being the only Alabama city in the loop, provided the second half of the league's name. Carrollton went by the moniker "Hornets" again, and was led by manager Lester Reeves. Reeves, who played on the 1934 Hornets squad, led the team to the first half of the season pennant. Mandeville Mills won the second half of the split season, thus the stage for an all-Carrollton league championship series was set. Carrollton won the final series that was greatly overshadowed by the local Junior American Legion baseball team, the Carrollton Farmers. The Farmers were tearing their way through any and all opponents in 1935 and became national champions of all Junior American Legion baseball teams. Charles "Red" Roberts starred in the infield for the Farmers, and he played briefly for the Hornets late in the season. Roberts was well on his way to becoming a baseball icon in the city of Carrollton.

In 1936, an independent, traveling team was organized to represent Carrollton at the ball yard, but only two games were played as most of the other teams in the area were involved in a regular league. A large percentage of area baseball fans were more interested in watching the Carrollton Farmers American Legion team go for another national title than any other team the city could provide. As a good-will gesture, the independent Carrollton team loaned their newly purchased uniforms to the Farmers to wear in the national Junior American Legion tournament.

For the next two years, the American Legion team dominated the spotlight on the Carrollton baseball diamond. No team was organized to represent the city in any other fashion in 1937 and 1938. The Farmers continued to play extremely well, but they never could go quite as far as the national championship team of 1935.

An industrial league known as the Northwest Georgia League sprouted up in 1939. The new circuit was made up of Caroline Mills of Carrollton, Temple, Villa Rica, Villa Rica CCC, Whitesburg, Banning, and Buchanan. Carrollton and Villa Rica CCC finished first and second in the regular season and met in the post-season league championship series. Villa Rica CCC won the series three games to none with the final game being a 14 to 6 waxing. Although Carrollton had a good team, much of the baseball attention in the city was paid again to the Carrollton Farmers American Legion team.

No baseball club was put together in Carrollton in 1940 and 1941. The main diamond entertainment in the city was the American Legion team that continued to provide fans with quite a good brand of baseball.

After the Japanese attack on Pearl Harbor on December 7, 1941, baseball was one of the last things on the minds of the citizens. War was declared on Japan the very next day bringing the United States into World War II, and baseball would be put on hold until after the end of the war on September 2, 1945.

1946

League Presidents: Carl W. East, Cliff Hall
Team Operated by Carrollton Baseball Club, Inc
Team President: Harvey J. Copeland
Secretary: Earl Stoples
Treasurers: Harvey J. Copeland and Earl Stoples
Manager(s): Luther Gunnells
Games played at City Athletic Field; seating capacity 3,250

Carrollton Hornets Roster

Player	G	HR	RBI	AVG	POS	W	L	ERA
Barkley, ---	4				P	2	1	
Bieser, Fred	24	1	6	.111	OF			
Borders, Aubrey	29	0	7	.267	P	7	6	3.82
(includes Newnan stats)								
Bosser, Mel	4				P	1	2	
Brock, Paul	12	0	7	.333	P	10	2	3.46
Cain, George	7				P	1	1	
Childs, Frank	39	0	11	.178	P, OF	0	3	
Colter, ---	1				P	0	0	
Condit, ---	18	0	1	.167	P	8	7	3.02
(includes Opelika stats)								
Crowson, Marv	6				P	3	1	
Dean, Harry	2				P	1	0	
Farr, Curtis	10-							
Fincher, Bob	10	1	4	.242				
Flowers, Burnice	10-							
Fraker, Dick	38	0	9	.263	OF			
Garner, Bob	67	12	35	.281	P, OF	3	4	6.10
Gulliver, Clark	90	1	20	.201	OF, P	0	0	
Gunnells, Luther	117	24	96	.381	M, SS, P	0	1	
Gurdy, ---	1				P	0	0	
Guyton, ---	24	0	6	.174	3B			
Hill, Jim	121	0	50	.257	C			
Hurley, ---	1				P	0	0	
Israel, Bill	30	0	5	.242	P	12	8	3.96
Kirschner, George	1				P	0	0	
Langley, Jim	19	0	10	.250	1B			
Little, Walt	2				P	1	1	
Marshall, Shorty	128	8	54	.273	2B			
Matthews, Bob	35	0	3	.107	P	16	13	6.88
Milo, ---	10-							
Oglesby, Hugh	26	1	5	.149	OF			
Patterson, Bill	10-							
Pittman, Al	12	0	0	.125	P	4	4	4.43
Reed, Jim	8				P	0	5	
(includes LaGrange stats)								
Roberts, Red	67	3	37	.308	3B, SS			
Robison, Roy	10-							
Seigler, Bill	26	0	5	.220	P	4	4	5.34
Shivers, ---	10-							
Snider, Floyd	38	3	16	.221	OF			
(includes Newnan stats)								
Souter, George	58	5	37	.321	3B, OF, P	1	2	
Spencer, Bill	1				P	0	0	
Sprayberry, Jim	2				P	0	0	
(includes Valley stats)								
Steel, ---	1				P	0	0	
Stoyle, Jim	90	7	83	.351	1B			
Terry, Horace	10-							
Thomas, Dallas	16	0	9	.254	OF			
Westbrook, John	16	0	1	.057	P	6	7	2.51
(includes Tallassee stats)								
Williams, Paul	39	0	14	.261	3B			
Yearty, Sam	6				P	1	0	
York, Lew	121	19	84	.302	1B, OF, P	0	0	

Georgia-Alabama League Final Standings

Team	W	L	Pct	GB	Affiliate
Carrollton Hornets	75	55	.577	----	Unaffiliated
Valley Rebels	72	58	.554	3.0	Unaffiliated
Tallassee Indians	71	59	.546	4.0	Pittsburgh
Newnan Brownies	68	62	.523	7.0	Unaffiliated
LaGrange Troupers	59	71	.454	16.0	Unaffiliated
Opelika Owls	45	85	.346	30.0	Unaffiliated

1946 Georgia-Alabama League Map

The Georgia-Alabama League made its way back to existence in 1946 following World War II. With the golden age of baseball and the baby-boom era taking shape, cities all over were eager to take part in America's favorite past time. Even the infamous ineligible class man scandal that broke up the league at the end of the 1930 season could not deter organizers from bringing back the west Georgia, east Alabama based circuit.

Former Carrollton manager Carl East from the 1930 season was named as president of the new and improved Georgia-Alabama League. The three teams from Georgia in the six team league were Carrollton, Newnan, and LaGrange, while Valley (Lanett), Tallassee, and Opelika made up the three Alabama clubs.

Former Atlanta Cracker and baseball veteran Luther Gunnells was chosen to manage and play shortstop for the Carrollton ball club that was now going by the moniker "Hornets." Getting prepared for the upcoming season, manager Gunnells auditioned players in exhibition games against teams such as the Dixie Cotton Mill of LaGrange, Silvertown of Thomaston, and the Yellow Cab team of Atlanta. Murray "Red" Howell, who played for Carrollton on the 1928 team, played first base for the Yellow Cab club. Gunnells would have to trim the club down to nineteen players before the season opener on Friday, April 26 when the Newnan Browns were coming to town.

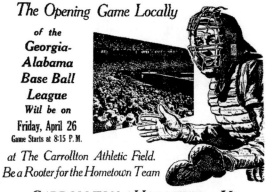

The Opening Game Locally

of the
Georgia-Alabama Base Ball League
Will be on
Friday, April 26
Game Starts at 8:15 P.M.

at The Carrollton Athletic Field.
Be a Rooter for the Hometown Team

CARROLLTON "HORNETS" VS THE NEWNAN "BROWNS" under powerful lights

On opening day, under the lights of the City Athletic Field in Carrollton, the Hornets hosted the Newnan Browns. Manager Gunnells sent veteran right-hander Bob Garner to the mound to do the pitching for the Hornets. Each team scored one run in the fourth, and great defense was played all around. In the eighth frame, Newnan scored four runs while Carrollton manufactured three on two hits, a walk, and an error. Down by one, the Hornets started to stage a rally, but it was quickly snuffed out by the Browns ending the game at 5 to 4 in favor of Newnan. The other two opening games in the league, Valley at LaGrange and Tallassee at Opelika, were called rained out.

At the end of the first week of the season, Opelika held the top spot in the standings with three wins and one loss. Carrollton, Newnan, and Tallassee were tied for second each with a three and two record. LaGrange was next with one win and three losses, and Valley took last place with a single victory and four defeats.

CHARLEY ROBERTS SIGNS WITH LOCALS

Charles "Red" Roberts, Carrollton's only native to ever play major league baseball, signed a contract to play for his hometown Hornets in the first week of May. Roberts played briefly for the Washington Senators in 1943 and had most recently played for the Louisville Colonels of the class-AA American Association before being hired by the Hornets.

The Carrollton team won all five ball games played in the second week of the season putting them in first place in the league standings. Defeating Tallassee twice and Opelika, Newnan, and LaGrange once each, the Hornets now boasted a record of eight wins and two losses.

"Shorty" Marshall And Stoyle Lead Carrollton Hitting

Four wins and one loss in week three of the season moved Carrollton even further into first place. Second baseman Shorty Marshall and first baseman Jim Stoyle were leading the team in hitting each with a .382 average. Lew York was not far behind with an average of .360. Pitcher Bob "Buck" Mathews had a record of two wins and no losses, and Bob Garner and Bill Seigler each had records of two and one from the mound.

"Buck" Matthews Does An Iron Man Stunt. Wins Two

On May 22, Buck Mathews pitched and won both sides of a double header at the Newnan ball yard. The Browns got only four hits off Mathews in game one that ended in a score of 3 to 1. Eight hits were surrendered by Buck in the second game of the night which the Hornets won narrowly 5 to 4.

After a full month of baseball in the 1946 season, Carrollton still held a fast lead over the rest of the league. With a record of twenty-four wins and nine losses, Carrollton was three and a half games ahead of second place Valley who had a twenty and twelve mark. Newnan was in a distant third with fourteen victories and seventeen defeats, and Opelika had the fourth position with eleven wins and sixteen losses. Tallassee was only a half game behind Opelika with eleven in the win column and seventeen in the loss, and LaGrange had sunken to the bottom winning only nine games in twenty-six games played.

Buck Mathews won his tenth game of the year on June 3 against the Tallassee Indians. Mathews' perfect 10-0 record was supported thus far by outstanding hitting of the Hornets. Six players were batting over .300 with manager Luther Gunnells leading the pack at .319.

Marriage on Field To Take Place on Saturday

Carrollton pitcher Bill Seigler married Miss Mildred Bradley of Augusta on the City Athletic Field pitchers mound before the game on Saturday, June 8. A capacity crowd packed the stands to witness the ceremony that was followed by Valley defeating the Hornets 8 to 2. Fortunately, the groom was not scheduled to pitch.

The Hornets held a four and a half game lead over the Valley Rebels in mid-June. By July 4, the lead was cut down to one game with Carrollton still slimly holding first place. Good baseball was being played by Carrollton, but better baseball was the brand of the Valley

Rebels. The lead the Hornets took early in the season was slowly being closed in upon.

During the same course of time between Flag Day and Independence Day, Gunnells' boosted his batting average from .325 to a second in the league .349. Jake Daniel, manager and first baseman for LaGrange and former Brooklyn Dodger, was leading the league with a .356 average. Jim Stoyle and Bob Garner were both also above the .300 batting mark for the Hornets with averages of .332 and .300 respectively.

Three Hornets Are Put On Newnan Herald All-Star League Team

Pitcher Bob Matthews, shortstop Luther Gunnells, and outfielder Lew York were all three named to the Newnan Herald newspaper's Georgia-Alabama League All-Star team. Matthews, who started the season winning eleven straight pitching starts, was the only player in the league to receive a unanimous nod from all in the electing body. Shorty Marshall was also named to the team as a utility player.

At the end of the second week of July, Carrollton was tied at the top of the league standings with Valley, both teams with forty-three wins and thirty losses. By the end of week three of the month, Valley took a half game lead and extended their lead over Carrollton to two games by week four. While manager Gunnells and the rest of team strove for the top spot, the Hornets only needed to be one of the top four teams in the league at the end of the

regular season to make the post-season, Shaughnessy-style playoffs.

Shaughnessy Playoff System

Prior to the 1930's, many minor league baseball leagues conducted no post-season championship series. The team with the best record at the end of the season was simply crowned champion of the league. Those that did have post-season play usually held a series between the winner of the first half of the season and the winner of the second half. Many teams suffered financially from lack of attendance during the final weeks of the seasons when it became apparent that the team would not be in contention for the post-season championship series. Frank "Shag" Shaughnessy, a former major league player and minor league player and manager, devised a system where more teams would have a chance of playing in the post-season and a chance of being the champion of the league. In the Shaughnessy system, the top four teams in the league standings at the end of the season advance to the playoffs. Usually, in the first round, the first place and the fourth place teams play each other in a best of five games series as do the second and third place teams. The winners of these two series meet to play a best of seven games series to determine the champion of the league. There were variations of which places played which and the number of games played in each series, but the concept remained the same. This system helped keep attendance and interest high as it gave more teams a chance to play in the coveted post-season games. Better attendance through the end of the season saved many teams from financial ruin.

LEAGUE PRESIDENT GIVES FANS WARNING ON BASEBALL BETTING

A warning against betting among fans was given by the National Association of Minor League Baseball president Judge

William G. Bramham. Wagers on anything from game scores to fly balls to pitches were being placed in the stands all around the league, and the high president called for it to stop immediately. Fans found in violation of the policy would be turned over to local authorities and prosecuted fully.

Cliff Hall of Carrollton was elected as the new president of the Georgia-Alabama League following the departure of Carl East from the position. Hall expressed that the final month of the season would test the endurance of the league. He urged fans to behave themselves in a sporting manner at games if they wanted to have a team and a league in the following season. The squabbles between fans and players of other teams and umpires coupled with the gambling problems would not be tolerated by organized baseball, Hall warned. Major league and higher minor league teams would not tolerate such behavior in class-D leagues and would consider disbanding them if these activities continued.

Hard-hitting first baseman Jim Stoyle was sold to the Montgomery Rebels of the class-B Southeastern League. He was still playing with Carrollton but on a twenty-four hour recall condition. The Hornets hoped to keep Stoyle as long as possible, but Montgomery decided to call him up immediately. His big bat was going to be missed in the stretch for another pennant at the City Athletic Field.

STANDINGS
(Including games through August 14)

	W	L	Pct.
Valley	64	44	.593
CARROLLTON	62	52	.544
Tallassee	59	53	.527
Newnan	55	53	.509
LaGrange	51	61	.455
Opelika	41	69	.369

Carrollton retook the lead in the first week of August, but Valley came right back the next week extending their lead to a wide five-game gap over Carrollton. The mid-August standings served as an early indicator that the playoff bound teams would most likely be Valley, Carrollton, Tallassee, and Newnan in order.

Gunnells And Hill On All-Star Team

The National Press Bureau announced its All-Star team of the Georgia-Alabama League naming Luther Gunnells and Jim Hill to the elite squad. Other Hornets Shorty Marshall, Lew York, Aubrey Borders, and Bill Seigler received honorable mention in the team selection.

Between August 14 and 21, Carrollton went from being five games behind Valley to being three games ahead. The Hornets went on a seven game winning streak during the week, and the Rebels dropped all seven games played. Ironically, the two teams did not play each other in the drastic turn of events. Unless another amazing win-loss streak coupling occurred with each team on the reverse end, Carrollton would easily coast into the top seed of the post-season playoffs.

Carrollton Wins Flag By Defeating Opelika

On Wednesday, August 28, the Hornets solidified their first place finish in the league standings with a 13 to 7 victory over the last place Opelika Owls. Carrollton surrendered four runs in the first inning at the Hornets nest, but the Owl pitching was easily feasted upon throughout the rest of the game. With five games left in the regular season, Carrollton could lose them all and still hold first place over Valley.

The first round of the Shaughnessy style playoffs were set to start on Monday, September 2 with Carrollton hosting whichever team came out in third place at the season's end. Five games would be played until one team had won three to advance to the championship series. The second and fourth place teams would also meet in a five game set. Then, the final series, also consisting of five games, would be played between the two winners of the first round series'.

Final Standings of Clubs In Ga.-Ala. League

	W	L	Pct.
Carrollton	75	55	.577
Valley	71	59	.546
Tallassee	71	59	.546
Newnan	70	60	.538
LaGrange	60	70	.462
Opelika	44	86	.338

At the end of the regular season, the figures in the standings initially reported were slightly mistaken. Once corrected,

Carrollton, who won twenty-three of their last twenty-eight games, held first place with a record of seventy-five wins and fifty-five losses. Valley was in second place with a seventy-two and fifty-eight record three games behind the Hornets. Third place was held by Tallassee with seventy-one victories and fifty-nine defeats, and Newnan came out in fourth with a sixty-eight and sixty-two mark. LaGrange was fifth with a fifty-nine and seventy-one record, and Opelika was in the back of the pack thirty games out of first place with forty-five in the win column and eighty-five in the loss. Carrollton was scheduled to play Tallassee in the first round of post-season action, and Valley was slated to take on Newnan.

Manager Luther Gunnells took the league batting title with a .373 average. Woodrow Bottoms of Newnan had an average of .405 but had not played in the necessary two-thirds of games scheduled during the season to be in consideration for the award. Jake Daniels, Gunnells' main competition in hitting during the season, came in second with a score of .355.

Carrollton Wins First Series Playoff Game

The Hornets took the first game of the five game series against the Indians by a 9 to 6 final. Manager Gunnells sent pitching ace Paul Brock to the mound to do the hurling hoping to get the early series lead. Carrollton batters swatted four home runs in the game including two by Red Roberts and one each by Shorty Marshall and Floyd Snider. All nine Carrollton runs were scored off of starting Tallassee pitcher Woodford Parks in the first three and one third innings. Brock gave up twelve hits on the mound but was able to hold the visitors to six runs. Having more rest than usual between starts prior to this game, Brock's arm was tight throughout the game preventing him from pitching as well as he had been during the regular season. The two teams would now travel to Tallassee for game two.

The second game of the first round series was won by Tallassee on their home diamond. Game three was won by the Hornets, and game four was again taken by the Indians. With the series now tied at two games each, the fifth and final game would be played at Carrollton's City Athletic Field.

Hornets Lose Final Game, 6-5, In Heartbreaking Finish

With the chance for advancement to the league championship series on the line, Tallassee jumped out to an early lead. Carrollton chased after the lead the whole game but was never able to come up with enough offense to overtake. Opportunity came knocking on the Hornets' door in the bottom of the ninth inning with the score 6 to 5 in favor of the Indians. Dick Fraker led off with a walk and was followed by Red Roberts. Carrollton native Roberts hit a long ball toward the fence that would either be a home run or at least fall in for a double. But Tallassee center fielder Walt Posey ran with winged sandals on his feet and

caught the ball against the wall. Fraker, thinking the ball would never be caught, was not able to return to first base before the throw to the bag and was doubled off for the second out. Posey's circus catch saved the game and the series for the visitors as George Souter made the third out on a sharp grounder to short. Tallassee took the series three games to two and would now advance to the league championship.

On the other side of round one of the Shaughnessy playoffs, Newnan and Valley went the distance before Newnan finally emerged victorious three games to two. Tallassee and Newnan met for the league championship five-game series which was won by Tallassee three games to two. Both semi-final series and the championship series appeared to be very evenly matched as all series went the maximum number of games.

The Shaughnessy system, which was new to most Carrollton fans, received harsh criticism. Carrollton won the regular season pennant having the best record at the end of the schedule but only finished third in the post-season playoffs. Tallassee, on the other hand, finished third in the regular season but was crowned league champion because they won the games that counted the most in the Shaughnessy system. Most fans consoled themselves by saying, "Just wait 'til next year!"

1947

League President: Arthur R. Decatur
Team Operated by Carrollton Baseball Club, Inc
Team President: Harvey J. Copeland
Vice-President / Secretary-Treasurer: R.E. Muse
Manager(s): Paul Crain, Charles "Red" Roberts
Games played at City Athletic Field; seating capacity 3,250
Total Regular Season Attendance: 52,245

Carrollton Hornets Roster

Player	G	HR	RBI	AVG	POS	W	L	ERA
Alexander, Bill	16	0	5	.125	P	3	4	5.42
(includes Griffin stats)								
Allen, John	83	1	23	.242	2B, OF			
Bozzuto, Bert	26	0	3	.113	P	10	6	3.09
Collins, Lee	47	1	22	.201	OF			
Crain, Paul	41	0	10	.205	M, P	19	14	2.93
(includes Valley stats)								
Dendinger, Jacob	23	2	12	.260	OF			
DiMasi, Joe	17	1	12	.246	OF			
Ello, Jim	89	1	30	.224	C			
(includes Griffin stats)								
Goicoechea, Leo	12	0	3	.160	P	5	2	3.46
Hill, Jim	90	0	47	.295	C			
Jones, Bill	70	0	27	.276	P	14	11	
(includes Newnan stats)								
Kelly, Dick	122	9	84	.303	3B			
Langley, Jim	89	18	64	.277	1B			
Little, Walt	10	0	1	.129	P	7	3	3.60
Marshall, Shorty	121	7	76	.330	2B, SS			
Matthews, Bob	40	0	3	.182	P	16	11	2.54
(includes Newnan stats)								
Monarchi, Pete	70	5	44	.270	2B, OF			
Murphee, Bill	39	1	15	.277	1B			
Padgett, Charles	17	0	5	.162	SS			
Patterson, Bill	81	3	30	.249	C, OF			
Roberts, Red	97	11	72	.385	M, SS, 3B			
Singley, Hulen	17	0	2	.091	P	9	4	4.45
Smith, ---					P	3	2	
Snider, Floyd	124	21	102	.307	OF			
Thomas, Dallas	107	11	72	.284	OF			
Tilley, Travis	28	0	7	.244	OF			
(includes LaGrange stats)								
Webb, Bill	31	2	16	.406	P	22	5	2.40

Georgia-Alabama League Final Standings

Team	W	L	Pct	GB	Affiliate
Carrollton Hornets	75	49	.605	----	Unaffiliated
Opelika Owls	76	50	.603	----	Unaffiliated
Valley Rebels	75	51	.595	1.0	Unaffiliated
Newnan Brownies	72	53	.576	3.5	Unaffiliated
Tallassee Indians	62	63	.496	13.5	Unaffiliated
Griffin Pimientos	53	68	.438	20.5	Unaffiliated
LaGrange Troupers	46	78	.371	29.0	Unaffiliated
Alexander City Millers	39	86	.312	36.5	Unaffiliated

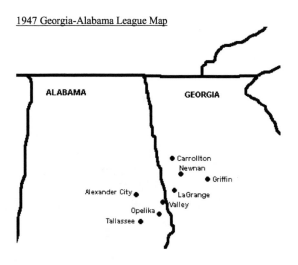

1947 Georgia-Alabama League Map

Dispute on Sunday Ball Here Grows

During the developmental stages of the 1947 Georgia-Alabama League schedule, a dispute arose among Carrollton fans on the issue of Sunday baseball games. In prior years, games were not played on Sundays in Carrollton. Under pressure of numerous citizens opposed to having games on the Sabbath, the Carrollton club notified the league directors that the thirteen games originally scheduled to be played in Carrollton on Sundays would have to be changed. These games were rescheduled to be played either on Saturday night or in an Alabama city in the league as Sunday baseball was not considered taboo in that state. The Griffin club decided to not have baseball in their city on Sundays either but instead move their Sunday games to the neutral, non-league city of Thomaston.

The 1947 Georgia-Alabama League was notably larger than the previous year. Comprised of six teams in the 1946 season, the league had now grown to eight clubs with Griffin, Georgia and Alexander City, Alabama joining the same six clubs that made up the league in the previous year.

Paul Crain, a pitcher for the class-AA Atlanta Crackers in 1946, was chosen to lead the Hornets into battle as manager for the 1947 season. Manager Crain worked to get his bunch into shape for the season in exhibition games against teams such as the famous, bearded House of David traveling team and the Cuban All-Star team.

Ga.-Ala. League To Open April 23; Hornets Play Here

With the newly rewritten schedule now ready to go, the 1947 season finally got under way. On Wednesday, April 23, pitcher Bill Webb led the Hornets to win number one in the opening game against the Alexander City Millers. At the City Athletic Field, the home field for Carrollton, Webb struck out twelve Miller batters and allowed only four hits. The Hornets' offensive efforts landed them only three hits, but Alexander City pitcher Ed Chitwood walked in the winning run in

the seventh inning to give Carrollton the 3 to 2 win.

Through the first week of the season, Carrollton was standing in an honorable third place in the league. Opelika was first followed by Valley. Newnan Tallassee, LaGrange, Alexander City, and Griffin were behind Carrollton in order to round out the circuit. The Hornets' four and three record included a 15 to 1 routing of the LaGrange Troupers.

Over the course of another week of the young season, the Hornets lost a manager, surrendered a no-hitter, and fell dramatically in the standings. Manager Paul Crain left his post as leader of the Carrollton club and showed up hurling for Valley a few days later. Catcher Jim Hill was given the manager's job on an interim basis until a full time manager could be named. On Saturday, May 3, Valley came to town and handed the Hornets a no-hitter from the arm of Bob Wiseman. The Rebels garnered twelve runs on thirteen hits, and Carrollton contributed with two boots in the field. Having won only one game and lost six over the past week, the Carrollton team was now in seventh place in the league leading only Alexander City in the standings.

HORNETS SHOW OLD-TIME FORM TO BEAT ALEX CITY

Several players from the regular season pennant winning 1946 club returned to the Carrollton lineup on Tuesday, May 13 in a game against Alexander City. Hometown hero Red Roberts returned from a stint with Charleston of the class-A South Atlantic League to play third base and was also named as the new manager of the club. Ace pitcher of the previous season, Buck Mathews, was also back in Hornets flannel. Buck coached third base in the game awaiting his turn in the pitching rotation. Finally, Jim Langley manned the initial sack on the Hornet infield to round out the prodigal returns. A hearty boost was given to the fans and the rest of the team in seeing these Hornets back at the home nest, and Carrollton defeated the Millers 12 to 8. Roberts, Shorty Marshall, and Floyd Snider each hit home runs in the game, the latter two sparking a seven run rally in the seventh frame. This win and a few more during the week allowed the Hornets to move up two notches in the standings to fifth place.

STANDINGS
(Includes Wednesday Games)

	W	L	Pct
Opelika	26	6	.813
CARROLLTON	20	15	.571
Newnan	20	15	.571
Valley	18	14	.563
Tallassee	17	17	.500
Griffin	11	21	.344
LaGrange	11	22	.313
Alex City	10	23	.303

Carrollton continued their winning ways continuously improving their status in the league standings. A month into the season, the Hornets had climbed up to fourth place from the dismal seventh position held a few weeks prior. And when the dust settled from the fast baseball played in the month of May, Carrollton was found to be in second place in the standings tied with Newnan. The Opelika Owls were the only team outpacing the Hornets at this juncture, but the gap was large at seven and a half games.

CHARLEY ROBERTS CAPTURES GA.-ALA. BAT LEAD WITH .397

By mid-June, manager Red Roberts had boosted his batting average up to .397 to lead the league in hitting. Roberts was accompanied by six other Hornets in the over .300 hitting club: Langley .375, Thomas .341, Hill .333, Marshall .328, Snider .325, and Patterson .311. The Carrollton pitching staff comprised of Mathews, Singley, Webb, Alexander, and Bozzuto all boasted a win-loss average of .600 or better. These two elements coupled together made a good formula to win ball games.

Roberts, Matthews And Webb Selected On All-Star Team

All-Star team selections were made just prior to Independence Day, and Red Roberts, Buck Mathews, and Bill Webb were all selected as starters on the team. Shorty Marshall was also selected as a utility player for the elite squad. Abe White, a Carrollton pitcher from 1928 through 1930 and now manager of the Griffin team, was nominated to serve as manager of the All-Star team. The mid-season game of league's best was played against the first place Opelika Owls on their home roosting ground. The All-Stars easily handled the Owls 3 to 0 with much credit going to Red Roberts' pair of triples that resulted in two of the three All-Star runs.

STANDINGS
(Does not include Monday's games)

	W	L	Pct.
Opelika	49	23	.681
Valley	39	29	.574
Carrollton	40	31	.563
Newnan	38	30	.559
Tallassee	37	34	.521
Griffin	33	38	.465
LaGrange	28	46	.381
Alex City	20	51	.282

At the mid-summer break, the Hornets held a firm grip on third place in the league standings with a forty and thirty-one record. Opelika led the league followed by Valley by an eight game margin. Carrollton was another game and a half behind Valley, and Newnan had fourth place by a game and a half margin behind Carrollton. The lower bracket of the loop had Tallassee, Griffin, LaGrange, and Alexander City in order. Alexander City was in the pit twenty-eight and a half games out of first place with fifty-two games left on the slate to try to make up lost ground.

For about a month following the All-Star break, the Georgia-Alabama League standings went virtually unchanged. Teams that had been winning were still winning, and teams that had been losing mostly kept their trend as well. The effect of this happening was a wider gap between the top four and the bottom four teams in the circuit.

Newnan Et Al Favor C Loop Over Carrollton's Protest

At a meeting of the Georgia-Alabama League directorate, Carrollton was the lone opposed vote to petitioning the National Association of Minor League Baseball for a bump up in classification to class-C baseball for the circuit. An increase from the current class-D to class-C baseball would raise the salary limit for each team and increase the number of higher class men that could play for each team. Higher salaries would most likely mean higher admission prices to games, and Carrollton's management was not in favor of charging fans more to get into games. The effort was led by Newnan, and most Carrollton fans said that Newnan wanted to shove Carrollton around at the conference table only because they've never been able to do so on the baseball diamond.

Roberts Hits .404, Webb Wins 15 Games

Top batsman in the league honors still belonged to Hornets manager Red Roberts in mid-August. Carrollton also employed the best pitcher in the league in the form of Bill Webb who had just won his fifteenth game of the season. With only two weeks left in the season, Carrollton rested in fourth place in the standings with a sixty and forty-four record. Opelika still hogged first place with sixty-eight wins and forty losses with Valley close behind at the sixty-two and forty-two mark. Newnan was only two-tenths of a percentage point behind Valley with sixty-three victories and forty-three defeats and a two game lead over Carrollton. Tallassee was in fifth in the league rankings with fifty wins and fifty-five losses followed by Griffin by a game and a half gap and a forty-eight and fifty-four record. LaGrange had thirty-seven wins and sixty-seven losses in the seventh spot, and Alexander City brought up the rear with a thirty-two and seventy-three record, thirty-three and a half games out of first place. Carrollton had a very good chance at making the post-season Shaughnessy playoffs, but another regular season pennant looked doubtful at this point.

Hornets Hold Even In Hot Baseball Race

In the third week of August, the Hornets showed promise of a strong finish in the regular schedule winning seven out of eight games played. Red Roberts' gang went from fourth place to second place, and four and a half games now separated them with first place Opelika. Carrollton closed the gap by another two games in the following week by winning four out of six games played. One of the losses was a hard-fought pitchers' dual in which Bert "Lefty" Bozzuto allowed only three hits but lost the game 1 to 0 on a ninth inning home run to Alexander City. Opelika dropped five games during the week including a 19 to 5 waxing at the hand of Bill Webb and the Hornets. It was Webb's twentieth win of the season, and the laugher of a game was called in the seventh inning with the consent of both managers. With one week of baseball left, the top four teams of the league, Opelika, Valley, Newnan, and Carrollton, had already secured playoff berths as the rest

of the league was now statistically out of the race.

Those Hornets Do It Again Win Pennant In Final Tilt

On Monday, September 1, the last day of the regular season, the Hornets celebrated Labor Day with victories in both games of a split double header against the Newnan Browns. The day game win at Newnan and the night game victory at the Carrollton home field coupled with Valley defeating Opelika in the final two games gave the Hornets a lead of two-tenths of a percentage point over Opelika. Once again, the Georgia-Alabama League pennant belonged to Carrollton.

Bill Webb pitched and won the first game of the twin bill for the Hornets making it his twenty-second win of the season. The final was 1 to 0 as Webb and former Hornet Buck Mathews on the mound for Newnan battled it out. Carrollton's only tally came in the first inning in the form of a long home run from the bat of Jim Langley. Leo Goicoechea pitched the second game for the Hornets which was the regular season finale at the City Athletic Field. A record crowd estimated at over 3,600 was on hand to see the Hornets down the Browns 7 to 3. Goicoechea helped his own cause by driving in two runs on a base hit in the game. Carrollton batters took six of their runs from Newnan pitcher and former Hornet Paul Brock. Brock was relieved by Krone after giving up the six runs, and he tipped his hat to his former fans as he left the game. Bill Webb came into the game to relieve Goicoechea in the eighth frame and finished the game in perfect fashion keeping the win in tact. With the regular season pennant in the bag, Carrollton, being the first place team, would now face third place Valley in a five game series in the first round of playoff action. Second place Opelika and fourth place Newnan would also face each other in a five game set.

Valley Wallops Hornets, 8-6, In First Game Of Playoffs; Players Are Tired

Game one of the playoffs was played on Tuesday, September 2, the very next day, on the Carrollton diamond. All the players appeared to be tired and lacked the fighting spirit witnessed during the heated pennant race of the final weeks of the season. Valley won the game 8 to 6 as both teams used several overworked pitchers in the contest. Jacob Dendinger had the offensive play of the day for the Hornets with one of the longest home runs ever seen at the City Athletic Field.

At Jennings Field in Lanett, Alabama, the Rebels made it a two to nothing series over the Hornets in the second meeting of the first round series. Carrollton had their hat handed to them with a 13 to 0 shutout placed inside. Jacob Dendinger, usually an outfielder, took the mound for the Hornets as none of the regular pitchers were rested enough to make a good start due to the pennant race. Paul Crain pitched for Valley and gave up only two hits in the contest that was called at seven innings by consensus of the managers. Carrollton would now come back home for game three and would have to win three straight from Valley to advance to the league championship series.

The third game of the series was rained out on Thursday, September 4 giving all the players on both teams a much needed rest. With the permission of Jupiter Pluvius, game three was played the next day under the lights of the Hornets nest in Carrollton. Pleasing to the home crowd, the Hornets kept hope alive with a 5 to 3 win over the Rebels. Walt Little pitched the complete game for Carrollton allowing only four hits and striking out ten.

HORNETS OUT REBELS FACE OPELIKA OWLS

Game four sealed the deal for Valley as they defeated Carrollton 5 to 4 at Jennings Field. Nobly, Bill Webb took the mound for the Hornets nursing a sore arm and was unable to find his usual form. The game was tied at four in the bottom of the ninth inning with one out when Valley loaded the bases. On an infield grounder, the ball was thrown home for out number two of the inning. Catcher Bill Patterson, trying to turn a double play, threw wide to first allowing the runner on second to score for the win.

In the other first round series of the league playoffs, Opelika defeated Newnan by a three games to one final as well. Valley took the best of seven games final series four games to two over Opelika.

Carrollton boasted the top offensive player in the league as Red Roberts' final hitting percentage of .385 was better than all the rest. The best pitcher also belonged to Carrollton as Bill Webb finished the season with an astounding twenty-two wins and five losses. Webb also batted .406 but did not have the necessary one hundred at bats to qualify for the batting crown. Shorty Marshall, Floyd Snider, and Dick Kelly each also finished the season batting over the .300 mark. Pitchers Bill Jones, Leo Goicoechea, Walt Little, Hulen Singley, and Bert Bozzuto all had winning pitching records over .500.

For the second year in a row, the third place team in the regular season was crowned as champion of the league, and the first place team went home in the initial round of the playoffs. Carrollton copped the regular season pennant in fine fashion, but once again fell victim to the Shaughnessy system in the post-season.

1948

League President: Arthur R. Decatur
Team Operated by Carrollton Baseball Club, Inc
Team President: Harvey J. Copeland
Secretary-Treasurer: William O. Cobb
Manager(s): Charles "Red" Roberts, Oliver Hill
Games played at City Athletic Field; seating capacity 3,250
Total Regular Season Attendance: 53,000

Carrollton Hornets Roster

Player	G	HR	RBI	AVG	POS	W	L	ERA
Arroyo, Blas	65	0	28	.210	P, 3B, OF	2	2	3.00
Bertha, Elmer	37	1	8	.183	1B			
Bozzuto, Bert	14	0	1	.100	P	5	5	3.84
Burke, Joe	15	0	2	.257	P	3	3	2.39
Cain, George	25	0	5	.157	P	8	6	4.29
Cichon, Frank	108	12	66	.266	OF			
Dendinger, Jacob	16	0	8	.283	OF			
Doerflinger, Gene	41	0	6	.182	P	23	11	2.13
Edwards, Hoyt	28	0	2	.091	P	8	6	4.34
(includes Newnan stats)								
Giombetti, Eddie	1				P	0	0	
Glover, Omer	49	0	8	.172	C			
(includes Alexander City stats)								
Hill, Jim	95	0	54	.239	C			
Hill, Oliver	12	0	4	.170	M, 3B			
Jefts, Virgil	12	0	2	.344	C			
Little, Walt	27	0	9	.177	P	13	7	3.92
Lovelady, Willard	15	0	2	.188	P	2	1	3.56
Marshall, Shorty	121	13	52	.307	2B			
Monarchi, Gene	111	0	38	.236	SS			
Monarchi, Pete					2B			
Nagle, Bob	32	1	6	.190				
Nasworthy, Luther	10	0	1	.120				
Nelson, Dick	26	1	1	.212	P	5	5	4.60
Przeworski, Ted	123	11	90	.246	3B, OF			
Revels, Bill	12	0	3	.192	P	4	5	2.81
Roberts, Red	86	4	64	.337	M, 3B, SS			
Roedel, Bob	12	0	2	.095	C			
Roman, Carl	23	0	5	.218	OF			
Russell, Bing	78	4	38	.255	OF			
Silverman, Jerome	77	0	32	.315	1B			
Snider, Floyd	48	6	34	.277	1B, OF			
Varner, Buck	66	9	35	.292	OF			
Williams, Bob	11	0	1	.167				

Georgia-Alabama League Final Standings

Team	W	L	Pct	GB	Affiliate
Valley Rebels	75	51	.595	----	Boston-A
Carrollton Hornets	73	53	.579	2.0	Unaffiliated
Newnan Brownies	68	58	.540	7.0	Unaffiliated
Alexander City Millers	63	63	.500	12.0	Unaffiliated
Opelika Owls	62	64	.492	13.0	Unaffiliated
Griffin Pimientos	55	71	.437	20.0	St Louis-A

LaGrange Troupers	54	72	.429	21.0	NY-A
Tallassee Indians	54	72	.429	21.0	St Louis-N

1948 Georgia-Alabama League Map

With all eight of the same teams returning to the Georgia-Alabama League for the 1948 season, managers were working hard to whip their men into ball players once again. Carrollton's Charles "Red" Roberts returned to manage the Hornets, and several familiar faces joined him on the team again. Herb "Shorty" Marshall, Jacob Dendinger, Floyd Snider, Bert Bozzuto, and Pete Monarchi all came back to play for Carrollton in the new season. Pete Monarchi also brought along his brother Gene and their uncle Eddie Giombetti. A fast team was predicted with the returning core group and newly acquired prospects.

Hornets Swamp Newnan Here In Opening Game By 13 to 5

The season opened on Tuesday, April 20 with Carrollton hosting the Newnan Browns at the packed City Athletic Field. Prior to the game, festivities were held to present Carrollton with the regular season pennant from the 1947 season. Major League Baseball Commissioner Happy Chandler was on hand to present the flag to Carrollton Hornets president Harvey Copeland. Georgia-Alabama League president Art Decatur was also there for the ceremonies as was former Georgia Governor Ellis G. Arnall. The Hornets easily won the game 13 to 5 behind a great hitting and the strong left arm of Bert Bozzuto. Newnan struck first with two runs in the second inning and two more in the third. Carrollton answered with six runs in the fourth frame followed by one, two, and four runs in the fifth, sixth, and seventh frames respectively. Although the entire Hornets line up hit the ball well, Shorty Marshall was the offensive star of the night with three doubles and a home run.

Win Opening Day Trophy

The fans of the Carrollton Hornets showed their pride well by having the largest opening day attendance in the circuit. An estimated 2,290 Hornet followers paid to see the home opener at the City Athletic Field. Newnan's first home game gave them second place in the race with approximately 1,900 in attendance.

At the end of the first week of play, Alexander City, who finished in last place in the prior season, jumped out to an early lead winning all of their first seven games. Griffin, Newnan, and LaGrange followed in the standings each with four wins and three losses each. Opelika was next with an even three and three record, and Carrollton trailed with a mark of three and five. Valley was a game behind

Carrollton with two victories and six defeats, and Tallassee rode in the caboose with only one win in six games played.

Injuries gave Red Roberts and the Hornets a rough start of the season. At one point in the first two weeks of the season, Carrollton was as low as seventh place in the standings. The addition of pitchers Gene Doerflinger and returning Walt Little improved the rotation from the mound. Catcher Jim Hill also returned to the lineup, and the boys pushed themselves up in the standings to fourth place.

GUNNELLS LEADS HITTERS, MARSHALL TOPS HOMERS

A full month into the season, former Carrollton manager and shortstop Luther Gunnells was leading the league in batting with an amazing .630 percentage. Gunnells, now managing the Opelika club, could probably have been playing in a higher class of baseball, but his managerial and developmental skills were much needed with the young players in class-D. The Hornets second sacker Shorty Marshall was leading the league in home runs with six and was one of the five players in the league batting over .400.

On Wednesday, May 26, the Hornets downed the Rebels of Valley in a 13 to 3 contest. Joe Burke pitched six-hit ball through seven innings when Gene Doerflinger came in to finish the job for Carrollton. Frank Cichon and Floyd Snider each went two for two, and Red Roberts got two hits in three at bats. Shorty Marshall hit safely twice in four trips to the plate, and Bing Russell hit the lone dinger of the night for Carrollton. This was the second win in a row over Valley who held third place in the standings just ahead of the Hornets.

GA.-ALABAMA LEAGUE

CLUBS	w.	l.	pct.	CLUBS	w.	l.	pct.
Valley	39	26	.600	Opelika	33	34	.493
Carrollton	38	27	.585	Griffin	29	38	.433
Newnan	38	28	.576	LaGrange	27	38	.415
Alex City	34	33	.507	Tallassee	27	41	.397

The Hornets played a hot brand of baseball during the month of June boosting their place in the standings up to second place. With nineteen wins and nine losses in the first summer month, Carrollton moved past Newnan and Alexander City and now sat only one game behind league leader Valley.

Mid-summer All-Star selections were made naming the best players in the league to the team. Carrollton players given the honor of being voted onto the squad were pitcher Gene Doerflinger, outfielder Frank Cichon, and second baseman Shorty Marshall. With three players on the team, Carrollton once again had more than their fair share of representation in the eight-team league's best of the best.

Newnan's Browns worked their way into the jockeying for the top position in the league standings after the All-Star break. During the rest of July, Newnan, Valley, and Carrollton took turns being in first place. A snapshot at the end of the month showed Valley in first place with fifty-five wins and thirty-nine losses. Newnan was in second at the time with a fifty-four and forty-two record. Carrollton was a half game behind them in third with fifty-three victories and forty-two defeats. In fourth place was Opelika with a fifty-one and forty-six mark. Early leader Alexander City had now dropped to fifth place with forty-eight wins and forty-seven losses, and LaGrange came next with forty-two in the win column and fifty-four in the loss. Griffin held on to the second from the bottom rung with thirty-nine wins and fifty-five losses, and Tallassee trailed by only three-tenths of a point with a forty and fifty-seven record.

A week into the month of August, Red Roberts was sidelined by a recurring injury he suffered during World War II in the battlefields of France. This injury was serious enough for hospitalization and would probably put him on the bench for the remainder of the season. This devastating blow struck the Hornets physically as well as mentally. Former Boston Brave and Atlanta Cracker Oliver Hill was called upon to manage the club and play third base in the absence of Roberts.

REVELS HURLS NO-HITTER BUT LOSES; 1 TO 0 AT LANETT AS DOUBLE-HEADER IS DIVIDED

With Carrollton, Newnan, and Valley still taking turns blocking the wind at the front of the league pack, a once in a lifetime baseball anomaly occurred for the Hornets. On Monday, August 16, newly acquired pitcher Bill Revels, formerly with Tampa of the class-C Florida International League, pitched a no hitter and lost the game. Revels struck out four and walked four in the game, and it was one of those walks that proved deadly to the new Carrollton pitcher. In the fifth inning, Valley left fielder Martini drew a walk and immediately broke in run for second. When the throw to second went wide and rolled into center field, Martini scampered to third. The next batter came

up, and Revels threw a pitch in the dirt for a passed ball allowing Martini to score the lone, winning run for Valley.

Doerflinger Wins 20th At Tallassee Sunday

Late in August, with the season winding down, and the race for the pennant heating up, Carrollton's ace pitcher Gene Doerflinger copped his twentieth win of the season. In the Sunday, August 22 game at Tallassee, Doerflinger gave up seven scattered hits as Carrollton won 5 to 3. This victory and every other win that could be garnered were needed if the Hornets were going to maintain their streak of winning regular season pennants.

On Monday, August 30, Carrollton and Valley were tied at the top of the league each with seventy-two wins and fifty-one losses. There were only three games for each left in the regular schedule, and two of them were facing each other.

VALLEY TRIPS HORNETS 6-1 WEDNESDAY; OVERFLOW CROWD SEES CRUCIAL CONTEST

On August 31, Carrollton easily handled the Alexander City Millers in a 4 to 1 game. Valley also defeated Newnan that day 11 to 3 keeping the tie in the standings. The crucial series for the Hornets to win another pennant was September 1 and 2 against Valley. Valley came to town and won the first game 6 to 1 over the Hornets giving the Millers a one game lead in the standings. Needing to win the second game of the two-game set to bring the tie back and force a playoff for the pennant, Carrollton fell victim again to the Rebels in the 5 to 3 season finale.

Although Carrollton was unable to win a third pennant in as many years in the Georgia-Alabama League, the cloud did have a silver lining. Carrollton had easily earned one of the four Shaughnessy playoff spots being in the top bracket of the league. Many Carrollton fans made it known that if the Hornets had had Red Roberts at the helm and on the third sack for the twenty-four games he missed, the outcome of the final season standings would have had Carrollton in the top position for the third consecutive year. First place Valley and third place Newnan would meet in the first round of post-season games as would second place Carrollton and fourth place Alexander City. The playoffs would begin immediately on Friday, September 3 at the Hornets nest.

Alex City Draws First Blood In Shaughnessy

In game one at the City Athletic Field, Alexander City defeated Carrollton by a 7 to 5 final. Manager Oliver Hill went with Hoyt Edwards to do the pitching for the Hornets, and the Millers liked the choice. Edwards gave up eight hits in four innings including a grand slam home run by Bill Culpepper in the fourth inning. Joe Yearty came in to relieve Edwards and pitched perfect baseball for the remaining five innings not allowing a single Miller batter to get on base. All of the Hornets runs were manufactured from base hits and walks except for Omer Glover's home run

in the fourth frame. The tired Carrollton players were ready for the much needed rest day on Saturday before game two would be played in Alexander City on Sunday.

REVELS GIVES ALEX CITY ONLY TWO SINGLES AS HORNETS COAST TO 8-0 SUNDAY VICTORY

On Sunday, September 5, Carrollton traveled to Alexander City and showed the Millers how baseball is supposed to be played. Bill Revels was on his game when he allowed only two base hits in the 8 to 0 shutout. Of the few that reached base, none of them made it past second in the very one-sided contest. Carrollton batters went through four Alexander City pitchers and scored seven of their eight runs in the fourth inning. Shorty Marshall got two hits, one of them a double, and drove in two runs. Gene Monarchi also drove in a run on a double, and Bill Revels contributed to his cause with a single and a run. With a tied series of one game each, game three was scheduled for Monday at Alexander City's Russell Park.

Game three turned out in favor of the Millers as Carrollton lost 7 to 1 on the road. Five errors by the Hornets and timely hitting by Alexander City gave the win to the home team. Carrollton had nine safe hits in the game, but they were scattered and unproductive. Walt Little, pitching for the Hornets, struck out four and allowed ten hits, all singles. Frank Cichon was Carrollton's leading hitter with a single and a double. The Hornets and Millers would now go to the Carrollton home field for game four.

CRUCIAL GAME ENDS IN 12th INNING FIASCO WITH FORFEIT TO HORNETS AFTER ARGUMENT

With a two games to one lead over Carrollton in the best of five game series, Alexander City came to the Hornets nest for game four of the first round. The 1 to 1 tie game went on for eleven and a half innings before it finally ended in a blowout between Alexander City and the umpires in the middle of the twelfth. Tempers flared when Miller Clifton Reach was struck out looking to end the top of the eleventh. Reach argued the call with Umpire Behrenbach using language unbecoming of a sportsman and was ejected from the game. Alexander City manager Luther Gunnells came out to defend his player using a few more expletives before Behrenbach told him to get his players onto the field for Carrollton's turn at bat. Before the Hornets got to bat, Arbiter Behrenbach handed a ball to Miller catcher Jim Ello, who played with Carrollton a few years prior. Ello was not satisfied with the quality of the ball given to him, so he threw it on the ground and demanded another one from Behrenbach. Balls had run short in the extra-inning game, and this ball was the best one left to play with. Behrenbach told Ello to pick up the ball, and Ello told Behrenbach to pick it up himself. After the two mules fought heatedly over who should pick up the turnip, Behrenbach pulled his watch and called the game for time limit issuing Alexander City a forfeiture for delaying the game.

Gene Doerflinger pitched the whole way for Carrollton giving up one run on four hits. The lone Hornet run came in the eighth inning when Ted Przeworski drew a walk, went to second then third on two straight sacrifices, and scored on Jim Hill's long single to left. Tied at two games apiece, the first round series would now see game five between Carrollton and Alexander City at the City Athletic Field in Carrollton.

REVELS CINCHES PLAY-OFF SERIES WEDNESDAY NIGHT BY SWAMPING ALEX CITY HERE 6 TO 2

The fifth and final game of the first round of the Shaughnessy playoff series was played on Wednesday, September 8 at the Carrollton home diamond. Bill Revels, on short rest, took the mound for the Hornets and got good run support from his teammates. Revels gave up only five hits to the Millers in the 6 to 2 win that gave Carrollton the game and the series. Luther Gunnells sent the usually dominating Paul Linsley to do the hurling for the Millers, but Carrollton batters were able to touch him for twelve hits. Gene Monarchi led the Hornet offense with three hits in four at bats, and two hits each were garnered by Shorty Marshall, Frank Cichon, Bing Russell, and Omer Glover.

Valley defeated Newnan three games to one in the other first round playoff series. Valley would now host Carrollton in the first game of the best of seven league championship series on Thursday, September 9.

Errors Cost Hornets Final Series Opener

In the initial game of the Georgia-Alabama League championship series, Valley emerged victorious 3 to 0 at their home ball yard. Errors gave the Millers all three of their runs in the game, while Carrollton left eight runners stranded on base unable to score any runs. Joe Yearty pitched for the Hornets allowing only four hits. The hits all came with good timing coupled with errors resulting in the three Valley runs.

The next day, Valley went to Carrollton for game two of the series. Again, the Millers defeated the Hornets as the Carrollton offense was unable to get into gear in the 5 to 1 contest. Carrollton's only run was scored by Shorty Marshall when he was driven in from first by Buck Varner.

Game three of the series was a pitcher's dual between Gene Doerflinger of the Hornets and Willis Eustice of the Millers. Both pitchers were well on their game at the Valley diamond, but the latter came out better in the 2 to 0 Miller victory. Carrollton now trailed the series three games to none and needed to win the remaining four straight if the league championship was to be had. The fourth game of the series was scheduled for Monday, September 13 in Carrollton.

VALLEY TAKES PLAY-OFF IN FOUR STRAIGHT BY WINNING FINAL 13-5 IN CITY PARK HERE

Valley took game four and the series from Carrollton in as many games to become the 1948 Georgia-Alabama League champions of the Shaughnessy post-season tournament. The Hornets, who had only scored one run total in the previous three games, crossed the plate five times in the final contest, but Valley scored thirteen runs before the small crowd of faithfuls who had gathered at the City Athletic Field. Credit was given to the Hornets for their never say die attitude

when three runs were scored in the bottom of the ninth inning.

Although the regular season pennant was not in the cards for the Hornets, the club went further in the Shaughnessy playoffs than ever before. In the two previous years in which the league used the system for the post-season games, Carrollton was ousted in the first round both times. Many fans voiced their opinions again that had Red Roberts been on the field to guide the Hornets, both the regular season and the post-season flags would be flying atop the pole at the City Athletic Field.

1949

League President: Arthur R. Decatur
Team Operated by Carrollton Baseball Club, Inc
Team President: William O. Cobb, P.L. Shaefer
Chairman of the Board: Harvey J. Copeland
Secretary-Treasurer: Eugene R. McGee
Treasurers: H.J. Copeland and Earl Stoples
Manager(s): Bill Seal, Jr., Bill Rucker
Games played at City Athletic Field; seating capacity 3,250
Total Regular Season Attendance: 36,029

Carrollton Hornets Roster

Player	G	HR	RBI	AVG	POS	W	L	ERA
Bartholomew, Jack	25	0	4	.219	2B			
Berman, Buddy	112	0	22	.227	2B			
Bobowski, Ed	33	0	5	.239	P	10	13	3.51
(includes LaGrange stats)								
Bozzuto, Bert	26	0	1	.186	P	5	14	5.12
(includes Alexander City stats)								
Burnstein, Leonard	17	0	2	.244	OF			
Calkins, Dick	1				OF			
Callen, Jim	4				OF			
Cichon, Frank	55	1	29	.276	OF			
Conhenney, Jim	94	0	32	.218	3B			
Fullington, ---	4	0	0	.500				
Hudson, Bill	24	1	14	.323	1B			
Hutchins, Bob	7				P	4	3	2.33
Jefts, Virgil	114	2	40	.241	C			
Jones, Casey	22	0	1	.136	P	4	3	2.57
Kuras, Walt	27	0	7	.266	P	12	8	2.77
Langemeier, Paul	14	0	4	.059	P	4	4	3.13
Little, Walt	12	0	0	.083	P	4	6	5.12
(includes Alexander City stats)								
Maloof, Joe	11	0	0	.188	P			
Matthews, Luther	8				P	3	3	2.52
Morelli, Jim	107	13	52	.259	OF			
Nasworthy, Luther	93	11	47	.244	SS, OF			
Nelson, Burel	22				P	5	8	
Poole, Buddy	12	0	0	.200	P	1	3	4.78
Ridenour, Roy	14	0	4	.132	SS			
Rucker, Bill	120	9	75	.279	M, 1B, OF			
Russell, Bing	11	0	2	.182	OF			
Seal, Bill Jr	85	23	97	.341	M, 2B, SS			
Shirley, Jim	85	7	44	.215	1B			
Thompson, Jim	19	2	13	.219	OF			
Tidwell, John	39	5	32	.316	OF			
Umscheid, Don	11	0	0	.000	P			
Wadewitz, Oswin	11	0	0	.087	P	2	7	1.88
Whited, Gerald	12	0	5	.200	1B			
Yarborough, Mack	4				SS			

Georgia-Alabama League Final Standings

Team	W	L	Pct	GB	Affiliate
Newnan Brownies	74	52	.587	----	Anniston
Alexander City Millers	69	57	.548	5.0	Unaffiliated
Tallassee Cardinals	66	60	.527	8.0	St Louis-N
LaGrange Troupers	65	61	.516	9.0	NY-A
Valley Rebels	62	64	.492	12.0	Boston-A
Opelika Owls	62	64	.492	12.0	Unaffiliated
Carrollton Hornets	56	70	.444	18.0	Vicksburg
Griffin Pimientos	50	76	.397	24.0	Unaffiliated

1949 Georgia-Alabama League Map

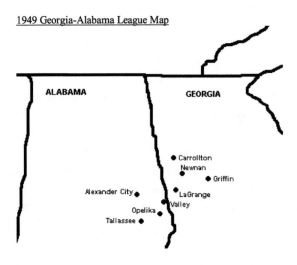

Newly appointed Carrollton manager Bill Seal worked to get his players in shape for the 1949 season as the club, for the first time, had a working relationship with another club in a higher classification of baseball. Now affiliated with the Vicksburg Billies of the class-B Southeastern League, Carrollton would have more support with a steady stream of talent. Being unaffiliated in all previous years in organized baseball, Carrollton would also have to deal with the new issue of prospects being pulled away to play on the higher class team when needed.

The same eight teams made up the Georgia-Alabama League as did in 1948. Former Carrollton manager Red Roberts was now the skipper of the Alexander City Millers and had started a rivalry with

Opelika manager Bubba Ball before the season even opened. Both managers were quoted making comments of how the other team was going to be left in the dust by the rest of the league.

Exhibition games were played against area semi-pro and amateur teams to give players time in the box and managers a feel for which players had what abilities. Carrollton was victorious in six out of eight of the practice games against teams such as Southern Railway, Vidalia, East Point Motors of Atlanta, and fellow Georgia-Alabama League team Alexander City.

In an interesting pre-season game, Carrollton hosted the Rome Romans of the North Georgia City League. Bert Bozzuto pitched well in the 6 to 1 Hornets victory. The game was pleasing to the home crowd throughout, but the most amusing occurrence was in the bottom of the fourth when a 'possum wandered out onto the field. Most of the players and fans watched stunned and entertained as the North American marsupial made his way out to center field completely nonchalant of the game going on. The Rome outfielders gave chase to the 'possum and soon cornered him against the left field fence where he was captured allowing the game to resume.

BROWNS SMOTHER HORNETS 11-1 TUESDAY NIGHT BEFORE OVERFLOW CROWD AT NEWNAN

The first game of the season for Carrollton was on the road at the Newnan diamond versus the Brownies on Tuesday, April 26. Manager Seal went with Bert Bozzuto to do the mound work for the Hornets. Bozzuto, who had been untouchable during exhibition outings,

was unable to get into a groove and gave up five runs in the first inning. Newnan continued to hit the ball freely until they had eleven tallies total. Carrollton finally scored one run and threatened to score more in the top of the ninth, but the Brownies quickly snuffed out any inkling of a rally.

In other opening day games, Opelika defeated Valley 7 to 3, LaGrange narrowly beat Griffin by a 2 to 1 final, and Tallassee was victorious over Alexander City 5 to 3 in a ten-inning affair.

BACK THE 1949
HORNETS
OPENING HOME GAME
Wednesday, April 27
Carrollton vs Newnan
CITY BALL PARK
8:15 p.m.

Before a packed house at the City Athletic Field, the Hornets hosted Newnan on Wednesday, April 27 in their home opener. Carrollton had the courtesy of giving their company a second victory in as many days as the Brownies won 8 to 4. The Hornets struck first scoring two in the second inning, but the Brownies answered with two in the fifth, three in the sixth, and three more in the eighth. Two more runs were scored by Carrollton late in the game, but it was too little too late. After two games played, the Hornets sat in the cellar of the circuit with a zero and two record.

HORNETS DROP 4-1 GAME TO TALLASSEE HERE MONDAY; MACK YARBOROUGH BREAKS ARM

On Monday, May 2, the Hornets lost their young prospect shortstop Mack Yarborough to a broken arm in an on-field collision with left fielder Jim Callen. Three pitches into the game against the Tallassee Cardinals at the Hornets nest, Tallassee leadoff man Bill Blackwell popped one up to shallow left field off of pitcher Burel Nelson. Callen hustled in from left after the ball, and Yarborough went gave chase from his position as well. Neither man was able to make the catch as they collided sending Yarborough to the grass. Callen was unhurt in the incident. The physician's assessment on the field indicated a severe fracture just below the shoulder on Mack's left arm. After about a forty-five minute delay, play resumed with Tallassee defeating Carrollton 4 to 1. Yarborough was sent to a bone specialist in Atlanta and was expected to be out for the season.

On the same day, the Opelika Owls and the Newnan Brownies squared off in a marathon contest that went nineteen long innings before Opelika finally rallied for three runs in the nineteenth frame and emerged victorious 7 to 4.

A week and a half into the season, numerous games had been postponed or cancelled due to rain throughout the league. In the games that Jupiter Pluvius had allowed to be played, Carrollton had won only two and lost six putting the club in a tie for sixth place in the league. Tallassee was in first place with a perfect five wins and no losses followed by Opelika with a four and two record. In third place came LaGrange with three in the win column and two in the loss, while Newnan was fourth with four victories and three defeats. Griffin was fifth with an even three and three mark followed by Carrollton and Valley tied for sixth. Alexander City was the only team in the loop yet to win a game in the five they had played putting them at the bottom of the list.

HORNETS PROTEST SATURDAY GAME; BROWNS WIN 3-2 BUT EXCEED LEAGUE SQUAD LIMIT

A protest of a game that Carrollton lost 3 to 2 to the Newnan Brownies on Saturday, May 28, resulted in a win after Carrollton disputed the game. In the seventh inning, Hornet skipper Bill Seal stepped into the batters box and noticed that seventeen men were in uniform for the Brownies. The league had instructed teams to cut squads to sixteen men by May 26, two days prior. Seal immediately announced to the home plate umpire that the rest of the game would be played under protest citing the player limit violation by Newnan as the reason. Upon review by league president Art Decatur, the Carrollton club was awarded the victory by an official score of 9 to 0. In addition to the loss, Newnan was also fined $50 as a reminder to follow the league rules.

LaGrange Manager Suspended Following Near Riot Thursday

LaGrange Troupers manager Bill Cooper was suspended by league president Decatur following an incident in LaGrange on June 2. During the game against the Tallassee Cardinals, a less than sober Troupers fan ran onto the field and attacked home plate umpire Luther Gunnells following a questionable call. Gunnells, a former Carrollton player and manager, was immediately assisted by the field arbiter, Merritt "Sugar" Cain, another former Carrollton player. Several more fans came onto the field and roughly man-handled both officials. There were only two policemen in the park at the time, and neither was brave enough to try to stop the ruckus. Manager Cooper and other LaGrange players intervened and halted the fuss, and, fortunately, neither umpire was seriously injured. The next day, Cooper was suspended for not providing adequate police protection at the ballpark.

By mid-June, Carrollton still had not gotten their record on the winning track. Despite a six-game winning streak that ended with a thirteen inning tie against Tallassee, the Hornets remained below .500 with twenty-two games won and twenty-four games lost. Tallassee was at the top of the heap with twenty-seven wins and nineteen losses. Carrollton was solidly in sixth place, five games behind the league leader with the mid-season mark quickly approaching.

Manager Bill Seal carried the big stick around the City Athletic Field as he was leading the club in home runs with seventeen. Among his dingers were three that came in one game where Carrollton crushed Opelika 16 to 3. Jim Morelli and Bill Rucker both brought their batting averages up to the .300 mark during the first half of June, and Frank Cichon was

pushing the toward the same number. Walt Kuras and Ed Bobowski were the hot hurlers for the Hornets. Bobowski proved to be too much for former major leaguer Rudy York who came to town with his Griffin Pimientos for a 6 to 2 defeat. Pitchers Bert Bozzuto and Walt Little were both released from the Carrollton squad. Bozzuto was immediately picked up by Red Roberts at Alexander City and got the best of his former team on the next two times he saw them. Little had been with the Hornets since the 1946 season.

SEAL, CICHON, KURAS AND MORELLI SELECTED TO ALL-STAR SQUAD FOR MONDAY'S GAME

Four players from the Carrollton team were selected to the All-Star team to represent Georgia in the mid-season exhibition game. Bill Seal, Frank Cichon, Walt Kuras, and Jim Morelli were named to the team that would take on the best players from the Alabama league cities at Jennings field in Lanett, Alabama on July 11. Seal was selected to play third base, Cichon to play right field, Kuras would be one of six pitchers, and Morelli was to be a utility outfielder. The Georgia aggregation of the best won the game by a 1 to 0 final. Kuras pitched the fourth, fifth, and sixth innings of the contest and allowed only one hit.

The standings looked more dismal than ever for the Hornets at the All-Star break. Newnan led the league with forty-two wins and thirty-one losses followed by tied Alexander City and LaGrange each with a thirty-seven and thirty-five record. Valley and Tallassee were next by a half game also tied with thirty-seven victories and thirty-six defeats each. Opelika was in sixth place with thirty-six in the win column and thirty-eight in the loss. Carrollton held seventh place in the eight-team circuit with a thirty-five and thirty-eight mark, and Griffin brought up the rear with thirty-one wins and forty-three losses. For the most part, the standings were tight with only two and a half games separating the second place and seventh place teams. First place Newnan had four and a half games over the second place Alexander City as an exception, and last place Griffin was eleven and a half games out of first.

SEAL IS SOLD TO ANNISTON FOR CASH AND PLAYER AND RUCKER TAKES HORNET REINS

During the last week of July, the Carrollton club sold for cash outfielder Frank Cichon to Greenville, Mississippi of the class-C Cotton States League. Days later on July 28, "Appreciation Day" at the City Athletic Field, the club also sold manager Bill Seal to Anniston of the class-B Southeastern League just prior to the start of the game. Infielder Bill Rucker was immediately named to take over the position for the remainder of the season. Following this news, the Hornets proceeded to play spoiler knocking Alexander City out of the league lead giving them a 5 to 3 defeat. Seal had been criticized in recent days for his less than disciplined managerial style and lack of firmness with young players.

With manager Seal gone, the Hornets had only one player left from spring training on the squad. Leadoff man Buddy Berman was the sole survivor on the Hornets roster from the original pre-season line up. Formerly a batboy for the Brooklyn Dodgers, Berman was evidence

of the Hornets' increased player turnover in the losing season thus far.

Hornets Play .533 Ball For Manager Rucker; Have 8 Games Left

Following the departure of manager Bill Seal and the assignment of Bill Rucker to the Carrollton helm, the Hornets began to play better baseball than ever during the season. Winning fourteen out of twenty four games, Carrollton climbed to within three games of the top bracket of the league. Talk began of the possibility of a post-season playoff berth. As soon as the word "playoff" was spoken, the Hornets dropped six straight games and went back to old familiar seventh place only ahead of Griffin. One of the losses was especially tough as Hornet pitcher Oswin Wadewitz was cruising through a no-hitter against LaGrange when it fell through in the ninth inning. Carrollton lost the game heartbreakingly 2 to 1. With only six games left in the regular season schedule, the post-season was now most certainly out of reach for the Hornets.

Hornets Drop Final Game Thursday; Owls Win 3-2 In Ninth

Carrollton finished the season with an all too familiar one run loss on Thursday, September 1. The 3 to 2 win for the Opelika Owls in the season's final game was enough to give them a fifth place tie with the Valley Rebels in the standings, but these two teams along with Carrollton and Griffin would not see any post-season action.

The four teams that did make the cut for the Shaughnessy style playoffs were Newnan, Alexander City, Tallassee, and LaGrange in order. First place Newnan and third place Tallassee would square off in the first round of the post-season, championship tournament as would second place Alexander City and fourth place LaGrange. Newnan and Tallassee went the limit on games before Newnan finally took the series three games to two. Alexander City defeated LaGrange three games to one on the other side of the bracket. The best of seven game championship series went only five games when Alexander City upset Newnan four games to one. Newnan had won the regular season pennant by five games over Alexander City. For the fourth straight year, the Georgia-Alabama League pennant winner fell victim to the Shaughnessy system and was not crowned as the ultimate champion of the loop.

Since the Carrollton club had a losing season, it was not certain whether or not a team would be representing the city in the Georgia-Alabama League in the following season. Financial difficulties were made public knowledge as gate receipts were only two-thirds of what they had been in the previous year.

1950

League President: Arthur R. Decatur
Team Operated by Carrollton Baseball Club, Inc
Team President: P.L. Shaefer
Vice Presidents: E.V. Folds, M.C. Roop
Secretary: William O. Cobb
Treasurers: Walter New
General Manager: Harvey J. Copeland
Manager(s): Herbert "Shorty" Marshall, Stanley Coulling
Games played at City Athletic Field; seating capacity 3,250
Total Regular Season Attendance: 26,365

Carrollton Hornets Roster

Player	G	HR	RBI	AVG	POS	W	L	ERA
Arroyo, Blas	33	2	10	.282	P, 3B, OF	9	7	5.37
Beasley, John	39	0	13	.200	SS			
(includes Rome stats)								
Beauchamp, Walt	27	0	11	.303	2B			
Berman, Buddy	18	0	8	.323	2B			
Bobowski, Ed	32	1	7	.169	P		17	7	4.96
Clark, Ray	119	12	77	.338	SS			
Cobiella, Ricardo	21	0	6	.212	2B			
Corrales, Reinaldo	32	0	15	.284				
Coulling, Stan	14	1	3	.182	P	3	3	4.59
Dennis, Jack	10	0	2	.333	P			
DeSouza, Fred	122	24	92	.299	3B			
Fernandez, Mike	4				P	1	3	
Fetner, Charles	16	0	11	.271	1B			
Gonzalez, Cotayo	8				P	4	2	4.19
Hutchins, Bob	24	0	2	.225	P	9	3	5.21
(includes Rome stats)								
Jones, Casey	34	0	3	.137	P	11	7	5.12
(includes Newnan stats)								
Kelly, Mason					P			
Lee, Fred	108	10	65	.260	OF			
Marshall, Shorty	80	10	64	.354	M, 2B			
Mazak, Leo	26	0	6	.208	P	4	9	6.24
Morelli, Jim	113	14	70	.291	OF			
Patterson, Bill	109	1	68	.233	C			
(includes Griffin, Valley, and Alexander City stats)								
Reach, Clifton	97	13	51	.202	2B, OF			
Shirley, Jim	105	17	71	.236	1B			
Shoemake, Claude	62	18	68	.342	OF			
Solt, Gene	119	38	151	.365	C, OF			
Victor, Ernie	1				P			
Weldon, Bill	27	1	6	.098	P	8	9	5.33
White, Curtis	16	0	2	.214	P	4	5	5.55

Georgia-Alabama League Final Standings

Team	W	L	Pct	GB	Affiliate
LaGrange Troupers	73	48	.603	----	NY-A
Alexander City Millers	73	53	.579	2.5	Unaffiliated
Carrollton Hornets	66	57	.537	8.0	Unaffiliated
Newnan Brownies	62	60	.508	11.5	Unaffiliated

Valley Rebels	58	65	.472	16.0	Unaffiliated
Griffin Tigers	57	64	.471	16.0	Unaffiliated
Opelika Owls	52	72	.419	22.5	Unaffiliated
Rome Red Sox	49	71	.408	23.5	Washington

1950 Georgia-Alabama League Map

The face of the Georgia-Alabama League changed slightly at the end of the 1949 season as the Tallassee Cardinals relinquished their franchise citing financial difficulties. Filling the vacancy, in stepped the city of Rome, Georgia with a team called the Red Sox, an affiliate of the Washington Senators organization of the American League.

An old friend was became the new manager of the Carrollton Hornets for the season. Herb "Shorty" Marshall, well-liked infielder on the 1946, 1947, and 1948 Hornets squads, had been appointed to lead the team and play second base. Marshall played in Stockton of the class-C California League and West Palm Beach of the class-B Florida International League in 1949. Expectations were high that Marshall would lead the club to a better finish than the previous year's seventh place in the league standings.

The Carrollton club severed its ties with the class-B Vicksburg team of the Southeastern League. It was decided that if an affiliation could not be arranged with a major league team, then the club would operate independently. Much of the misfortune of the previous season was blamed on the higher-class Vicksburg pulling players out of Carrollton and not replacing them with any real talent. With a losing team on the field, financial difficulties were an almost certainty. Vicksburg did not provide the needed financial or player support to Carrollton that a major league club would have given in times of trouble.

Spring practice had been hampered by unseasonably cold weather for April. Most of the pitchers remained stiff and unable to completely loosen up enough to pitch to their fullest ability. Through the preseason, exhibition games, manager Marshall had narrowed his roster down to the necessary twenty-one men ready for the season to get underway.

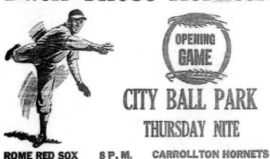

The season opened for the Hornets as the new kid on the block, the Rome Red Sox, came to town on Thursday, April 27. Prior to the game at the City Athletic Field, a parade was held through town with dignitaries from both teams participating. Approximately three thousand fans turned out for the first game that started with Carrollton Mayor Hubert Griffin throwing out the ceremonial first pitch. Carrollton welcomed Rome to the league with a 17 to 6 demolishing. Skipper Marshall went with left-hander Cotayo Gonzalez to do the hurling. Gonzalez cruised to the easy victory behind excellent run support that included home runs by Freddie DeSouza and Fred Lee, and Shorty Marshall created much excitement when he stole home in the fifth inning. Rome used five pitchers in the game including regular third baseman Johnny Stowe.

Carrollton traveled to Rome the next day to be guests at the Red Sox home opener. Rome reciprocated the results of the previous day's game and defeated the Hornets by a 14 to 9 final. Rome also copped the league opening day attendance trophy with over three thousand eight hundred paid patrons. Carrollton's three thousand fans at their home opener earned the club second place in the attendance contest.

Just over a week into the new season, the Hornets were sitting in the same spot as they finished in 1949, seventh place. Alexander City was in the lead in the standings with seven wins and two losses. Newcomer Rome was second with an eight and three record, and Newnan held third with a mark of six and four. Fourth place was occupied by LaGrange with four victories and five defeats, while Opelika and Griffin were tied in fifth each with a four and six record. Carrollton had three wins and five losses, and Valley was last in the league with three in the win column and eight in the loss.

Among the three victories for the Hornets was a 17 to 6 routing of the Opelika Owls. Gene Solt and Jim Morelli each had four hits and a homer in the game, and every Carrollton player in the game garnered at least one safe hit. The knowledge of the rule book was tested by the officials as three unusual plays occurred in the game. In the first incident, a base runner was rounding first after hitting the ball and was tripped by the first baseman allowing him a free pass to second. The second incident involved the third base coach and the third baseman on a fly ball in foul territory on the third base side. When the third base coach failed to get out of the way of the third baseman giving chase to the ball, the batter was called out automatically. Unusual incident number three was when a ground ball grazed a base runner between second and third putting him out automatically and giving the batter first base only. It was believed that three such out of the ordinary plays had never occurred in the same game before in the Georgia-Alabama League.

Hornets Average 12 Runs Per Home Game; Minus Road Victory

By mid-May, the Carrollton club still had a losing record of seven wins and nine losses. Ironically, all of the six games played at home were won, and all except one of the road games played were lost. Furthermore, Carrollton had accumulated eighty-nine runs in the seven games won to their opponents total of thirty-six. The large number of runs was mostly coming from the big bats of Freddie De Souza and Gene Solt, both of whom had just hit two over the fence in one game that Carrollton took from Opelika 21 to 1. Ray Clark, Fred Lee, and manager Shorty Marshall were also hitting their fair share of long balls in the Hornets nest batting displays.

DECATUR RESIGNS; NEW LOOP PRESIDENT EXPECTED BY MAY 31

Georgia-Alabama League president Art Decatur resigned the position at the end of May. George Cahall of LaGrange, vice president of the circuit, acted as interim president until the league directors could name a replacement. Decatur's resignation came after a ruling he made concerning a protested game received much dissension among other league officials. The game in question was between Carrollton and Valley at the Valley home field on Friday, May 12. During the game, an argumentative discussion developed among the umpires and the managers of each team concerning a wild pitch. Valley general manager Hoyt King, wearing civilian clothes, made his way onto the field to try to speed the discussion along and have play resumed. Team officials not in uniform were not allowed onto the playing field during a game, so Hornet manager Shorty Marshall called a protest. Valley won the contest 10 to 7 in regulation, and Decatur denied the Carrollton protest allowing the victory to stay on the record of Valley. Decatur commented that his departure from the presidency was for the "good of the

league." Less than a week later, the league's directors voted seven to one to reinstate Decatur back to the position.

Alex City Millers Adopt New T-Shirt, Shorts 'Uniforms'

With summer's arrival and the temperatures heating up, the Alexander City Millers decided to dress down their uniforms to shorts and t-shirts in lieu of the traditional flannels. Mobile, Alabama of the class-AA Southern Association and Hollywood, California of the class-AAA Pacific Coast League had both gone to short pants for the hotter games. It was not known if the Millers, led by manager Red Roberts, would dawn their new skivvies on the road as numerous sarcastic cat-calls and wolf-whistles would be inevitable.

MARSHALL'S .423 BATTING MARK IS TOPS IN LEAGUE; SOLT LEADS IN HOME RUNS WITH 19

Manager Shorty Marshall had the best bat in the league at the end of the second week of June. Batting .423, Marshall was seventeen points ahead of second place Jack Bearden, manager the of Griffin club. Big Gene Solt was leading the circuit in home runs with nineteen at this point of the season. Over the next week, Solt got five more dingers to add to his quickly mounting total. Freddie DeSouza was second on the Carrollton roster in homers with eleven. The Hornets were also ahead of the rest of the league in team batting average with a .297 percentage. Griffin was the closest competitor in this category with a .289 score. Carrollton's hot bats moved the team into fifth place in the league standings with a record of twenty-six and twenty-four.

Weds Hornet Pitcher

On-field nuptials were held for Carrollton pitcher Bill Weldon on Thursday, June 29 prior to the game against the Alexander City Millers at the City Athletic Field in Carrollton. Weldon took as his bride Miss Olene Hill of Waverly, Alabama with Reverend H.B. Benson conducting the ceremony. Carrollton narrowly won the game over the Millers 10 to 9 by overcoming a deficit of seven runs. Blas Arroyo pitched the complete game for the Hornets and got the win as he struck out ten Millers batters. Offensively, the Hornets were safe on eighteen hits including a home run by Jim Morelli.

A three-way tie for first place came about on July 5 when LaGrange, Alexander City, and Griffin all had records of forty wins and twenty-nine losses. Newnan was a game and a half behind the threesome with a thirty-eight and thirty record, and Carrollton, only three games out of first, was closing in on the top bracket with thirty-six in the win column and thirty-one in the loss. Valley was sixth in the standings with a thirty-three and thirty-eight mark followed by Rome with twenty-eight victories and forty defeats. Opelika was the league whipping post with nineteen wins and forty-seven losses having won less than twenty-five percent of their games.

FIVE HORNETS ON EASTERN ALL-STAR SQUAD; FREDDIE DESOUZA LONE ROOKIE SELECTED

All-Star team selections were made for the mid-season classic to be held in Griffin on Monday, July 10 when the best players of the eastern half of the league, consisting of Rome, Griffin, Newnan, and Carrollton, would meet the best of the western half, consisting of Alexander City, LaGrange, Valley, and Opelika. Carrollton players selected to the elite team were catcher Gene Solt, pitchers Bob Hutchins and Bill Weldon, outfielder Jim Morelli, and third baseman Freddie DeSouza. Hard-hitting DeSouza had the distinction of being the only rookie selected for the eastern squad. The west won the hard-fought, evenly matched game by a score of 4 to 3 in thirteen innings. Bob Hutchins and Bill Weldon both pitched in the game, and neither of them allowed any hits.

GENE SOLT TIES HOME RUN MARK WITH 30TH; MORELLI, DESOUZA ALSO HOMER IN 14-3 WIN

Saturday night, July 15, saw Carrollton catcher Gene Solt tie the Georgia-Alabama single season home run record. Solt hit his thirtieth dinger of the season at the City Athletic Field tying the mark previously set by Jake Daniels in 1946. With a month and a half of baseball left to be played, it was certain that Solt would get the one more homer needed to set a new record. Jim Morelli and Freddie DeSouza each also hit one over the wall in the 14 to 3 crushing of the Newnan Browns.

Hornets batters were hitting the ball well enough for three of them to be among the top six batters in the league. Solt was batting .390, second in the circuit, Shorty Marshall was third in the league with a .379 average, and Ray Clark was hitting .351 ranking him sixth among top league batters. Outfielder Claude Shoemake and third sacker Freddie DeSouza were both also above the .300 batting mark with percentages of .323 and .316 respectively. Even pitcher and part-time utility man Blas Arroyo got his swing into a groove and was hitting .280 with one home run.

Browns Drop Pair To "Iron Man" Bobowski And Slugging Hornets

Hornets hurler Ed Bobowski turned in an iron man stunt against the Newnan Browns on Monday, July 24 as he pitched and won both games of a double header. With final scores of 7 to 5 and 9 to 1, Bobowski got good run support from the Hornets offense. For good measure, "Bobo" hit a home run in the second game of the night.

On the last day of July, the Hornets finally cracked the top bracket of the league standings with a split double header against Opelika coupled with a Newnan loss to LaGrange. Carrollton sat in fourth place with forty-eight wins and forty-three losses, a half game ahead of Newnan. LaGrange led the league followed by Alexander City by three and a half games. Griffin was in third place two games behind Alexander City, and Carrollton clung onto fourth place two games back of Griffin. Newnan came next by a half game, and Valley trailed Newnan by five and a half games. Rome was in seventh place, three and a half

games behind Valley, and Opelika was in the cellar, twenty-two games out of first place. With a month of baseball left in the season, Carrollton now had a good chance harnessing one of the four Shaughnessy playoff berths given to the top four teams of the league.

Boston Braves Get Gene Solt for $3,500; Finishes Year Here

Scouts of the higher baseball echelon were sitting up and taking notice of the hot bat of Hornets catcher Gene Solt. The Boston Braves bought Solt from the Carrollton club for the sum of $3,500, a figure that was thought to be a steal for the Braves. Part of the agreement was that Solt would finish the year in Carrollton since the Hornets were making a run at the post-season playoffs. It was expected that Solt would play in class-A the following season, and possibly as high as class-AA. The twenty-one year old catcher had just hit his thirty-first home run of the season for the Hornets making him the new single season home run king of the Georgia-Alabama League.

Pitcher's Second Iron Man Stunt Pushes Hornets Into Third Place; Crowd Small

Ed Bobowski completed his second iron man pitching feat on Wednesday, August 2 before a scattered crowd of two hundred twenty-three fans. The Hornets shutout the Valley Rebels in the first game of the twin bill 5 to 0 with Bobo only allowing three hits. Ray Clark provided his team's pitcher some breathing room with his grand-slam home run in the bottom of the first inning. The work horse pitcher cruised in the second game as Carrollton easily won 14 to 4. These two victories were Bobowski's sixth and seventh in a row and his fourteenth and fifteenth of the season. Most importantly, the two wins moved Carrollton past Griffin by a game into third place in the standings. Griffin lost two games to LaGrange on the same day.

At the end of the first week of August, the Hornets moved into second place in the standings with LaGrange only four and a half games ahead in first. There was a half game margin over third place Alexander City for Carrollton, and Griffin and Newnan sat three and a half back of Alexander City tied for fourth. With twenty games left to go, the races for the regular season pennant and the four coveted playoff positions were beginning to heat up.

1,100 GREET OLD TIMERS; HORNETS KEEP NEAR SECOND WITH TWO WINS OVER TIGERS

Carrollton old-timers night was held at the City Athletic Field on Saturday, August 12 at half time of a double header against the Griffin Tigers. Between the two games, former Carrollton players were honored for their contributions to the city's teams of yesteryear. Ex-players in attendance from the 1928-30 era were pitchers Abe White, Carl Davis, Homer Carter, and Merritt "Sugar" Cain, outfielder Henry "Pat" Patton, catcher G.E. "Cheese" Goggans, shortstop Colon Sappenfield, and former club president A.W. "Andy" Ford. Representing the 1946-48 years were catcher Jim Hill and current Hornets manager Shorty Marshall.

Abe White, the current manager of the visiting Griffin team, led the players of the past in a pre-game "warm-up" much to the enjoyment of the fans that turned out to see them.

The old-timers were not the only entertainment of the evening. Carrollton won both games of the twin bill from Griffin 7 to 6 and 14 to 1. Newly acquired pitcher Stan Coulling, who came from the recently defunct Gadsden team of the Southeastern League, pitched the complete first game and added to the offense with a two-run homer. Freddie DeSouza also hit a two-run shot in the seventh inning that gave the Hornets the runs needed for the win. Carrollton batted a round in each of the second and third innings in game two scoring eleven runs. Hornets pitcher Roy "Casey" Jones, with his arm trademarkedly completely bathed in heat balm, enjoyed the comfortable lead on his cruise to the easy victory.

Marshall Suspended And Club Fined $300 In Row

With the club well entrenched in third place in the league standings, the Hornets were nearing the end of the baseball season when an irate fan caused manager Shorty Marshall to be suspended for the remainder of the 1950 season. The prelude to the fracas occurred about mid-way through the game when the home plate umpire threw Carrollton third baseman DeSouza out of the game for an unapparent reason. Manager Marshall, who was positioned unusually in left field, came in and asked the umpire what the player said to deserve the ejection. Marshall became irate when the official gave his reasons that remained undisclosed, but play was soon resumed. At the end of the game, Marshall and the arbiter got into a heated debate in front of the Carrollton dugout. It was during this argument that a fan came from the stands and punched the umpire in the face sending him to the dirt. The ruckus was stopped by Marshall, several players, and other fans, and the downed official was tended to for injuries. Upon review of the incident, league president Art Decatur indefinitely suspended skipper Marshall and fined him $300 for not providing adequate police protection for the umpire. New Carrollton pitcher Stan Coulling was named to take over as manager for the rest of the season.

FERNANDEZ TOSSES 2-HITTER IN FINAL HOME GAME; GENE SOLT HITS 38th IN 6-1 VICTORY

The Hornets played their final regular season home game on Friday, September 1 and copped a 6 to 1 victory over the Opelika Owls. Mike Fernandez pitched for his only win of the season for the Hornets and Gene Solt etched in stone his place in the record book with his thirty-eighth home run. The same two teams met the next day, and Opelika won this time 6 to 4 in the only game of the day and the final game of the season in the Georgia-Alabama League.

An uneventful pennant race that started off hot but quickly cooled off trudged its way through August with the team rankings being practically the same at the end of the month as they were at the beginning. The top bracket of four teams now advanced to the post-season, Shaughnessy style playoffs. LaGrange, the first place team and regular season

pennant winner, was slated to face third place finisher Carrollton in a best two of three game first round series. Second place Alexander City would take on fourth place Newnan for three games on the other side of the playoff bracket.

Bessant's No-Hitter Helps Troupers Beat Hornets In Fiayoff

In game one of the playoff series between Carrollton and LaGrange at the LaGrange home field, the Troupers no-hit the Hornets behind the arm of rookie pitcher Don Bessent. Not only were the Hornets not allowed a single hit in the Monday, September 4 game but the Troupers scored fourteen runs on twenty-one hits against the combined pitching of Ed Bobowski and Leo Mazak. With the shorter than usual first round playoff series, Carrollton was already in jeopardy of being eliminated after only one game.

TROUPERS BUMP HORNETS FROM PLAYOFF IN 15 INNING PITCHER'S DUEL HERE TUESDAY

On Tuesday, September 5, following an embarrassing shutout by LaGrange, the Hornets were eliminated from the post-season games in a fifteen-inning 6 to 4 Troupers win. Carrollton scored all four runs in the third inning, while LaGrange got one in the first, two in the fourth, and one more to tie the game in the fifth. Mike Fernandez, on the hill for the Hornets, and Gerald Wallis, the Troupers pitcher, both went the full distance in the three and a half hour, marathon contest. LaGrange finally broke the tie in the top of the fifteenth frame and held on for the win through Carrollton's turn at bat.

LaGrange advanced to the league championship series against Alexander City, the winner of the other side of the first round. Newnan bowed down in two straight games to Alexander City just like Carrollton did to LaGrange. As the final championship series was shortened to five games instead of the traditional seven, LaGrange needed all five to take it from Alexander City by an exciting three games to two score. The LaGrange Troupers were now the supreme champions of the Georgia-Alabama League owning the regular season pennant and the post-season championship flag.

SOLT, BOBOWSKI MAKE SCORERS' ALL-STAR TEAM; LaGRANGE PLACES 5 MEN ON SQUAD

An All-Star team was named at the end of the season at the request of league president Art Decatur recognizing the best players throughout the year. Carrollton players Gene Solt and Ed Bobowski were named to this team that would not play any games but was named just to go in the record book. Solt set three new single-season league records during the year with his 38 home runs, 151 runs batted in, and 308 total bases. Bobowski turned two iron man stunts during the season, winning both games of two double headers, and finished with a record of seventeen wins and seven losses.

"HORNETS IN LEAGUE NEXT YEAR," DECATUR SAYS; CLUB OFFICIALS ON FINANCIAL FENCE

Georgia-Alabama League president Art Decatur was quoted as saying that Carrollton would definitely play in the league in 1951. Six of the eight teams sent word to the president before the end of the season that they would be playing next season. The two that did not make the commitment were Newnan and Carrollton. Although the Hornets had a winning season and made the playoffs, attendance was lower than ever before including the previous, losing season. The president's optimism did not pan out, and neither Carrollton nor Newnan put a team into the league in the following year. The Georgia-Alabama League played with the six remaining teams in 1951, but the circuit ceased to exist any longer after that. The Carrollton Hornets last game in organized baseball was the heart breaking, fifteen-inning loss to the LaGrange Troupers in the first round of the 1950 post-season.

Post-1950

Following the 1950 season, Carrollton did not have a baseball team to represent the city on the minor league or semi-pro level for over ten years. Although a lot of great ball was played by the American Legion teams during those years, it was not until the Carrollton Lakers emerged in 1961 as part of the West Georgia Association of Semi-pro Baseball that a higher level of baseball was seen in Carrollton.

Playing at the Lakeshore ballpark across the street from Lake Carroll, the Lakers, under the leadership of Jelp Robinson, won every game they played against other teams in the West Georgia Association in 1961. The perfect record earned the Lakers the honor of hosting the league All-Star game and facing a team comprised of the best players in the circuit. Other teams in the semi-pro league included Bowdon, Haralson, Pepsi of Newnan, Sargent, Bonnell, Corinth, and Jake. Joe Arp was the pitching ace of the Carrollton club, and Harry Shadrix batted .525 over the course of the season.

In 1962, the Carrollton Lakers returned to the West Georgia Association and again dominated the league. The Lakers repeated in earning the honor of taking on the All-Stars of the league. A winning streak of seventeen consecutive games in 1962 was enjoyed by the Lakers until it finally ended on August 26 when Jake defeated Carrollton 6 to 0. Carrollton had won over thirty consecutive league games when those from the previous season were included in the streak. A new team called the Southwire Sparks entered the league adding to the competition for the Lakers and giving the home crowd another team to call their own.

Southwire was the home team for Carrollton in 1963, as the Lakers did not enter the West Georgia Association. The Lakers did, however, organize a team in time to enter the Georgia State Semi-pro Baseball Tournament held at the Lakeshore ballpark in July and August. One by one, teams were eliminated from the tournament until it came down to the final two: the Carrollton Lakers and the Johnson Chicks of Macon. Johnson took the final game from the Lakers by a 12 to 2 final to cop the crown of this tournament for the eighth year in a row.

When the 1964 West Georgia Association season began, the Carrollton Lakers were officially back in the loop after their one-year sabbatical. Narrowly winning the first half of the split season over the hot Southwire Sparks, the Lakers earned a berth in the post-season championship series. Jake took the second half of the season and became the opponent of Carrollton for the league title. In the three game series, the Lakers won the first game on September 6. The following week, on September 13, the two teams squared off for a double header to decide who would be the champion of the league. Jake won the first game 5 to 3, but Carrollton blanked Jake in the second game 10 to 0 and garnered the big trophy.

The final year of play for the Carrollton Lakers and the West Georgia Association was 1965. It was another good season of baseball as the best-in-the-league Lakers faced and defeated the circuit's All-Stars 3 to 2. Jimmy Blackwell was the ace pitcher for the

Lakers who finished their astounding run of our national pastime on a high note with yet another winning season.

As organized minor league baseball was revamped in 1963 eliminating classes B, C, and D, most of the small to moderate size towns lost their teams. Much of the interest in the lower baseball leagues began to wane in the mid-1950's as the television became an increasingly popular form of family entertainment.

Many great ballplayers passed took the field for the Carrollton minor league teams. Fourteen of these players graduated on to play in the major leagues, some for only one game, and some for many years. Four former major league players also wore a Carrollton uniform, and one player, pitcher Bob Hasty, briefly stopped in Carrollton between major league assignments.

During the seasons that Carrollton had teams in organized baseball, much success was had. Of ten different teams, seven had winning records, five won regular season pennants, and two won post-season championship series'.

Photographs

Following are pages of photographs collected depicting Carrollton baseball players, baseball games, and a few other interesting images pertaining to the city's baseball history. Some of the pictures were taken by fans and players, but many of the photographs were taken by Mr. B.M. Long who realized the importance of recording local history in the area. The photographs taken by Mr. Long used in the pages following now belong to the Annie Belle Weaver Special Collections of the Ingram Library of the State University of West Georgia.

Other collections kind enough to loan photographs to the following compilation include that of Blas Arroyo, Bert Bozzuto, John Crawford, Eddie Giombetti, Herb Marshall, Gene Monarchi, Pete Monarchi, Edwin Roberts, Mrs. Jelp Robinson, and the Times-Georgian newspaper.

Present day look at where the City Athletic Field, Carrollton's home field from 1928-30 and 1946-50, was located. Note the concrete section of the stands that remains on the hillside.

Left: 1920 Carrollton Baseball Team that won the Georgia State League Pennant that year. Front row left to right: Pop Shaw, Red Reese, Frank Pratt, and P.P. Swann. Middle row: Harry Allen and Jules Watson. Back row: Jess Craven, Goat Brandon, Manager Charlie Bell, Lefty Sutton, and Bill McKinnon. This photo was taken in front of the grand-stand at the South Street Ballpark.

Below: Another shot of the 1920 Carrollton Baseball Team in front of the third base side bleachers.

Above: (1920) Carrollton's Jess Craven prepares to step into the batters box.
Below: (1920) Left to right: Pop Shaw, Goat Brandon, and Ed Chaplin.

Above: (1920) Carrollton Manager Charlie Bell poses before a game.

Above: (1920) Visiting Team batting, possibly Cedartown.

Right: (1920) Jules Watson of Carrollton stops at third at the South Street Ballpark during a game against rival Cedartown.

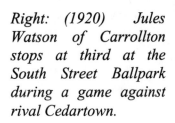

Above: (1920) Carrollton's Ed Chaplin slides into second base.
Below: (1920) Carrollton catcher Red Reese.

Above: (1920) Carrollton battery Red Reese, left, and Albert Bonifay, right.
Below: (1920) Visiting team batting at the "Pickle Factory."

Left: (1920) View of the bleachers on the third base side of the field at the South Street Ballpark This section was open-air, not covered as was the grand-stand behind home plate.

Above: (1920) Carrollton players Ed Chaplin, right, and Red Reese, left, pose in front of the South Street Ballpark grandstand.

Above two photos: (1920) Game action at the South Street Ballpark. Below: (1920) Carrollton player-manager Charlie Bell awaits game time.

Above: (1920) Carrollton players prepare to take their turn at bat. Left to right are Lefty Sutton, Goat Brandon, and Bill McKinnon.

Above: 1928 Carrollton Frogs Baseball Team, Champions of the Georgia-Alabama League. Left to right are Grimes, Manager Paul Fittery, Brant Boswell, Dick Taliaferro, Fob James, Miller Huggins, Cheese Goggans, Lacey, Jo-Jo White, Abe White, Kemp Wicker, Red Howell, and Bob Rowe.

Below: (1928) Carrollton's Jo-Jo White rounds third base after hitting one of his 27 home runs during his first season in professional baseball.

Above: (1928) Paul Fittery, manager and pitcher for Carrollton prior to a game at the newly constructed City Athletic Field.

Above: (1928) Red Howell of Carrollton takes a swing for the camera warming up for a game.

1928 Carrollton Frogs photos, clockwise from top left. (1) Paul Fittery, left, and Jo-Jo White, right. (2) Left to right: Red Howell, Cheese Goggans, and Jo-Jo White. (3) Bob Rowe. (4) Dick Taliaferro. (5) Game action at the City Athletic Field. (6) Kemp Wicker.

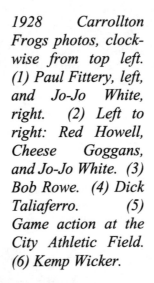

Above: 1929 Carrollton Champs Baseball Team, Champions of the Georgia-Alabama League. Front row left to right: Manager Paul Fittery, Squirt Holsomback, Henry Patton, Cheese Goggans, Benny Freedman, Bob Ezzell, and Abe White. Back row: Eddie Reese, Bill McGhee, Red Justiss, Colon Sappenfield, Ralph Stanfield, Marion Anderson, and Hoyt Crowe.

Left: (1929) Five players of the Carrollton Champs pose for a picture prior to a game at the City Athletic Field. Shown left to right are Marion Anderson, Edie Reese, unidentified player, Squirt Holsomback, and Bob Ezzell.

1946 Carrollton Hornets Baseball Team. Front row left to right: Dallas Thomas, Aubrey Borders, Fred Bieser, Team President Harvey Copeland, Manager Luther Gunnells, Shorty Marshall, George Souter, Bill Patterson, and Al Pittman. Back row: Bill Israel, Condit, Floyd Snider, Red Roberts, Paul Brock, Jim Hill, Lew York, Bob Mathews, and Dick Fraker.

Above: (1946) Carrollton manager Luther Gunnells and President Harvey Copeland receive gifts before a game in Carrollton.
Left: (1946) Phyllis Langley Young, niece of Red Roberts, pictured in front of the Carrollton team bus.

Above: (1946) Carrollton players left to right: Charlie "Red" Roberts, Luther Gunnells, Shorty Marshall, and Lew York.
Right: (1947) Carrollton pitcher Bert Bozzuto.

1947 Carrollton Hornets Baseball Team. Front row left to right: Jacob Dendinger, Bill Jones, Bill Webb, Shorty Marshall, Team President Harvey Copeland, Manager Red Roberts, Bert Bozzuto, and Leo Goicoechea. Back row: Dick Kelly, Donnie Muse, Glen Thomas, Walt Little, Bill Patterson, Floyd Snider, and Jim Hill. Batboy in front is Richard Mahaffy.

1947 Carrollton Hornets photos at the City Athletic Field, clockwise from top left. (1) John Allen. (2) Pete Monarchi. (3) Bill Patterson. (4) Dallas Thomas. (5) Front row left to right: Bert Bozzuto and Leo Goicoechea. Back row: Walt Little, Bill Webb, and Bill Jones.

1948 Carrollton Hornets baseball team during spring training from the April 15, 1948 edition of the Carroll County Times. Top row left to right: Elmer Bertha, Bob Bess, Bert Bozzuto, and Eddie Giombetti. Second row: Pete Kurowski, Shorty Marshall, Gene Monarchi, and Pete Monarchi. Third row: Corbet Newton, Bernie Povanda, Manager Red Roberts, and Bob Roedel. Fourth row: Carl Roman, Gilbert Sanchez, Don White, and Bob Williams. Bottom left: Team President Harvey Copeland.

Above: (1948) Ceremonies at the beginning of the 1948 season presenting the 1947 Georgia-Alabama League Pennant to the Carrollton Hornets. Far right presenting the flag is Baseball Commissioner Happy Chandler. Receiving the flag is Carrollton Team President Harvey Copeland. Georgia-Alabama League President Art Decatur is shown at the far left of the photo.

Left: Georgia-Alabama League President Art Decatur addresses the Carrollton crowd following the 1947 league pennant presentation. Pictured at the far left of the photo is Baseball Commissioner Happy Chandler. To Chandler's left is former Georgia Governer Ellis Arnall.

Clockwise from top left: (1) 1948 Ticket to Carrollton's opening day game. (2) 1948 Carrollton pocket schedule. (3) Carrollton spring training photo of Eddie Giombetti, left, and Gilbert Sanchez, right. (4) Letter from F.M. Kline of the Crape Myrtle Hotel to Gene Monarchi's girlfriend.

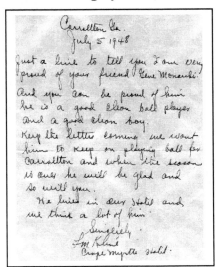

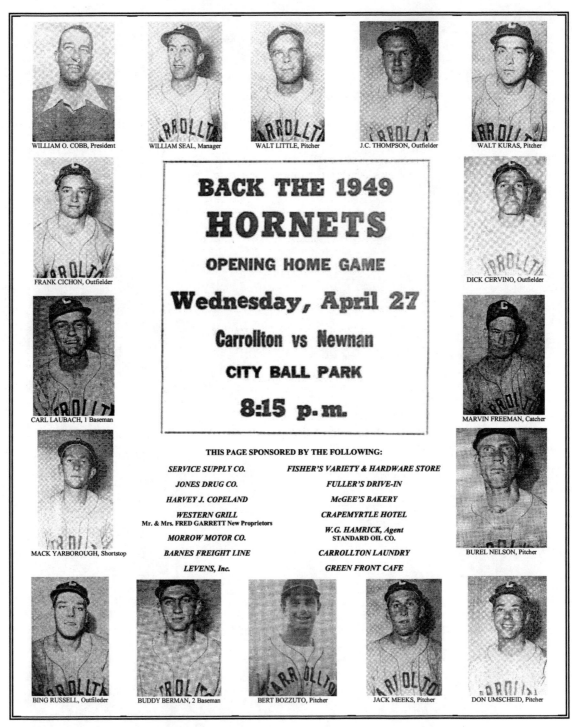

WILLIAM O. COBB, President

WILLIAM SEAL, Manager

WALT LITTLE, Pitcher

J.C. THOMPSON, Outfielder

WALT KURAS, Pitcher

FRANK CICHON, Outfielder

DICK CERVINO, Outfielder

CARL LAUBACH, 1 Baseman

MARVIN FREEMAN, Catcher

MACK YARBOROUGH, Shortstop

BUREL NELSON, Pitcher

BING RUSSELL, Outfielder

BUDDY BERMAN, 2 Baseman

BERT BOZZUTO, Pitcher

JACK MEEKS, Pitcher

DON UMSCHEID, Pitcher

BACK THE 1949 HORNETS

OPENING HOME GAME

Wednesday, April 27

Carrollton vs Newnan

CITY BALL PARK

8:15 p. m.

THIS PAGE SPONSORED BY THE FOLLOWING:

SERVICE SUPPLY CO.

JONES DRUG CO.

HARVEY J. COPELAND

WESTERN GRILL
Mr. & Mrs. FRED GARRETT New Proprietors

MORROW MOTOR CO.

BARNES FREIGHT LINE

LEVENS, Inc.

FISHER'S VARIETY & HARDWARE STORE

FULLER'S DRIVE-IN

McGEE'S BAKERY

CRAPEMYRTLE HOTEL

W.G. HAMRICK, Agent
STANDARD OIL CO.

CARROLLTON LAUNDRY

GREEN FRONT CAFE

Reproduction of April 26, 1949 Times-Free Press Ad for Carrollton Hornets baseball.

Above: 1950 Carrollton Hornets Baseball Team. Front row left to right: Cotayo Gonzalez, Jim Shirley, Fred DeSouza, Reggie Corrales, Manager Shorty Marshall, Jim Morelli, Ray Clark, Blas Arroyo, and Fred Lee. Back row: Cliff Reach, Curtis White, Buddy Berman, Leo Mazak, Jack Dennis, Mason Kelly, Ernie Victor, Gene Solt, and Bill Weldon. Below: Same team in a different pose.

Right: (1950) Carrollton crowd of approximately 3,000 fans at the City Athletic Field ballpark for the Hornets home opener on April 27, 1950.

Left: (1950) Carrollton pitcher and utility man Blas Arroyo pitching from the mound at the City Athletic Field.

Right: (1950) Carrollton players left to right: Blas Arroyo, Reggie Corrales, and Fred DeSouza.

Left: (1950) Close up view of the scoreboard at the City Athletic Field in Carrollton.

Above: 1961 Carrollton Lakers Baseball Team. Front row left to right: Pat Cain, Richard Wiggins, Leroy Robinson, and Bobby Ray Harris. Middle row: J.P. Preston, Duell Robinson, Wayne Robinson, W.L. Copeland, and Joe Arp. Back Row: Rube Prater, Elbert Eason, Harry Shadrix, Jerry Lanier, Reuben Walker, and Coach Jelp Robinson. Below left: 1961 West Georgia Association championship trophy won by the above Carrollton Lakers team.

Below right: 1962-63 Carrollton Lakers banquet. Front row left to right: Wayne Robinson, Jerry Lanier, Johnny Daniels, Pat Cain, and Billy Bell. Back row: Coach Jelp Robinson, Bobby Ray Harris, Skeeter Robinson, Donnie Sinft, Jimmy Blackwell, Frankie Jordan, Reuben Walker, Duell Robinson, and Fleming Wiggins.

Player Statistics

The following pages contain statistics for Carrollton players while they played in a Carrollton uniform. Many listings contain gaps where stats are missing, and there are several reasons for these gaps. In some cases, certain statistics, such as runs batted in, were not kept by the scorekeepers of the league or team. Thus, these numbers may very well never be recovered. There were numerous players who had a "cup of coffee" stint with the Carrollton team. Most of these players did not spend enough time to get their name in the official league record book in the year they played, so no statistical entry was made for them. Every attempt has been made using the best available information sources to compile the most accurate and complete statistics for each player listed here.

Statistics abbreviations and definitions:

General terms:
Yr = Year played
Team = Location of the team

Batting Statistics:
G = Games played in
AB = At Bats
R = Runs scored
H = Hits

2B = Doubles
3B = Triples
HR = Home Runs
RBI = Runs Batted In
SB = Stolen Bases
BB = Base on Balls or Walks
SO = Strikeouts
AVG = Batting Average – calculated as H/AB

Fielding Statistics:
POS = Positions played
PO = Putouts
A = Assists
E = Errors
FA = Fielding Average – calculated as (A+PO) / (A+PO+E)

Pitching Statistics:
G = Games pitched in
W = Wins
L = Losses
PCT = Winning Percentage – calculated as W / (W+L)
IP = Innings Pitched
H = Hits allowed
R = Runs allowed
ER = Earned runs allowed
SO = Strikeouts issued
BB = Base on Balls or Walks issued
ERA = Earned Run Average – calculated as (9 x ER) / IP

ALEXANDER, BILL — William V. Alexander

YR	TEAM	G	AB	R	H	2B	3B	HR	RBI	SB	BB	SO	AVG	POS	PO	A	E	FA	Pitching: G	W	L	PCT	ERA	IP	H	R	ER	SO	BB
1930	Carrollton	85	335	81	115	26	5	5		17	47	24	.343	2B, SS, OF	145	157	32	.904											

ALEXANDER, BILL — William Alexander B:R

YR	TEAM	G	AB	R	H	2B	3B	HR	RBI	SB	BB	SO	AVG	POS	PO	A	E	FA	Pitching: G	W	L	PCT	ERA	IP	H	R	ER	SO	BB
1947	*Carrollton	16	32	4	4	2	0	0	5	0	2	16	.125	P	4	10	2	.875	16	3	4	.429	5.42	78	98	53	47	40	31

*stats include 14 games played in Carrollton and 2 games played in Griffin during season

ALLEN, HARRY — Harry K. Allen

YR	TEAM	G	AB	R	H	2B	3B	HR	RBI	SB	BB	SO	AVG	POS	PO	A	E	FA	Pitching: G	W	L	PCT	ERA	IP	H	R	ER	SO	BB
1920	Carrollton	93		5	10									.108	P, OF															
1921	Carrollton	28		2	1									.036	P															

ALLEN, JOHN — John R. Allen T:R B:R

YR	TEAM	G	AB	R	H	2B	3B	HR	RBI	SB	BB	SO	AVG	POS	PO	A	E	FA	Pitching: G	W	L	PCT	ERA	IP	H	R	ER	SO	BB
1947	Carrollton	83	310	55	75	12	8	1	23	6	65	37	.242	2B, OF	172	44	11	.952											

ANDERSON, MARION

YR	TEAM	G	AB	R	H	2B	3B	HR	RBI	SB	BB	SO	AVG	POS	PO	A	E	FA	Pitching: G	W	L	PCT	ERA	IP	H	R	ER	SO	BB
1929	Carrollton	74	274	41	96	20	6	0		3	29	14	.350	2B	167	224	21	.949											

ARDIS, --------

YR	TEAM	G	AB	R	H	2B	3B	HR	RBI	SB	BB	SO	AVG	POS	PO	A	E	FA	Pitching: G	W	L	PCT	ERA	IP	H	R	ER	SO	BB
1920	Carrollton	3	0	0	0	0	0	0			0		.000																	

ARROYO, BLAS — Blas M. Arroyo "Lala" Born: October 8, 1924 in Cuba T:R B:L Height 5' 10" Weight 155

YR	TEAM	G	AB	R	H	2B	3B	HR	RBI	SB	BB	SO	AVG	POS	PO	A	E	FA	Pitching: G	W	L	PCT	ERA	IP	H	R	ER	SO	BB
1948	Carrollton	65	214	35	45	7	1	0	28	13	29	48	.210	P, 3B, OF	77	43	16	.882	7	2	2	.500	3.00	48	49	20	16	24	20
1950	Carrollton	33	71	15	20	3	0	2	10	0	7	6	.282	P	6	12	1	.947	18	9	7	.563	5.37	104	105	83	62	52	72

ATCHLEY, LOY

YR	TEAM	G	AB	R	H	2B	3B	HR	RBI	SB	BB	SO	AVG	POS	PO	A	E	FA	Pitching: G	W	L	PCT	ERA	IP	H	R	ER	SO	BB
1928	*Carrollton	61	185	29	59	8	2	4		4	8	20	.319	P, OF	82	31	4	.966	17	3	6	.333	3.52	92	98	63	36	29	19

*stats include play in Anniston and Cedartown during season

AVERY, --------

YR	TEAM	G	AB	R	H	2B	3B	HR	RBI	SB	BB	SO	AVG	POS	PO	A	E	FA	Pitching: G	W	L	PCT	ERA	IP	H	R	ER	SO	BB
1928	Carrollton	5	21	1	4								.190																	

BAILEY, --------

YR	TEAM	G	AB	R	H	2B	3B	HR	RBI	SB	BB	SO	AVG	POS	PO	A	E	FA	Pitching: G	W	L	PCT	ERA	IP	H	R	ER	SO	BB
1928	Carrollton	5													P, OF					5	0	0	.000	12.00	9	23	13	12	2	8

BALES, --------

YR	TEAM	G	AB	R	H	2B	3B	HR	RBI	SB	BB	SO	AVG	POS	PO	A	E	FA	Pitching: G	W	L	PCT	ERA	IP	H	R	ER	SO	BB
1920	Carrollton	60		3	16									.267																

BARBER, --------

YR	TEAM	G	AB	R	H	2B	3B	HR	RBI	SB	BB	SO	AVG	POS	PO	A	E	FA	Pitching: G	W	L	PCT	ERA	IP	H	R	ER	SO	BB
1921	Carrollton		319	62	108									.339	OF															

BARKLEY, -------- T:R B:R

YR	TEAM	G	AB	R	H	2B	3B	HR	RBI	SB	BB	SO	AVG	POS	PO	A	E	FA	Pitching: G	W	L	PCT	ERA	IP	H	R	ER	SO	BB
1946	Carrollton	4													P					4	2	1	.667		31	24	14		16	5

BARNES, --------

YR	TEAM	G	AB	R	H	2B	3B	HR	RBI	SB	BB	SO	AVG	POS	PO	A	E	FA	Pitching: G	W	L	PCT	ERA	IP	H	R	ER	SO	BB
1921	Carrollton	10-													P															

BARTHOLOMEW, JACK T:R B:R

BEASLEY, JOHN T:R B:R

BEAUCHAMP, WALT Walter Beauchamp T:R B:R

BECK, -----

BELL, CHARLIE Charles J. Bell

BERMAN, BUDDY Norman Berman T:R B:S

BERTHA, ELMER "Bates" Born: October 29, 1927 in Jessup, Pennsylvania T:R B:R Height: 6' 1" Weight: 135

BETTISON, -----

BIESER, FRED T:R B:R

BOBOWSKI, ED Edward Bobowski "Bobo" T:R B:R

BONIFAY, ALBERT Albert L. Bonifay T:L B:L

BORDERS, AUBREY T:R B:L

BOSSER, MEL Melvin Edward Bosser Born: February 8, 1914 in Johnstown, Pennsylvania Died: March 26, 1986 in Crossville, Tennessee T:R B:R Height: 6' 0" Weight: 173

BOSWELL, BRANT

YR	TEAM	G	AB	R	H	2B	3B	HR	RBI	SB	BB	SO	AVG	POS	PO	A	E	FA	Pitching: G	W	L	PCT	ERA	IP	H	R	ER	SO	BB
1949	Carrollton	25	64	16	14	0	0	0	4	3	20	8	.219	2B	30	37	7	.905											
1950	*Carrollton	39	130	19	26	6	0	0	13	4	16	41	.200	SS	48	95	13	.917											
1950	Carrollton	27	89	18	27	7	3	0	11	2	31	13	.303	2B	43	32	10	.882											
1920	Carrollton		43	9	5								.116	P, OF															
1920	Carrollton		343	68	109								.318	M, SS, 2B, 3B, P															
1949	Carrollton	112	396	69	90	12	0	0	22	9	71	76	.227	2B	306	252	21	.964											
1950	*Carrollton	18	62	13	20	1	1	0	8	4	13	9	.323	2B	38	35	4	.948											
1948	Carrollton	37	126	13	23	2	1	8	0	1	15	28	.183	1B	278	7	6	.979											
1930	Carrollton	10-												C															
1946	Carrollton	24	54	8	6	1	0	1	6	0	5	19	.111	OF	10	1	1	.917											
1949	*Carrollton	33	67	8	16	1	1	0	5	1	9	20	.239	P	10	28	2	.950	33	10	13	.435	3.51	187	187	116	73	74	112
1950	*Carrollton	32	83	12	14	2	0	1	7	0	7	31	.169	P					27	17	7	.708	4.96	176	182	114	97	100	118
1920	Carrollton		71	6	15								.211	P															
1946	*Carrollton	29	60	7	16	6	0	0	7	0	8	9	.267	P	4	27	2	.939	25	7	6	.538	3.82	132	115	64	56	84	34
1946	Carrollton	4											.333	P					4	1	2	.333		18	20	11		3	7
1928	Carrollton	88	357	79	97	19	2	12		14	52	38	.272	2B	201	269	28	.944											

*BEASLEY — stats include 35 games played in Rome and 4 games played in Carrollton during season

*BERMAN — stats include 3 games played in Carrollton and 15 games played in Alexander City during 1950 season

*BOBOWSKI — stats include 13 games played in LaGrange and 20 games played in Carrollton during 1949 season

*BORDERS — stats include 13 games played in Newnan and 16 games played in Carrollton during season.

BOZZUTO, BERT — Albert Bozzuto   Born: March 7, 1927 in Hamden, Connecticut   Height: 5' 9"   Weight: 160   T:L B:L

YR	TEAM	G	AB	R	H	2B	3B	HR	RBI	SB	BB	SO	AVG	POS	PO	A	E	FA	Pitching: G	W	L	PCT	ERA	IP	H	R	ER	SO	BB
1947	Carrollton	26	62	2	7	0	0	3	0	0	26		.113	P	0	11	3	.786	24	10	6	.625	3.09	140	137	53	48	99	33
1948	Carrollton	14	30	4	3	1	0	0	1	0	1	12	.100	P	1	13	3	.824	14	5	5	.500	3.84	82	78	40	35	56	29
1949	*Carrollton	26	43	1	8	0	0	1	0	1	12		.186	P	4	13	2	.895	26	5	14	.263	5.12	137	159	93	78	78	70

*stats include 9 games played in Carrollton and 17 games played in Alexander City during 1949 season

BRANDON, GOAT — C.N. Brandon

YR	TEAM	G	AB	R	H	AVG	POS
1920	Carrollton		284	52	87	.306	OF

BRINSON, ------

YR	TEAM	G	POS
1920	Carrollton	10-	SS

BROCK, PAUL   T:R B:R

YR	TEAM	G	AB	R	H	2B	3B	HR	RBI	SB	BB	SO	AVG	POS	PO	A	E	FA	Pitching: G	W	L	PCT	ERA	IP	H	R	ER	SO	BB
1946	Carrollton	12	36	8	12	2	0	0	7	0	1	9	.333	P	7	22	1	.967	12	10	2	.833	3.46	91	92	30	35	56	32

BRUNER, B.E.

YR	TEAM	G	AB	R	H	AVG	POS
1921	Carrollton		104	7	14	.135	SS

BUFORD, RED

YR	TEAM	G	AB	R	H	AVG	POS
1929	Carrollton		13	0	1	.077	OF

BURKE, JOE — Joseph Burke   T:R B:R

YR	TEAM	G	AB	R	H	2B	3B	HR	RBI	SB	BB	SO	AVG	POS	Pitching: G	W	L	PCT	ERA	IP	H	R	ER	SO	BB
1948	Carrollton	15	35	5	9	1	0	0	2	0	3	7	.257	P	9	3	3	.500	2.39	49	52	24	13	23	33

BURNSTEIN, LEONARD   T:R B:R

YR	TEAM	G	AB	R	H	2B	3B	HR	RBI	SB	BB	SO	AVG	POS
1949	Carrollton	17	41	7	10	1	0	0	2	0	6	2	.244	OF

BUTTS, ------

YR	TEAM	G	AB	R	H	2B	3B	HR	RBI	SB	BB	AVG	POS	PO	A	E	FA
1928	Carrollton	15	6	7	7	0	0	0	0	0	2	.467	1B	17	0	0	1.000

CAIN, GEORGE   T:L B:R

YR	TEAM	G	AB	R	H	2B	3B	HR	RBI	SB	BB	SO	AVG	POS	PO	A	E	FA	Pitching: G	W	L	PCT	ERA	IP	H	R	ER	SO	BB
1946	Carrollton	7												P					7	1	1	.500		20	26	20	7	7	10
1948	Carrollton	25	52	2	8	0	0	0	5	0	3	11	.154	P	4	21	3	.893	22	8	6	.571	4.29	128	141	78	31	55	54

CAIN, SUGAR — Merritt Patrick Cain   Born: April 5, 1907 in Macon, Georgia   Died: April 3, 1975 in Atlanta, Georgia   T:R B:L   Height: 5' 11"   Weight: 190

YR	TEAM	G	AB	R	H	2B	3B	HR	RBI	SB	BB	SO	AVG	POS	Pitching: G	W	L	PCT	ERA	IP	H	R	ER	SO	BB
1930	Carrollton	35	106	14	30	5	0	0	9	0	9	24	.283	P	21	8	10	.444	4.80	163	185	124	87	103	58

CALDARA, ------

YR	TEAM	G	POS	Pitching: G	W	L	PCT	ERA	IP	H	R	ER	SO	BB
1930	Carrollton	1	P	1	0	1	.000	18.00	2	6	4	4	2	1

CALKINS, DICK

YR	TEAM	G	POS
1949	Carrollton	1	OF

CALLEN, JIM

YR	TEAM	G	POS
1949	Carrollton	4	OF

"PICKLE IT!" Minor League Baseball of Carrollton, Georgia

YR	TEAM	G	AB	R	H	2B	3B	HR	RBI	SB	BB	SO	AVG	POS	PO	A	E	FA	Pitching: G	W	L	PCT	ERA	IP	H	R	ER	SO	BB
CANNON, SHORTY (D.T. Cannon)																													
1921	Carrollton	195		37	59								.303	OF, SS															
CARMICHAEL, ------																													
1921	Carrollton	14		1	8								.571																
CARTER, HOMER (Homer A. Carter)																													
1928	*Carrollton	28	71	8	18	3	1	1		0	4	8	.253	P, OF	11	25	4	.900	19	9	8	.529	4.00	126	151	75	56	47	23
*stats include play in Gadsden during season																													
1930	Carrollton	20			3								.150	P															
CARTER, RUSS (Russ B. Carter)																													
1920	Carrollton	10-												OF															
CHAPLIN, ED (Bert Edgar Chaplin (born Bert Edgar Chapman) Born: September 25, 1893 in Pelzer, South Carolina Died: August 15, 1978 in Sanford, Florida T:R B:L Height: 5'7" Weight: 158																													
1920	Carrollton	281		73	87								.310	OF, C															
CHATHAM, HAPPY (C.B. Chatham)																													
1920	Carrollton	109		12	28								.257	3B, SS, 2B															
CHILDS, FRANK T:R B:R																													
1946	*Carrollton	39	129	6	23	3	1	0	11	1	3	13	.178	OF, P	48	2	3	.943	7	0	3	.000		20	30	26		16	25
*stats include 36 games played in Newnan and 3 games played in Carrollton during season																													
CHRISTIANSEN, ------																													
1929	Carrollton	34		6	11								.324																
CICHON, FRANK T:R B:L																													
1948	Carrollton	108	410	67	109	13	9	12	66		30	67	.266	OF	182	12	28	.874											
1949	Carrollton	55	196	41	54	5	3	1	29		8	26	23	.276	OF	86	12	6	.942										
CLARK, RAY (Raymond Clark T:R B:R)																													
1950	Carrollton	119	459	82	155	38	2	12	77	6	56	48	.338	SS	152	253	38	.914											
COBIELLA, RICARDO T:R B:R																													
1950	Carrollton	21	66	10	14	1	0	0	6	0	16	8	.212	2B	60	48	4	.964											
COKER, E.R.																													
1930	Carrollton	34			9								.265	SS															
COLLINS, LEE B:R																													
1947	*Carrollton	47	164	14	33	7	0	1	22	0	19	21	.201	OF	58	2	4	.938											
*stats include 13 games played in Tallassee, 4 games played in Carrollton, 7 games played in Newnan, and 23 games played in Alexander City during season																													
COLTER, ------																													
1946	Carrollton	1												P					1	0	0	.000		2					

92

CONDIT, ------ T:R B:R

CONHENNEY, JIM James Conhenney T:R B:R

COOMBS, ------

CORNELIUS, RUSTY

CORRALES, REINALDO "Reggie" T:R B:R

COSBY, ------

COULLING, STAN Stanley H. Coulling Born: June 4, 1921 in Rocky Mount, North Carolina T:R B:R Height: 6'3" Weight: 190

CRAIN, PAUL T:R B:R

CRAVEN, JESS Jesse C. Craven

CROWE, HOYT

CROWSON, MARV Marvin Crowson T:R B:R

DAVENPORT, ------

DAVENPORT, ------

DAVIS, CARL

YR TEAM	G	AB	R	H	2B	3B	HR	RBI	SB	BB	SO	AVG	POS	PO	A	E	FA	Pitching: G	W	L	PCT	ERA	IP	H	R	ER	SO	BB
CONDIT, ------																													
1946 *Carrollton	18	48	2	8	0	0	1	0	3	7	.167	P	5	24	0	1.000	18	8	7	.533	3.02	134	119	51	45	70	42
CONHENNEY, JIM																													
1949 Carrollton	94	294	56	64	7	3	0	32	15	59	70	.218	3B	85	174	29	.909											
COOMBS, ------																													
1921 Carrollton	10-												P																
CORNELIUS, RUSTY																													
1921 Carrollton	10-												P																
CORRALES, REINALDO																													
1950 Carrollton	32	95	24	27	6	0	0	15	0	31	16	.284																
COSBY, ------																													
1928 *Carrollton	15	58	7	17	4	0	0	0		5	10	.293																
COULLING, STAN																													
1950 Carrollton	14	33	4	6	0	0	1	3	0	7	4	.182	M, P					8	3	3	.500	4.59	51	66	33	26	27	8
CRAIN, PAUL																													
1947 *Carrollton	41	112	10	23	6	0	0	8	0	8	13	.205	M, P	19	48	5	.931	33	19	14	.576	2.93	261	225	114	85	152	54
CRAVEN, JESS																													
1920 Carrollton		325	52	87								.268	OF, 1B															
CROWE, HOYT																													
1929 Carrollton	21	53	2	10	1	0	0	1	2	5		.188	P	6	33	0	1.000	22	8	7	.533		135	145	81	49	35	
CROWSON, MARV																													
1946 Carrollton	6												P					6	3	1	.750		35	26	16	16	16	18
DAVENPORT, ------																													
1921 Carrollton		103	10	24								.233	2B																
DAVENPORT, ------																													
1930 Carrollton	10			1								.100																	
DAVIS, CARL																													
1929 Carrollton		19	3	2								.105	P																
1930 Carrollton	10-												P																

CONDIT: stats include 11 games played in Opelika and 7 games played in Carrollton during season

COSBY: stats include play in Lindale during season

CRAIN: stats include 3 games played in Carrollton and 38 games played in Valley during season

93

YR	TEAM	G	AB	R	H	2B	3B	HR	RBI	SB	BB	SO	AVG	POS	PO	A	E	FA	Pitching: G	W	L	PCT	ERA	IP	H	R	ER	SO	BB
DEAN, HARRY James Harry Dean Born: May 12, 1915 in Rockmart, Georgia Died: June 1, 1960 in Rockmart, Georgia T:R B:R Height: 6' 4" Weight: 185														P					2	1	0	1.000		9	10	8		7	2
1946	Carrollton 2																												
DENDINGER, JACOB T:R B:R																													
1947	Carrollton	23	77	16	20	6	1	2	2	12	18	14	.260	OF	26	0	2	.929											
1948	Carrollton	16	46	4	13	5	0	0	3	8	12	6	.283	OF	23	0	2	.920											
DENNIS, JACK B:R																													
1950	Carrollton	10	12	3	4	0	0	0	2	0	3	2	.333	P															
DESOUZA, FRED Federico DeSouza T:R B:R																													
1950	Carrollton	122	421	149	126	33	6	24	92	6	165	92	.299	3B	137	239	27	.933											
DIMASI, JOE Joseph DiMasi T:L B:L																													
1947	Carrollton	17	57	11	14	3	1	1	12	3	12	14	.246	OF	20	2	1	.957											
DOERFLINGER, GENE Eugene Doerflinger T:R B:R																													
1948	Carrollton	41	88	9	16	1	0	0	6	0	14	14	.182	P	14	35	2	.961	37	23	11	.676	2.13	253	180	90	60	233	123
DUGAN, --------														P															
1920	Carrollton 10-																												
DUMAS, OTTO Otto B. Dumas																													
1928	Carrollton	20	84	7	25	9	0	1		2	4	10	.298	OF	27	3	3	.909											
EAST, CARL Carlton William East Born: August 27, 1894 in Marietta, Georgia Died: August 27, 1953 in Whitesburg, Georgia T:R B:L Height: 6' 2" Weight: 178														M, OF															
1930	Carrollton 190 86												.453																
EDWARDS, HOYT T:R B:R																													
1948	*Carrollton	28	33	1	3	0	0	0	2	0	4	11	.091	P	6	22	3	.903	27	8	6	.571	4.34	110	120	67	53	50	49
	*stats include 6 games played in Newnan and 22 games played in Carrollton during season																												
ELLO, JIM James Ello T:R B:R																													
1947	*Carrollton	89	281	26	63	11	2	1	30	5	20	47	.224	C	378	56	14	.969											
	*stats include 3 games played in Carrollton and 86 games played in Griffin during season																												
EZZELL, BOB Robert A. Ezzell																													
1929	Carrollton	95	355	82	131	32	5	13		15	40	21	.369	1B	961	27	15	.985											
1930	Carrollton	84	346	75	108	20	5	20		18	36	24	.312	1B	835	28	15	.982											
FARR, CURTIS "Red"																													
1946	Carrollton 10-																												
FERNANDEZ, MIKE Miguel Fernandez T:R B:R														P															
1950	Carrollton 4																		4	1	3	.250						29	

YR	TEAM	G	AB	R	H	2B	3B	HR	RBI	SB	BB	SO	AVG	POS	PO	A	E	FA	Pitching: G	W	L	PCT	ERA	IP	H	R	ER	SO	BB

FETNER, CHARLES T:L B:L

| 1950 | Carrollton | 16 | 59 | 2 | 16 | 1 | 1 | 0 | 11 | 3 | 4 | 4 | .271 | 1B | 127 | 1 | 3 | .977 | | | | | | | | | | | |

FINCHER, BOB Robert Fincher B:R

| 1946 | Carrollton | 10 | 33 | 3 | 8 | 0 | 0 | 1 | 4 | 1 | 2 | 7 | .242 | | | | | | | | | | | | | | | | |

FINNEY, LOU Louis Klopsche Finney Born: August 13, 1910 in Buffalo, Alabama Died: April 22, 1966 in Lafayette, Alabama T:R B:L Height: 6'0" Weight: 180

| 1930 | Carrollton | 55 | 234 | 43 | 91 | 17 | 2 | 7 | | 7 | 4 | 14 | .388 | OF | 124 | 8 | 6 | .956 | | | | | | | | | | | |

FISHER, ————

| 1930 | Carrollton | 19 | 67 | 13 | 19 | 1 | 0 | 1 | | 1 | 6 | 3 | .283 | 2B | 34 | 56 | 13 | .873 | | | | | | | | | | | |

FITTERY, PAUL Paul Clarence Fittery Born: October 10, 1887 in Lebanon, Pennsylvania Died: January 28, 1974 in Cartersville, Georgia T:L B:S Height: 5'8" Weight: 156

| 1928 | Carrollton | 33 | 220 | 33 | 50 | | | | | | | | .227 | M, P, OF | 85 | 73 | 6 | .963 | 28 | 21 | 2 | .913 | 1.60 | 225 | 194 | 64 | 40 | 137 | 29 |
| 1929 | Carrollton | 39 | 108 | 16 | 23 | 2 | 3 | 2 | | 1 | 16 | 23 | .213 | M, P | 45 | 58 | 3 | .972 | 23 | 16 | 2 | .889 | 1.81 | 174 | 165 | 56 | 35 | 89 | 30 |

FLOWERS, BURNICE

| 1946 | Carrollton | 10- | | | | | | | | | | | | | | | | | | | | | | | | | | | |

FRAKER, DICK Richard Fraker T:R B:R

| 1946 | Carrollton | 38 | 137 | 19 | 36 | 3 | 0 | 0 | 9 | 3 | 10 | 7 | .263 | OF | 63 | 2 | 2 | .970 | | | | | | | | | | | |

FRAKES, BEN

| 1928 | *Carrollton | 20 | 49 | 4 | 4 | 0 | 0 | 0 | 0 | 0 | 1 | 14 | .082 | P | 10 | 29 | 1 | .975 | 17 | 5 | 9 | .357 | 2.62 | 117 | 152 | 80 | 24 | 35 | 32 |

*stats include play in Gadsden during season

FREEDMAN, BENNY

| 1929 | Carrollton | 88 | 333 | 67 | 104 | 14 | 2 | 15 | | 9 | 37 | 46 | .312 | OF, C | 189 | 13 | 15 | .931 | | | | | | | | | | | |

FULLER, BERTRAM

| 1920 | Carrollton | 45 | 6 | 9 | | | | | | | | | .200 | SS | | | | | | | | | | | | | | | |

FULLINGTON, ————

| 1949 | Carrollton | 4 | 2 | 0 | 1 | 0 | 0 | 0 | 0 | 0 | 0 | 0 | .500 | | | | | | | | | | | | | | | | |

GALLAGHER, ————

| 1921 | Carrollton | 10- | | | | | | | | | | | | OF | | | | | | | | | | | | | | | |

GALLIVAN, PHIL Philip Joseph Gallivan Born: May 29, 1907 in Seattle, Washington Died: November 24, 1969 in St. Paul Minnesota Height: 6'0" Weight: 170

| 1930 | Carrollton | 7 | | | | | | | | | | | | P | | | | | 7 | 1 | 2 | .333 | 4.05 | 60 | 51 | 30 | 27 | 10 | 11 |

GARNER, BOB Robert Garner T:R B:R

| 1946 | Carrollton | 67 | 210 | 31 | 59 | 11 | 0 | 12 | 35 | 4 | 19 | 35 | .281 | OF, P | 81 | 7 | 7 | .926 | 10 | 3 | 4 | .429 | 6.10 | 59 | 73 | 48 | 40 | 29 | 31 |

GARRETT, TIGE H.L. Garrett

| 1928 | Carrollton | 30 | 124 | 21 | 24 | 6 | 0 | 1 | | 3 | 7 | 14 | .193 | 3B | 45 | 44 | 9 | .906 | | | | | | | | | | | |

GARVEY, --------
1921 Carrollton 10-

GIOMBETTI, EDDIE
Edward Giombetti   Born: October 24, 1923 in Jessup, Pennsylvania   T:R   B:R   Height: 5' 8"   Weight: 160

GLOVER, OMER   T:R   B:R
*stats include 27 games played in Alexander City and 22 games played in Carrollton during season

GOGGANS, G.E.   "Big Cheese"

GOICOECHEA, LEO
Leonardo Goicoechea   T:L   B:R

GONZALEZ, COTAYO   T:L   B:L

GOODE, --------

GRIFFITH, --------

GRIMES, --------
*stats include play in Lindale during season

GULLIVER, CLARK   T:R   B:R

GUNNELLS, LUTHER   T:R   B:R

GURDY, --------

GUYTON, --------   T:R   B:R

HARDWICK, GEORGE

YR TEAM	G	AB	R	H	2B	3B	HR	RBI	SB	BB	SO	AVG	POS	PO	A	E	FA
GARVEY — 1921 Carrollton	10-																
GIOMBETTI — 1948 Carrollton	1												P				
GLOVER — 1948 *Carrollton	49	116	9	20	1	0	8	2	16	25		.172	C	165	26	8	.960
GOGGANS — 1928 Carrollton	87	340	53	105	24	1	14	4	6	26		.309	C	302	67	19	.951
GOGGANS — 1929 Carrollton	92	335	37	96	12	2	6	6	12	24		.287	C	374	60	16	.971
GOGGANS — 1930 Carrollton	10-												C				
GOICOECHEA — 1947 Carrollton	12	25	2	4	0	0	0	3	0	3		.160	P	2	5	3	.700
GONZALEZ — 1950 Carrollton	8												P				
GOODE — 1930 Carrollton	19	76	7	14	5	0	0	1	7	11		.184	SS	44	55	11	.900
GRIFFITH — 1930 Carrollton	19	48	12	11	1	0	1	0	0	9		.229	P				
GRIMES — 1928 *Carrollton	10	42	6	16	5	0	0	1	1	4		.380	SS	15	16	9	.775
GULLIVER — 1946 Carrollton	90	344	52	69	12	2	1	20	8	31	20	.201	OF, P	193	8	3	.985
GUNNELLS — 1946 Carrollton	117	402	89	153	27	2	24	96	31	46	26	.381	M, SS, P	180	326	40	.927
GURDY — 1946 Carrollton	1												P				
GUYTON — 1946 Carrollton	24	69	9	12	3	0	0	6	1	9	11	.174	3B	9	19	4	.875
HARDWICK — 1930 Carrollton	12	36	6	12	1	0	0	0	1	3		.333	P				

Pitching:

Player / Year	G	W	L	PCT	ERA	IP	H	R	ER	SO	BB
GIOMBETTI 1948	1	0	0	.000		4					
GOICOECHEA 1947	12	5	2	.714	3.46	65	59	32	25	65	35
GONZALEZ 1950	8	4	2	.667	4.19	58	66	35	27	27	24
GRIFFITH 1930	15	5	5	.500	7.07	98	136	94	77	30	32
GULLIVER 1946	1	0	0	.000							
GUNNELLS 1946	3	0	1	.000		5	8	4		1	1
GURDY 1946	1	0	0	.000		2					
HARDWICK 1930	11	3	5	.375	6.46	71	104	61	51	23	24

YR	TEAM	G	AB	R	H	2B	3B	HR	RBI	SB	BB	SO	AVG	POS	PO	A	E	FA	Pitching: G	W	L	PCT	ERA	IP	H	R	ER	SO	BB
HARRISON, ------																														\
1929	Carrollton	16	55	8	17	2	1	1		1	4	12	.309	OF	33	1	1	.971											

HASTY, BOB Robert Keller Hasty Born: May 3, 1896 in Canton, Georgia Died: May 28, 1972 in Dallas, Georgia T:R B:R Height: 6' 3" Weight: 210

1921	Carrollton	10-												P															

HATHAWAY, R.H.

1921	Carrollton	110	20	18									.164	P															

HAWKINS, CY H.E. Hawkins

1921	Carrollton	108	7	23									.213	M, OF															

HENDERSON, HAP H.L. Henderson

1920	Carrollton	40	7	8									.200	P, OF															

HICKS, R.E.

1921	Carrollton	56	7	14									.250	1B, P															

HILL, JIM James William Hill T:R B:R

1946	Carrollton	121	401	45	163	9	1	0	50	3	36	31	.257	C	553	61	22	.965											
1947	Carrollton	90	308	41	91	20	0	0	47	0	8	18	.295	C	459	35	7	.986											
1948	Carrollton	95	330	30	79	4	0	0	54	1	23	12	.239	C	503	44	20	.965											

HILL, OLIVER John Clinton Hill Born: October 16, 1909 in Powder Springs, Georgia Died: September 20, 1970 in Decatur, Georgia T:R B:R Height: 5' 11" Weight: 178

1948	Carrollton	12	47	2	8	3	0	0	4	0	3	1	.170	M, 3B	12	28	4	.909											

HOLCOMB, HOT

1930	Carrollton	2												P					2	1	1	.500	7.71	14	27	14	12	3	6

HOLSOMBACK, SQUIRT Leonard Holsomback

1929	Carrollton	98	405	59	109	17	1	8		11	46	58	.269	3B	111	196	28	.916											
1930	Carrollton	84	348	78	105	20	6	7		7	48	27	.301	3B	104	170	23	.922											

HOLTZ, RED

1920	Carrollton	13	3	4									.308	1B															

HOWELL, RED Murray Donald Howell "Porky" Born: January 29, 1909 in Atlanta, Georgia Died: October 1, 1950 in Greenville, South Carolina T:R B:R Height: 6' 0" Weight: 215

1928	Carrollton	93	372	83	146					14	0	5	19	.392	OF	139	21	3	.982										

HUDSON, BILL William C. Hudson T:R B:R

1949	Carrollton	24	62	12	20	3	2	1		1	14	19	.323	1B	70	1	2	.973											

HUGGINS, MILLER

1928	*Carrollton	79	304	41	76	4	1	1		9	13	16	.250	3B	98	162	25	.912											

*stats include play in Gadsden during season

YR	TEAM	G	AB	R	H	2B	3B	HR	RBI	SB	BB	SO	AVG	POS	PO	A	E	FA	Pitching: G	W	L	PCT	ERA	IP	H	R	ER	SO	BB
HUMPHRIES, ------																													
1930	Carrollton	10-												OF															
HURLEY, ------																													
1946	Carrollton	1												P					1	0	0	.000		3					
HUTCHINS, BOB Robert L. Hutchins "Lefty" T:L B:L																													
1949	Carrollton	7												P	5	10	0	1.000	7	4	3	.571	2.33	54	51	21	14	34	19
1950	Carrollton	24	40	8	9	1	0	0	2	0	5	5	.225	P					24	9	3	.750	5.21	102	129	83	59	60	49
*stats include 15 games played in Rome and 9 games played in Carrollton during 1950 season																													
INGRAM, JIMMY																													
1920	Carrollton		7	1	1								.143	P															
ISRAEL, BILL William Israel T:R B:R																													
1946	Carrollton	30	62	3	15	2	0	0	5	0	1	10	.242	P	3	23	3	.897	24	12	8	.600	3.96	134	149	81	59	60	54
JAMES, FOB Forrest Hood James																													
1928	Carrollton	73	305	44	89	13	0	1		3	20	20	.292	1B	733	29	12	.985											
JEFTS, VIRGIL Virgil Robert Jefts T:R B:R																													
1948	Carrollton	12	32	3	11	1	0	0	2	0	2	3	.344	C	62	5	1	.985											
1949	Carrollton	114	377	48	91	18	1	2	40	0	71	47	.241	C	550	71	26	.960											
JESMER, W.H.																													
1921	Carrollton		142	17	40								.282	1B															
JONES, BILL William C. Jones T:R B:R																													
1947	Carrollton	70	203	31	56	6	3	0	27	0	11	24	.276	P	4	41	3	.938	36	14	11	.560							
*stats include 54 games played in Newnan and 16 games played in Carrollton during season																													
JONES, CASEY Roy L. Jones T:R B:R																													
1949	Carrollton	22	22	3	3	0	0	0	1	0	5	10	.136	P	5	20	3	.893	21	4	3	.571	2.57	77	65	38	22	48	39
1950	Carrollton	34	51	4	7	0	0	0	3	1	9	21	.137	P	3	35	0	1.000	32	11	7	.611	5.12	137	162	102	78	78	78
*stats include 21 games played in Newnan and 13 games played in Carrollton during season																													
JUSTISS, RED L.L. Justiss																													
1929	Carrollton	29	71	9	16	7	0	0	7	0	0	8	.225	P	3	35	3	.926	26	10	12	.454		184	211	109		95	53
1930	Carrollton		52		15								.288	P															
KELLY, DICK Richard W. Kelly T:R B:R																													
1947	Carrollton	122	524	95	159	15	5	9	84	16	17	28	.303	3B	132	251	53	.878											
KELLY, MASON T:R B:R																													
1950	Carrollton	1	0	0	0	0	0	0	0	0	0	0	.000	P					1	0	0	.000		1	1	0	0	1	0

YR	TEAM	G	AB	R	H	2B	3B	HR	RBI	SB	BB	SO	AVG	POS	PO	A	E	FA	Pitching: G	W	L	PCT	ERA	IP	H	R	ER	SO	BB
KIRSCHNER, GEORGE																													
1946	Carrollton													P					1	0	0	.000		4					
KITTS, CLAUDE																													
1921	Carrollton		56	9	9								.161	P															
KURAS, WALT Walter Kuras T:L B:L																													
1949	Carrollton	27	64	11	17	0	0	0	7	0	6	12	.266	P	6	21	2	.931	25	12	8	.600	2.77	159	144	80	49	101	92
LACEY, --------																													
1928	Carrollton	6	15	3	2								.133	P															
1929	Carrollton		18	3	4								.222	P															
1930	Carrollton	10-												P															
LAIRD, RED Green Flake Laird																													
1928	Carrollton	32	101	9	24	4	1	1	0	8	13		.237	P, OF	26	20	3	.939	15	9	4	.692	4.80	120	149	78	64	30	20
LANGEMEIER, PAUL T:R B:R																													
1949	Carrollton	14	17	2	1	0	0	0	4	0	9	4	.059	P	5	18	3	.885	14	4	4	.500	3.13	69	62	36	24	31	32
LANGLEY, JIM James D. Langley "J.D." T:L B:R																													
1946	Carrollton	19	68	7	17	1	0	0	10	5	1	13	.250	1B	96	3	1	.990											
1947	Carrollton	89	346	73	96	19	3	18	64	17	34	58	.277	1B	771	34	17	.979											
LASSETTER, ROY																													
1920	Carrollton		8	1	2								.250																
LEE, FRED L. Fred Lee B:L																													
1950	Carrollton	108	384	68	100	23	3	10	65	3	54	64	.260	OF	143	4	10	.936											
LEHMAN, OTTO																													
1921	Carrollton		20	1	2								.100	P															
LITTLE, --------																													
1921	Carrollton	10-												SS															
LITTLE, WALT Walter Little T:R B:R																													
1946	Carrollton	2	10	4	4	0	0	0	1	0	1	9	.129	P	0	7	2	.778	2	1	1	.500		17	19	5		8	4
1947	Carrollton	10	31	1	11	1	0	0	0	0	7	15	.177	P	1	12	3	.813	10	7	3	.700	3.60	80	75	39	32	68	24
1948	Carrollton	27	62	1	11	1	0	0	9	0			.083	P					27	13	7	.650	3.92	154	151	89	67	99	85
1949	*Carrollton	12	24	2	2	0	0	0	2	0	7	7		P					12	4	6	.400	5.12	58	63	46	33	53	39
LONG, H.L.																													
1920	Carrollton		29	6	0								.000	P															
1921	Carrollton		6	0	1								.167	P															

*stats include 10 games played in Carrollton and 2 games played in Alexander City during 1949 season

YR	TEAM	G	AB	R	H	2B	3B	HR	RBI	SB	BB	SO	AVG	POS	PO	A	E	FA	Pitching: G	W	L	PCT	ERA	IP	H	R	ER	SO	BB
LOPEZ, --------																													
1929	Carrollton	19	70	18	17	2	0	1	4		13	10	.243	OF	32	5	1	.974											
LOVELADY, WILLARD	T:L B:R																												
1948	Carrollton	15	16	0	3	0	0	0	2	0	0	3	.188	P	1	8	0	1.000	15	2	1	.667	3.56	48	40	24	19	18	31
MALOOF, JOE	Joseph Maloof T:R B:R																												
1949	Carrollton	11	16	1	3	0	0	0	0	0	1	4	.188	P	1	10	1	.917											
MANNING, --------																													
1930	Carrollton	2													P					2	0	1	.000	6.75	8	9	6	6	1	4
MARKS, MAX																													
1929	Carrollton	4		0	1								.250	P															
MARSHALL, SHORTY	Herbert R. Marshall Born: March 31, 1921 in Washington County, Georgia T:R B:R Height: 5'6" Weight: 135																												
1946	Carrollton	128	524	88	143	28	3	8	54	20	29	38	.273	2B	306	316	27	.958											
1947	Carrollton	121	518	99	171	29	7	7	76	16	38	20	.330	2B, SS	285	305	33	.947											
1948	Carrollton	121	495	99	152	32	3	13	52	20	60	16	.307	2B	360	334	38	.948											
1950	Carrollton	80	305	70	108	19	3	10	64	4	30	14	.354	M, 2B	117	121	13	.948											
MARTIN, S.R.																													
1921	Carrollton	101		11	25								.248																
MARTIN, AMOS																													
1930	Carrollton	27	117	22	39	6	0	5	2	6		7	.333	2B, SS	37	80	11	.914											
MATHEWSON, --------																													
1928	Carrollton	12		2	3								.250																
MATTHEWS, BOB	Robert Matthews "Buck" T:R B:R																												
1946	Carrollton	35	75	8	8	0	0	0	3	1	6	9	.107	P	4	52	1	.982	35	16	13	.552	6.88	123	227	111	94	111	50
1947	*Carrollton	40	99	15	18	1	1	0	3	0	8	14	.182	P	7	52	2	.967	38	16	11	.593	2.54	248	229	85	70	114	45

*stats include 23 games played in Carrollton and 17 games played in Newnan during season

YR	TEAM	G	AB	R	H	2B	3B	HR	RBI	SB	BB	SO	AVG	POS	PO	A	E	FA	Pitching: G	W	L	PCT	ERA	IP	H	R	ER	SO	BB
MATTHEWS, LUTHER	T:R																												
1949	Carrollton	8													P					8	3	3	.500	2.52	50	57	23	14	19	9
MAZAK, LEO	Leonard Mazak (also spelled Mierzejek) T:L B:L																												
1950	Carrollton	26	77	8	16	5	0	0	6	0	2	13	.208	P	7	15	4	.846	19	4	9	.308	6.24	124	157	106	86	53	61
MCGHEE, BILL	William Mac McGhee "Willie" or "Fibber" Born: September 5, 1905 in Shawmut, Alabama Died: March 10, 1984 in Decatur, Georgia T:L B:L Height: 5'10" Weight: 185																												
1929	Carrollton	61	222	26	69	9	2	0	2	14	19		.311	OF, 1B	165	12	7	.962											
1930	Carrollton	19	61	5	11	5	2	0	0	5	7		.180	SS	24	26	12	.645											

d: Nov 14, 2004

YR	TEAM	G	AB	R	H	2B	3B	HR	RBI	SB	BB	SO	AVG	POS	PO	A	E	FA	Pitching: G	W	L	PCT	ERA	IP	H	R	ER	SO	BB
MCKINNEY, _____																													
1928	*Carrollton	41	148	17	42	9	1	2	5	4		10	.284	C	174	27	9	.957											
	*stats include play in Lindale during season																												
MCKINNON, BILL																													
1920	Carrollton		25	4	7								.280	P															
MILNER, HOLT	B. Holt Milner																												
1930	Carrollton 10-																												
MILO, _____																													
1946	Carrollton 10-																												
MONARCHI, GENE	Eugene L. Monarchi — Born: June 11, 1925 in Jessup, Pennsylvania — T:R B:R Height 5'7" Weight: 150																												
1948	Carrollton	111	322	55	76	9	0	0	38	1	88	48	.236	SS	154	264	44	.905											
MONARCHI, PETE	Peter A. Monarchi — Born: February 13, 1927 in Jessup, Pennsylvania — T:R B:R Height: 5'10" Weight: 170																												
1947	Carrollton	70	230	42	62	16	3	5	44	0	47	48	.270	2B, OF	100	42	6	.959											
1948	Carrollton													2B															
MOORE, CLEM	H. Clem Moore																												
1921	Carrollton		95	21	38								.400	OF															
MOORE, J.																													
1928	Carrollton	8	20	2	3								.150	P					8	1	2	.333	5.85	40	45	30	26	14	21
MORELLI, JIM	James Morelli — T:R B:L																												
1949	Carrollton	107	401	86	104	16	3	13	52	15	71	41	.259	OF	257	11	14	.950											
1950	Carrollton	113	422	112	123	19	5	14	70	10	109	38	.291	OF	228	15	8	.968											
MURPHEE, BILL	William Murphee — T:L B:L																												
1947	Carrollton	39	112	23	31	2	3	1	15	1	31	22	.277	1B	315	13	6	.982											
NAGLE, BOB	Robert Nagle — B:L																												
1948	Carrollton	32	79	11	15	1	0	1	6	2	15	19	.190																
NASWORTHY, LUTHER	T:R B:R																												
1948	Carrollton	10	25	0	3	1	0	0	1	0		9	.120	SS, OF	152	156	27	.919											
1949	Carrollton	93	320	43	78	13	1	11	47	5		87	.244																
NELSON, BUREL																													
1949	Carrollton	22												P					22	5	8	.385		106				51	
NELSON, DICK	Richard Nelson — T:R B:R																												
1948	Carrollton	26	33	4	7	1	1	1	0	1		6	.212	P	1	9	1	.909	26	5	5	.500	4.60	88	85	62	45	32	61

YR	TEAM	G	AB	R	H	2B	3B	HR	RBI	SB	BB	SO	AVG	POS	PO	A	E	FA	Pitching: G	W	L	PCT	ERA	IP	H	R	ER	SO	BB
NETTLES, HOKE																													
1929	Carrollton	6	18	7	10								.556	OF															
OGLESBY, HUGH T:R B:R																													
1946	Carrollton	26	87	9	13	1	1	1	5	0	8	22	.149	OF	35	2	4	.902											
PADGETT, CHARLES T:R B:L																													
1947	Carrollton	17	68	9	11	1	0	0	5	1	5	13	.162	SS	23	53	12	.864											
PATTERSON, BILL William E. Patterson T:R B:L																													
1946	Carrollton	10-																											
1947	Carrollton	81	197	34	49	7	0	3	30	6	61	38	.249	OF, C	282	26	9	.972											
1950	*Carrollton	109	322	44	75	11	0	1	68	3	80	48	.233	C	469	50	15	.972											

*stats include 1 game played in Carrollton, 88 games played in Griffin, 4 games played in Valley, and 16 games played in Alexander City during 1950 season

YR	TEAM	G	AB	R	H	2B	3B	HR	RBI	SB	BB	SO	AVG	POS	PO	A	E	FA	Pitching: G	W	L	PCT	ERA	IP	H	R	ER	SO	BB
PATTON, HENRY M. Henry Patton																													
1929	Carrollton	99	379	84	108	30	5	12		17	58	51	.285	OF, SS	198	8	7	.920											
PITTMAN, AL T:R B:R																													
1946	Carrollton	12	25	1	3	0	0	0		0	2	4	.125	P	1	13	0	1.000	12	4	4	.500	4.43	69	89	44	34	26	22
POOLE, BUDDY T:R B:R																													
1949	Carrollton	12	15	2	3	0	0	0		0	1	7	.200	P	5	7	2	.857	12	1	3	.250	4.78	49	36	38	26	29	52
POWERS, ------																													
1921	Carrollton	10-												SS															
PRATT, FRANK Francis Bruce Pratt "Trackhorse" Born: August 24, 1897 in Blocton, Alabama Died: March 8, 1974 in Centreville, Alabama B:L T:R Height: 5' 10" Weight: 155																													
1920	Carrollton		205	29	60								.293	P, OF, SS															
PRESSLEY, BABE Omer V. Pressley "Press"																													
1920	Carrollton		112	20	35								.313	UT															
PRZEWORSKI, TED Theodore Przeworski T:R B:R																													
1948	*Carrollton	123	406	84	100	18	5	11	90	7	107	118	.246	3B, OF	157	51	19	.916											

*stats include 77 games played in LaGrange and 46 games played in Carrollton during season

YR	TEAM	G	AB	R	H	2B	3B	HR	RBI	SB	BB	SO	AVG	POS	PO	A	E	FA	Pitching: G	W	L	PCT	ERA	IP	H	R	ER	SO	BB
PULLIAM, J.C.																													
1920	Carrollton		33	6	4								.121	SS															
REACH, CLIFTON T:R B:L																													
1950	Carrollton	97	337	55	68	12	1	13	51	6	63	90	.202	2B, OF	193	25	20	.916											
REED, JIM James Reed T:R B:R																													
1946	*Carrollton	8												P					8	0	5	.000		43	57	41	34	24	

*stats include 7 games played in LaGrange and 1 game played in Carrollton during season

YR	TEAM	G	AB	R	H	2B	3B	HR	RBI	SB	BB	SO	AVG	POS	PO	A	E	FA	Pitching: G	W	L	PCT	ERA	IP	H	R	ER	SO	BB
REESE, EDDIE — Edward Reese																													
1929	Carrollton	37	162	14	45	12	0	4		3	3	24	.278	SS	70	126	12	.942											
1930	Carrollton		47		12								.255	SS															
REESE, RED																													
1920	Carrollton		144	21	32								.222	C, 2B															
REGISTER, ------																													
1920	Carrollton		85	16	31								.365	1B, OF, P															
REIS, ------																													
1921	Carrollton		52	7	9								.173	P															
REVELS, BILL — William Revels T:R B:R																													
1948	Carrollton	12	26	1	5	1	0	0	3	0	1	5	.192	P	4	17	1	.955	10	4	5	.444	2.81	64	63	32	20	50	39
RICHARDS, BABE — J.W. Richards																													
1921	Carrollton		166	23	60								.361	OF, P															
RIDENOUR, ROY T:R B:R																													
1949	Carrollton	14	38	5	5	1	0	0	4	0	9	12	.132	SS	29	41	6	.921											
ROBERTS, RED — Charles Emory Roberts Born: August 8, 1918 in Carrollton, Georgia Died: December 2, 1998 in Atlanta, Georgia T:R B:R Height: 6' 0" Weight: 170																													
1946	Carrollton	67	227	57	70	13	3	3	37	16	43	16	.308	3B, SS	69	131	20	.909											
1947	Carrollton	97	351	75	135	24	5	11	72	10	53	21	.385	M, 3B	169	297	27	.945											
1948	Carrollton	86	300	66	101	17	2	4	64	10	71	15	.337	M, 3B, SS	109	191	21	.935											
ROBERTSON, ------																													
1920	Carrollton	10-												P, OF															
ROBISON, ROY																													
1946	Carrollton	10-																											
ROEDEL, BOB — Robert Roedel T:R B:R																													
1948	Carrollton	12	42	4	4	1	0	0	2	0	2	6	.095	C	54	11	1	.985											
ROMAN, CARL T:R B:R																													
1948	Carrollton	23	55	0	12	3	0	0	5	2	5	10	.218	OF	36	5	1	.976											
ROWE, BOB																													
1928	*Carrollton	68	250	27	79	10	4	6		0	15	18	.316	OF	121	3	5	.961											
	*stats include play in Gadsden during season																												
RUCKER, BILL — William Rucker T:R B:R																													
1949	Carrollton	120	427	56	119	10	1	9	75	2	41	49	.279	M, 1B, OF	323	8	12	.965											

YR	TEAM	G	AB	R	H	2B	3B	HR	RBI	SB	BB	SO	AVG	POS	PO	A	E	FA	Pitching: G	W	L	PCT	ERA	IP	H	R	ER	SO	BB
RUSSELL, BING	Neil Russell Born: 1928 in New Hampshire T:R B:R Height: 6' 2"																												
1948	Carrollton	78	263	57	67	11	4	4	38	5	44	64	.255	OF	121	0	6	.953											
1949	Carrollton	11	33	2	6	0	0	0	2	0	4	7	.182	OF	15	1	0	1.000											
SAPPENFIELD, COLON																													
1929	Carrollton	54	229	40	74	5	4	4		2	8	20	.323	SS	89	150	23	.912											
SCHULTE, J.																													
1921	Carrollton		108	12	24								.222	OF															
SEAL, BILL	William A. Seal, Jr. T:R B:R																												
1949	Carrollton	85	293	68	100	22	2	23	97	15	75	17	.341	M, 2B, SS	165	185	25	.933											
SEIGLER, BILL	William Seigler T:R B:R																												
1946	Carrollton	26	41	4	9	2	0	0	5	0	5	2	.220	P	7	14	2	.913	23	4	4	.500	5.34	91	102	58	54	46	31
SESSIONS, PETE	E.E. Sessions																												
1921	Carrollton	10-												3B															
SHAW, POP	E.N. Shaw																												
1920	Carrollton		111	17	30								.270	OF															
SHIRLEY, JIM	James Shirley T:L B:L																												
1949	Carrollton	85	265	35	57	9	2	7	44	5	41	74	.215	1B	645	28	19	.973											
1950	Carrollton	105	369	67	87	13	3	17	71	5	72	80	.236	1B	672	44	11	.985											
SHIVERS, ------																													
1946	Carrollton	10-																											
SHOEMAKE, CLAUDE	T:L B:L																												
1950	Carrollton	62	234	54	80	6	0	18	68	3	27	6	.342	OF	60	2	3	.954											
SILVERMAN, JEROME	T:L B:R																												
1948	Carrollton	77	289	47	91	17	1	0	32	3	31	6	.315	1B	663	29	7	.990											
SINGLEY, HULEN	T:R B:R																												
1947	Carrollton	17	44	2	4	1	0	0	2	0	1	6	.091	P	2	15	2	.893	16	9	4	.692	4.45	93	96	55	46	41	47
SMITH, ------																													
1947	Carrollton	5												P					5	3	2	.600							
SMITH, J.																													
1921	Carrollton		174	15	36								.207	C															
SMITH, REUBEN																													
1930	Carrollton	10-												C															

YR	TEAM	G	AB	R	H	2B	3B	HR	RBI	SB	BB	SO	AVG	POS	PO	A	E	FA	Pitching: G	W	L	PCT	ERA	IP	H	R	ER	SO	BB
SNIDER, FLOYD "Smokey" T:R B:L																													
1946	*Carrollton	38	122	24	27	8	2	3	16	3	28	24	.221	OF	55	0	6	.902											
1947	Carrollton	124	463	95	142	22	9	21	102	12	90	85	.307	OF	228	10	15	.941											
1948	Carrollton	48	166	34	46	7	2	6	34	3	44	28	.277	1B, OF	158	3	5	.970											
*stats include 17 games played in Newnan and 21 games played in Carrollton during 1946 season																													
SOLT, GENE James Eugene Solt "Jim" T:R B:R																													
1950	Carrollton	119	460	106	168	27	1	38	151	6	65	38	.365	C, OF	433	69	30	.944											
SOUTER, GEORGE T:R B:R																													
1946	Carrollton	58	193	43	62	16	4	5	37	13	48	28	.321	3B, OF, P	63	35	7	.933	4	1	2	.333		19	18	12		12	10
SOWARD, JIM James E. Soward																													
1930	Carrollton	55			15								.273	P															
SPENCER, BILL Willard R. Spencer																													
1946	Carrollton	1												P					1	0	0	.000		2					
SPRAYBERRY, JIM James Sprayberry																													
1946	*Carrollton	2												P					2	0	0	.000		4					
*stats include 1 game played in Valley and 1 game played in Carrollton during season																													
STANFIELD, RALPH																													
1929	Carrollton	26	30	11	10	1	1	1	1		2	12	.167	P	7	43	2	.961	21	8	8	.500		135	155	84		43	27
1930	Carrollton		111		36								.324	P, OF															
STEEL, ------																													
1946	Carrollton	1												P					1	0	0	.000		1					
STOYLE, JIM James Stoyle T:R B:R																													
1946	Carrollton	90	336	70	118	22	3	7	83	15	28	28	.351	1B	947	27	23	.977											
STRICKLAND, ------																													
1929	Carrollton	11		3	2								.182	OF															
SUMMERLIN, FRITZ																													
1920	Carrollton	10-												OF															
SURATT, CLYDE																													
1921	Carrollton	10-												P															
SUTTON, LEFTY T:L																													
1920	Carrollton	7		1	2								.286	P															
SWANN, P.P. "Ducky"																													
1920	Carrollton	26		1	0								.000	P															

YR	TEAM	G	AB	R	H	2B	3B	HR	RBI	SB	BB	SO	AVG	POS	PO	A	E	FA	Pitching: G	W	L	PCT	ERA	IP	H	R	ER	SO	BB
TALIAFERRO, DICK	Clark Taliaferro "Tolly"																												
1928	Carrollton	70	306	61	120	20	8	9	8	10	33		.392	SS	141	189	24	.932											
TATE, J.R.																													
1929	Carrollton		214	28	53								.248	2B															
TAYLOR, ZACHERY																													
1930	Carrollton	55	193	35	68	14	4	4	4	16	15		.352	C	211	35	7	.972											
TAYLOR, BILL	J.W. Taylor																												
1921	Carrollton		285	37	77								.270	3B															
TERRY, HORACE																													
1946	Carrollton	10-																											
THOMAS, DALLAS	Dallas Glenn Thomas T:L B:L																												
1946	Carrollton	16	63	14	16	2	1	0	9	0	8	11	.254	OF	31	2	2	.943											
1947	Carrollton	107	416	79	118	24	5	11	72	14	53	107	.284	OF	206	12	18	.924											
THOMPSON, ERSKINE																													
1930	Carrollton	28	103	7	28	2	0	0	1		3	12	.271	M, C	99	13	5	.957											
THOMPSON, JIM	James C. Thompson T:R B:R																												
1949	Carrollton	19	73	10	16	4	2	2	13	0	5	22	.219	OF	29	2	1	.969											
TIDWELL, JOHN	"Little John" Born: August 1, 1928 in Fairfax, Alabama T:R B:R Height: 6'1" Weight: 180																												
1949	Carrollton	39	136	22	43	7	2	5	32	7	15	15	.316	OF	61	3	3	.955											
	*stats include 22 games played in LaGrange and 6 games played in Carrollton during season																												
TILLEY, TRAVIS	T:R B:L																												
1947	*Carrollton	28	90	12	22	3	4	0	7	1	9	10	.244	OF	40	4	4	.917											
	*stats include 5 games played in Carrollton and 6 games played in Griffin during season																												
TURK, ------																													
1930	Carrollton	17	2										.118	C															
TURNER, ------																													
1930	Carrollton	10-												P															
UMSCHEID, DON	Donald Umscheid T:L B:L																												
1949	*Carrollton	11	13	0	0	0	0	0	0		2	2	.000	P	4	7	0	1.000											
	*stats include 5 games played in Carrollton and 6 games played in Griffin during season																												
VARNER, BUCK	Glenn Gann Varner Born: August 17, 1930 in Hixson, Tennessee T:R B:L Height: 5'10" Weight: 170																												
1948	Carrollton	66	240	52	70	9	3	9	35	3	44	33	.292	OF	140	4	5	.966											
VICTOR, ERNIE																													
1950	Carrollton	1												P					1										

Column headers: YR · TEAM · G · AB · R · H · 2B · 3B · HR · RBI · SB · BB · SO · AVG · POS · PO · A · E · FA · Pitching: G · W · L · PCT · ERA · IP · H · R · ER · SO · BB

WADEWITZ, OSWIN — T:L B:L

YR	TEAM	G	AB	R	H	2B	3B	HR	RBI	SB	BB	SO	AVG	POS	PO	A	E	FA	P:G	W	L	PCT	ERA	IP	H	R	ER	SO	BB
1949	Carrollton	11	23	0	2	0	0	0	0	0	0	4	.087	P	0	9	2	.818	11	2	7	.222	1.88	67	61	37	14	34	44

WALTON, BATTLEAXE — O.C. Walton

YR	TEAM	AB	R	H	AVG	POS
1921	Carrollton	139	14	39	.281	C, OF, 3B

WATSON, JULES — "Old Folks"

YR	TEAM	AB	R	H	AVG	POS
1920	Carrollton	224	22	62	.277	2B, OF
1921	Carrollton	199	19	39	.196	M, 2B

WEBB, BILL — William Franklin Webb Born: December 12, 1913 in Atlanta, Georgia Died: June 1, 1994 in Mableton, Georgia T:R B:R Height: 6' 2" Weight: 180

YR	TEAM	G	AB	R	H	2B	3B	HR	RBI	SB	BB	SO	AVG	POS	PO	A	E	FA	P:G	W	L	PCT	ERA	IP	H	R	ER	SO	BB
1947	Carrollton	31	96	16	39	8	0	2	16	0	16	5	.406	P	15	44	0	1.000	28	22	5	.815	2.40	229	196	72	61	131	38

WELDON, BILL — William Weldon T:R B:R

YR	TEAM	G	AB	R	H	2B	3B	HR	RBI	SB	BB	SO	AVG	POS	PO	A	E	FA	P:G	W	L	PCT	ERA	IP	H	R	ER	SO	BB
1950	Carrollton	27	51	7	5	1	0	1	6	0	6	10	.098	P	5	30	3	.921	26	8	9	.471	5.33	130	147	105	77	69	78

WESLEY, _____

YR	TEAM
1930	Carrollton 10-

WESTBROOK, JOHN — T:L B:L

YR	TEAM	G	AB	R	H	2B	3B	HR	RBI	SB	BB	SO	AVG	POS	PO	A	E	FA	P:G	W	L	PCT	ERA	IP	H	R	ER	SO	BB
1946	*Carrollton	16	35	4	2	0	0	0	1	0	1	6	.057	P	4	18	2	.917	16	6	7	.462	2.51	104	96	48	29	67	30

*stats include 5 games played in Tallassee and 11 games played in Carrollton during season

WHITE, ABE — Adel White Born: May 16, 1904 in Winder, Georgia Died: October 1, 1978 in Atlanta, Georgia T:L B:R Height: 6' 0" Weight: 185

YR	TEAM	G	AB	R	H	2B	3B	HR	RBI	SB	BB	SO	AVG	POS	PO	A	E	FA	P:G	W	L	PCT	ERA	IP	H	R	ER	SO	BB
1928	Carrollton	29	82	6	14	1	0	0	1		2	18	.171	P	11	35	5	.902	29	13	10	.565	3.36	206	217	109	77	141	49
1929	Carrollton	31	85	7	22	3	0	0	0		1	17	.259	P	6	34	4	.909	31	10	11	.476		199	214	110		101	62
1930	Carrollton		8		1								.125	P															

WHITE, CURTIS — T:R B:R

YR	TEAM	G	AB	R	H	2B	3B	HR	RBI	SB	BB	SO	AVG	POS	PO	A	E	FA	P:G	W	L	PCT	ERA	IP	H	R	ER	SO	BB
1950 45	Carrollton	16	28	3	6	1	0	0	2	0	2	3	.214	P	1	5	0	1.000	16	4	5	.444	5.55	60	70	47	37	35	

WHITE, H.

YR	TEAM	G	AB	R	H	2B	3B	HR	RBI	SB	BB	SO	AVG	POS	PO	A	E	FA
1930	Carrollton	23	84	12	22	5	0	0	0	0	14	7	.261	2B, SS	31	38	3	.958

WHITE, JO-JO — Joyner Clifford White Born: June 1, 1909 in Red Oak, Georgia Died: October 9, 1986 in Tacoma, Washington T:R B:L Height: 5' 11" Weight: 165

YR	TEAM	G	AB	R	H	2B	3B	HR	RBI	SB	BB	SO	AVG	POS	PO	A	E	FA
1928	Carrollton	96	364	92	120	14	8		27	18	42	54	.330	OF	183	21	7	.967

WHITED, GERALD — T:R B:R

YR	TEAM	G	AB	R	H	2B	3B	HR	RBI	SB	BB	SO	AVG	POS	PO	A	E	FA
1949	Carrollton	12	40	2	8	1	0	0	5	0		15	.200	1B	77	3	1	.988

WICKER, KEMP — Kemp Caswell Wicker Born: August 13, 1906 in Kernersville, North Carolina Died: June 11, 1973 in Kernersville, North Carolina T:L B:R Height: 5' 11" Weight: 182

YR	TEAM	AB	H	AVG	POS
1928	Carrollton	7	1 2	.500	P

WILLIAMS, BOB — Robert Williams B:L

YR	TEAM	G	AB	R	H	2B	3B	HR	RBI	SB	BB	SO	AVG
1948	Carrollton	11	24	2	4	0	0	0	1	0	3	7	.167

YR	TEAM	G	AB	R	H	2B	3B	HR	RBI	SB	BB	SO	AVG	POS	PO	A	E	FA	Pitching: G	W	L	PCT	ERA	IP	H	R	ER	SO	BB
WILLIAMS, LUKE Luke A. Williams																													
1920	Carrollton		42	3	7								.167	SS															
WILLIAMS, PAUL T:R B:R																													
1946	Carrollton	39	119	15	31	2	1	0	14	5	11	16	.261	3B	33	53	12	.878											
WILSON, JACK																													
1920	Carrollton		85	8	18								.212	OF, 3B, 2B, SS															
WINN, BREEZY																													
1929	Carrollton		12	0	3								.250	OF, P															
YARBOROUGH, MACK																													
1949	Carrollton	4												SS															
YEARTY, SAM Samuel Yearty T:R B:R																													
1946	Carrollton	6												P					6	1	0	1.000		20	26	17		3	3
YORK, LEW Louis York T:R B:R																													
1946	Carrollton	121	427	71	129	19	0	19	84	11	37	52	.302	1B, OF, P	444	12	24	.950	1	0	0	.000		1					

Player Register

The following is a list of Carrollton players and the different teams they played with in baseball. Most of the lists for players only contain established baseball teams on which the player played, but there are a few that contain independent and semi-pro teams. The asterisk by many of the players' names indicates that a complete playing record could not be compiled for that player and the listing may not be complete.

The team listing for players are by year played and team played for. In parentheses is the league abbreviation and the class of minor league baseball that league played in that particular year.

*ALEXANDER, BILL
28 Lindale (Ga-Ala D)
29 Lindale (Ga-Ala D)
30 Carrollton (Ga-Ala D)
31 Chattanooga (SA A)

ALEXANDER, BILL
47 Carrollton (Ga-Ala D)
    Griffin (Ga-Ala D)
48 Kinston (Coastal Plain D)

*ALLEN, HARRY

20 Carrollton (Georgia St D)
21 Carrollton (Georgia St D)
    Greenville (South Atl B)

ALLEN, JOHN

46 LaGrange (Ga-Ala D)
47 LaGrange (Ga-Ala D)
    Carrollton (Ga-Ala D)
48 Seaford (Eastern Shore D)
    Griffin (Ga-Ala D)
51 Valley (Ga-Ala D)
    Alexander City (Ga-Ala D)

ANDERSON, MARION

29 Carrollton (Ga-Ala D)
30 Lindale (Ga-Ala D)
    Augusta (South Atl B)
    Greenville (South Atl B)
    Tampa (Southeastern B)
    Omaha (Western A)
31 Waterloo (Miss Valley D)
32 Quincy (I.I.I. B)
    Des Moines (Western A)
34 Bartlesville (West Assoc C)
35 Americus (Ga-Fla D)
36 Rogers (Ark-Mo D)

*ARDIS, ------
20 Carrollton (Georgia St D)

ARROYO, BLAS

48 Tampa (Florida Int C)
    Carrollton (Ga-Ala D)
49 Palatka (Florida St D)
50 Gainesville (Florida St D)
    Carrollton (Ga-Ala D)
51 Palatka (Florida St D)
52 Burlington (I.I.I. B)
53 Rock Hill (Tri-St B)

*ATCHLEY, LOY
28 Carrollton (Ga-Ala D)
    Anniston (Ga-Ala D)
    Cedartown (Ga-Ala D)
31 High Point (Piedmont C)
37 Newport (Appalachian D)
38 Newport (Appalachian D)
    Evansville (I.I.I. B)

*AVERY, ------
28 Carrollton (Ga-Ala D)

*BAILEY, ------
28 Carrollton (Ga-Ala D)
    Anniston (Ga-Ala D)

*BALES, ------
20 Carrollton (Georgia St D)

*BARBER, ------
21 Carrollton (Georgia St D)

BARKLEY, ------
46 Carrollton (Ga-Ala D)

*BARNES, ------
21 Carrollton (Georgia St D)

BARTHOLOMEW, JACK
48 Salisbury (N Carolina St D)
49 Salisbury (N Carolina St D)
    Carrollton (Ga-Ala D)
    New Iberia (Evangeline D)
50 New Iberia (Evangeline D)
53 Meridian (Cotton St C)
    Cordele (Ga-Fla D)
    Jesup (Georgia St D)
    St Hyacinthe (Provincial C)

BEASLEY, JOHN
48 Enterprise (Alabama St D)
49 Enterprise (Alabama St D)
50 Dothan (Alabama St D)
    Houma (Evangeline C)
    Rome (Ga-Ala D)
    Carrollton (Ga-Ala D)

BEAUCHAMP, WALT
49 Vidalia (Georgia St D)
    High Point-Thomasville (N Carolina St D)
50 Carrollton (Ga-Ala D)
    Vidalia-Lyons (Georgia St D)
51 Douglas (Georgia St D)

*BECK, ------
20 Carrollton (Georgia St D)

*BELL, CHARLIE

20   Carrollton (Georgia St D)

BERMAN, BUDDY

46   Cambridge (Eastern Shore D)
     Valdosta (Ga-Fla D)
48   Lenoir (W Carolina D)
49   Carrollton (Ga-Ala D)
50   Carrollton (Ga-Ala D)
     Alexander City (Ga-Ala D)
     Bridgeport (Colonial B)
     Abbeville (Evangeline C)

BERTHA, ELMER

48   Carrollton (Ga-Ala D)

*BETTISON, ------
30   Carrollton (Ga-Ala D)
31   Greensboro (Piedmont C)

BIESER, FRED

46   Carrollton (Ga-Ala D)

BOBOWSKI, ED
48   Newark (Ohio-Ind D)
     LaGrange (Ga-Ala D)
49   LaGrange (Ga-Ala D)
     Carrollton (Ga-Ala D)
50   Carrollton (Ga-Ala D)

*BONIFAY, ALBERT

20   LaGrange (Georgia St D)
     Carrollton (Georgia St D)
21   Columbia (South Atl B)
23   Richmond (Virginia B)

BORDERS, AUBREY

46   Newnan (Ga-Ala D)
     Carrollton (Ga-Ala D)

BOSSER, MEL
38   Dover (Eastern Shore D)
39   Thomasville (Ga-Fla D)
     Spartanburg (South Atl B)
40   Thomasville (Ga-Fla D)
41   Selma (Southeastern B)
45   Syracuse (IL AA)
     Cincinnati (National League)
46   Carrollton (Ga-Ala D)
     Memphis (SA AA)
49   Burlington (Carolina B)
     Lumberton (Tobacco St D)
52   Augusta (South Atl A)

*BOSWELL, BRANT

28   Carrollton (Ga-Ala D)
29   Buffalo (International AA)
30   Jacksonville (Southeastern B)

BOZZUTO, BERT

47   Carrollton (Ga-Ala D)
48   Carrollton (Ga-Ala D)
49   Carrollton (Ga-Ala D)
     Alexander City (Ga-Ala D)

*BRANDON, GOAT

20   Carrollton (Georgia St D)
21   Greenwood (Cotton St D)

*BRINSON, ------
20   Carrollton (Georgia St D)

BROCK, PAUL

42   Pensacola (Southeastern B)
     Petersburg (Virginia D)
44   Louisville (AA AA)
     Atlanta (SA A1)
45   Columbus (AA AA)
46   Carrollton (Ga-Ala D)
47   Newnan (Ga-Ala D)
48   Sparta (Georgia St D)
49   Sparta (Georgia St D)
     Charlotte (Tri-St B)

*BRUNER, B.E.
21   Carrollton (Georgia St D)
     LaGrange (Georgia St D)

*BUFORD, RED
29   Carrollton (Ga-Ala D)

BURKE, JOE
48   Carrollton (Ga-Ala D)

BURNSTEIN, LEONARD
46   Wilmington (Tobacco St D)
     Sanford (Tobacco St D)
49   Carrollton (Ga-Ala D)

*BUTTS, ------
28   Carrollton (Ga-Ala D)

CAIN, GEORGE
46   Pittsfiled (Canad-Amer C)
     Carrollton (Ga-Ala D)
     Charlotte (Tri-St B)
48   Carrollton (Ga-Ala D)

*CAIN, SUGAR

30   Carrollton (Ga-Ala D)
31   Harrisburg (NY-P B)
32   Philadelphia (American League)
     Baltimore (IL AA)
33   Philadelphia (American League)
34   Philadelphia (American League)
35   Philadelphia (American League)
     St Louis (American League)
36   St Louis (American League)
37   Chicago (American League)
38   St Paul (AA AA)
     Chicago (American League)
39   St Paul (AA AA)
40   Knoxville (SA A1)
41   Knoxville (SA A1)
42   Anniston (Southeastern B)
43   Birmingham (SA A1)

*CALDARA, ------
30   Carrollton (Ga-Ala D)

CALKINS, DICK
49   Carrollton (Ga-Ala D)
     Ft Lauderdale (Florida Int C)

CALLEN, JIM
49   Carrollton (Ga-Ala D)

*CANNON, SHORTY
21   Carrollton (Georgia St D)
23   Austin (Texas Assoc D)

*CARMICHAEL, ------
21   Carrollton (Georgia St D)

*CARTER, HOMER
28   Carrollton (Ga-Ala D)
     Gadsden (Ga-Ala D)
30   Carrollton (Ga-Ala D)
     Anniston (Ga-Ala D)
     Huntsville (Ga-Ala D)

*CARTER, RUSS
20   Carrollton (Georgia St D)
21   Albany-Decatur (Ala-Tenn D)

*CHAPLIN, ED

19	Sanford (Florida St D)
20	Carrollton (Georgia St D)
	Boston (American League)
21	Boston (American League)
22	Boston (American League)
23	Mobile (SA A)
27	Meridian (Cotton St D)
29	Pensacola (Southeastern B)

*CHATHAM, HAPPY
20	Carrollton (Georgia St D)

CHILDS, FRANK
46	Carrollton (Ga-Ala D)
	Newnan (Ga-Ala D)
47	Griffin (Ga-Ala D)
48	Montgomery (Southeastern B)

*CHRISTIANSEN, ------
29	Carrollton (Ga-Ala D)

CICHON, FRANK

48	Carrollton (Ga-Ala D)
49	Carrollton (Ga-Ala D)
	Greenville (Cotton St C)

CLARK, RAY

48	Valley (Ga-Ala D)
49	Valley (Ga-Ala D)
50	Carrollton (Ga-Ala D)
52	Joplin (West Assoc C)
55	Albuquerque (W Texas-NM B)

COBIELLA, RICARDO
50	Palatka (Florida St D)
	Carrollton (Ga-Ala D)
51	Laredo (Gulf Coast B)
	Ardmore (Sooner St D)
	Seminole (Sooner St D)

*COKER, E.R.
30	Carrollton (Ga-Ala D)
	Columbia (South Atl B)

COLLINS, LEE
47	Tallassee (Ga-Ala D)
	Carrollton (Ga-Ala D)
	Newnan (Ga-Ala D)
	Alexander City (Ga-Ala D)

COLTER, ------
46	Carrollton (Ga-Ala D)

CONDIT, ------

46	Carrollton (Ga-Ala D)

CONHENNEY, JIM
49	Carrollton (Ga-Ala D)

*COOMBS, ------
21	Carrollton (Georgia St D)

*CORNELIUS, RUSTY
19	Charlotte (South Atl C)
20	Charlotte (South Atl C)
	Lindale (Georgia St D)
21	Carrollton (Georgia St D)

CORRALES, REINALDO

49	Palatka (Florida St D)
50	Ft Lauderdale (Florida Int B)
	Miami Beach (Florida Int B)
	Carrollton (Ga-Ala D)
51	Edenton (Virginia D)
52	Big Spring (Longhorn C)
53	Maryville (Mountain St D)
	Morristown (Mountain St D)
55	Portsmouth (Piedmont B)
	Norfolk (Piedmont B)
	Rock Hill (Tri-St B)

*COSBY, ------
28	Carrollton (Ga-Ala D)
	Lindale (Ga-Ala D)

COULLING, STAN

41	Moultrie (Ga-Fla D)
42	Moultrie (Ga-Fla D)
46	Centreville (Eastern Shore D)
47	Montgomery (Southeastern B)
48	Montgomery (Southeastern B)
49	Montgomery (Southeastern B)
50	Montgomery (Southeastern B)
	Gadsden (Southeastern B)
	Carrollton (Ga-Ala D)
51	Ft Lauderdale (Florida Int B)

CRAIN, PAUL
37	Mayodan (Bi-St D)
38	Mayodan (Bi-St D)
	Hopkinsville (Kitty D)
39	Mayodan (Bi-St D)
	Lynchburg (Virginia D)
40	Erwin (Appalachian D)
41	Owensboro (Kitty D)
	Canton (Mid-Atl C)
42	Nashville (SA A1)
46	Atlanta (SA AA)
47	Carrollton (Ga-Ala D)

Valley (Ga-Ala D)

*CRAVEN, JESS

13	Newnan (Ga-Ala D)
14	Carrollton (Independent)
15	Carrollton (Independent)
16	LaGrange (Ga-Ala D)
	Anniston (Ga-Ala D)
20	Carrollton (Georgia St D)
21	Greenwood (Cotton St D)

*CROWE, HOYT

28	Lindale (Ga-Ala D)
29	Carrollton (Ga-Ala D)
30	Rock Island (Miss Valley D)

CROWSON, MARV
46	Carrollton (Ga-Ala D)

*DAVENPORT, ------
21	Carrollton (Georgia St D)

*DAVENPORT, ------
30	Carrollton (Ga-Ala D)
	Columbus (Southeastern B)
	Des Moines (Western A)
31	St Joseph (Western A)

*DAVIS, CARL
27	Springfield (Western Assoc C)
28	Cedartown (Ga-Ala D)
29	Carrollton (Ga-Ala D)
	Springfield (I.I.I. B)
30	Richmond (Central B)
	Carrollton (Ga-Ala D)
	Talladega (Ga-Ala D)
	Chattanooga (SA A)
	St Joseph (Western A)
	Topeka (Western A)

DEAN, HARRY
39	Sanford (Florida St D)
40	Charlotte (Piedmont B)
41	Washington (American League)
	Greenville (South Atl B)
	Fargo-Moorhead (Northern C)
42	Superior (Northern C)
46	Carrollton (Ga-Ala D)

DENDINGER, JACOB

46	Burlington (Carolina C)
	Roanoke (Piedmont B)
47	Tampa (Florida Int C)
	Carrollton (Ga-Ala D)
48	Carrollton (Ga-Ala D)

DENNIS, JACK

41	Cambridge (Eastern Shore D)
46	Portland (New England B)
47	Portland (New England B)
50	Carrollton (Ga-Ala D)

DESOUZA, FRED

50	Carrollton (Ga-Ala D)
51	Shelby (W Carolina D)
52	Lafayette (Evangeline C)
53	Columbus (South Atl A)
54	Columbus (South Atl A)
	Omaha (Western A)
57	Elmira (NY-P D)

DIMASI, JOE

47	Carrollton (Ga-Ala D)
	Concord (N Carolina St D)
	Reidsville (Tri-St B)

DOERFLINGER, GENE

47	Alexander City (Ga-Ala D)
48	Carrollton (Ga-Ala D)
49	St Petersburg (Florida Int B)

*DUGAN, ------

20	Carrollton (Georgia St D)

*DUMAS, OTTO

27	Chattanooga (SA A)
28	Carrollton (Ga-Ala D)
29	Mobile (SA A)
30	Winston-Salem (Piedmont C)
	Mobile (SA A)
	Nashville (SA A)

EAST, CARL

12	Lindale (Independent)
	Rome (Southeastern D)
13	Rome (Appalachian D)
	Montgomery (SA A)
14	Montgomery (SA A)
	Thomasville (Georgia St D)
15	Little Rock (SA A)
	St. Louis (American League)
16	Lincoln (Western A)
17	Lincoln (Western A)
19	Sioux City (Western A)
	Wichita (Western A)
20	Wichita (Western A)
21	Wichita (Western A)
22	Wichita (Western A)
23	Minneapolis (AA AA)
24	Washington (American League)
28	Minneapolis (AA AA)
29	Chattanooga (SA A)
30	Carrollton (Ga-Ala D)

	Anniston (Ga-Ala D)
31	Florence (Palmetto D)

EDWARDS, HOYT

48	Carrollton (Ga-Ala D)

ELLO, JIM

47	Baton Rouge (Evangeline D)
	Carrollton (Ga-Ala D)
	Griffin (Ga-Ala D)
48	Griffin (Ga-Ala D)
	Alexander City (Ga-Ala D)
49	Alexander City (Ga-Ala D)
50	Houma (Evangeline C)

*EZZELL, BOB

29	Carrollton (Ga-Ala D)
30	Carrollton (Ga-Ala D)
32	Monroe (Cotton St D)

FARR, CURTIS

46	Carrollton (Ga-Ala D)

FERNANDEZ, MIKE

48	Roseville (Far West D)
49	Klamath Falls (Far West D)
50	Carrollton (Ga-Ala D)
51	Ft Lauderdale (Florida Int B)

FETNER, CHARLES

49	Ozark (Alabama St D)
50	Ozark (Alabama St D)
	Carrollton (Ga-Ala D)

FINCHER, BOB

38	Gainesville (Florida St D)
39	Opelousas (Evangeline D)
41	Ocala (Florida St D)
	Gainesville (Florida St D)
46	Ozark (Alabama St D)
	Dothan (Alabama St D)
	Carrollton (Ga-Ala D)
	Montgomery (Southeastern B)

FINNEY, LOU

28	Talladega (Ga-Ala D)
29	Gadsden (Ga-Ala D)
30	Carrollton (Ga-Ala D)
31	Harrisburg (NY-P B)
	York (NY-P B)
	Philadelphia (American League)
32	Portland (PCL AA)
33	Montreal (IL AA)
34	Philadelphia (American League)
35	Philadelphia (American League)
36	Philadelphia (American League)
37	Philadelphia (American League)
38	Philadelphia (American League)
39	Philadelphia (American League)
	Boston (American League)
40	Boston (American League)
41	Boston (American League)
42	Boston (American League)
44	Boston (American League)
45	Boston (American League)

	St Louis (American League)
46	St Louis (American League)
	Opelika (Ga-Ala D)
	Valley (Ga-Ala D)
47	St Petersburg (Florida Int C)
	Philadelphia (National League)
48	St Petersburg (Florida Int C)
49	West Palm Beach (Florida Int B)
50	Temple (Big State B)

*FISHER, ------

30	Carrollton (Ga-Ala D)
	Macon (South Atl B)
	Jacksonville (Southeastern B)

*FITTERY, PAUL

12	Anderson (Carolina Assoc D)
14	Cincinnati (National League)
15	Salt Lake City (PCL AA)
17	Philadelphia (National League)
18	Los Angeles (PCL AA)
19	Los Angeles (PCL AA)
20	Sacramento (PCL AA)
21	Sacramento (PCL AA)
23	Sacramento (PCL AA)
24	St Paul (AA AA)
28	Carrollton (Ga-Ala D)
29	Carrollton (Ga-Ala D)
30	Anniston (Ga-Ala D)

FLOWERS, BURNICE

46	Carrollton (Ga-Ala D)

FRAKER, DICK

42	Dothan (Ga-Fla D)
43	Little Rock (SA A1)
46	Carrollton (Ga-Ala D)
	Tampa (Florida Int C)
	Lakeland (Florida Int C)
47	Lakeland (Florida Int C)
	St Petersburg (Florida Int C)
	Greenville (Coastal Plain D)

*FRAKES, BEN

28	Carrollton (Ga-Ala D)
	Gadsden (Ga-Ala D)

*FREEDMAN, BENNY

29	Carrollton (Ga-Ala D)

*FULLER, BERTRAM

20	Carrollton (Georgia St D)

FULLINGTON, ------

49	Carrollton (Ga-Ala D)

*GALLAGHER, ------
21   Carrollton (Georgia St D)

*GALLIVAN, PHIL
27   Waco (Texas A)
29   Macon (South Atl B)
30   Carrollton (Ga-Ala D)
      Macon (South Atl B)
31   Hartford (Eastern A)
      Brooklyn (National League)
32   Chicago (American League)
      Jersey City (IL AA)
33   Buffalo (IL AA)
34   Chicago (American League)
35   Indianapolis (AA AA)

GARNER, BOB
38   Salisbury (Eastern Shore D)
39   Charlotte (Piedmont B)
42   Chattanooga (SA A1)
43   Utica (Eastern A)
      Birmingham (SA A1)
44   Nashville (SA A1)
      Mobile (SA A1)
46   Carrollton (Ga-Ala D)
      Anniston (Southeastern B)

*GARRETT, TIGE
15   Talladega (Ga-Ala D)
20   Griffin (Georgia St D)
23   Mayfield (Kitty D)
28   Carrollton (Ga-Ala D)

*GARVEY, ------
21   Spartanburg (South Atl B)
      Carrollton (Georgia St D)

GIOMBETTI, EDDIE

48   Carrollton (Ga-Ala D)

GLOVER, OMER
48   Alexander City (Ga-Ala D)
      Carrollton (Ga-Ala D)
50   Headland (Alabama St D)
51   Headland (Ala-Fla D)
52   Graceville (Ala-Fla D)
      Panama City (Ala-Fla D)
      Jesup (Georgia St D)

*GOGGANS, G.E.

28   Carrollton (Ga-Ala D)
29   Carrollton (Ga-Ala D)
30   Carrollton (Ga-Ala D)
      Anniston (Ga-Ala D)
31   Elmira (NY-P B)
      York (NY-P B)
32   York (NY-P B)
      Scranton (NY-P B)

GOICOECHEA, LEO

44   Kingsport (Appalachian D)
      Chattanooga (SA A1)
45   Chattanooga (SA A1)
      Williamsport (Eastern A)
47   Carrollton (Ga-Ala D)
48   St Petersburg (Florida Int C)
49   St Petersburg (Florida Int C)
      Hartford (Eastern A)
50   Memphis (SA AA)
51   Ft Lauderdale (Florida Int B)
53   Tyler (Big State B)
      Greenville-Bryan (Big State B)

GONZALEZ, COTAYO

50   Carrollton (Ga-Ala D)

*GOODE, ------
30   Carrollton (Ga-Ala D)

*GRIFFITH, ------
30   Hagerstown (Blue Ridge D)
      Carrollton (Ga-Ala D)

*GRIMES, ------

28   Carrollton (Ga-Ala D)
      Lindale (Ga-Ala D)

GULLIVER, CLARK
46   Carrollton (Ga-Ala D)

GUNNELLS, LUTHER

36   Enterprise (Ala-Fla D)
38   Andalusia (Ala-Fla D)
41   Dothan (Alabama St D)
42   Meridian (Southeastern B)
      Pensacola (Southeastern B)
43   Memphis (SA A1)
44   Atlanta (SA A1)
45   Atlanta (SA A1)
46   Carrollton (Ga-Ala D)
47   Opelika (Ga-Ala D)
48   Opelika (Ga-Ala D)
      Alexander City (Ga-Ala D)

GURDY, ------
46   Carrollton (Ga-Ala D)

GUYTON, ------
46   Carrollton (Ga-Ala D)

*HARDWICK, GEORGE
29   Lindale (Ga-Ala D)
30   Carrollton (Ga-Ala D)

*HARRISON, ------
29   Carrollton (Ga-Ala D)

*HASTY, BOB
19   Mobile (SA A)
      Philadelphia (American League)
20   Mobile (SA A)
      Philadelphia (American League)
21   Carrollton (Georgia St D)
      Philadelphia (American League)
22   Philadelphia (American League)
23   Philadelphia (American League)
24   Philadelphia (American League)
29   Birmingham (SA A)
30   Birmingham (SA A)
31   Birmingham (SA A)
32   Birmingham (SA A)
      Atlanta (SA A)
33   Atlanta (SA A)
      Jersey City (IL AA)

*HATHAWAY, R.H.
21   Carrollton (Georgia St D)
23   Morristown (Appalachian D)

*HAWKINS, CY
20   Rome (Georgia St D)
21   Carrollton (Georgia St D)
      Griffin (Georgia St D)

*HENDERSON, HAP
20   Carrollton (Georgia St D)
27   Chattanooga (SA A)

*HICKS, R.E.
21 Carrollton (Georgia St D)
      Griffin (Georgia St D)

HILL, JIM

42   Pensacola (Southeastern B)
46   Salisbury (Eastern Shore D)
      Carrollton (Ga-Ala D)
      Allentown (Inter-St B)
47   Carrollton (Ga-Ala D)
48   Carrollton (Ga-Ala D)

HILL, OLIVER
35   Akron (Mid-Atl C)
      Joplin (West Assoc C)
      Atlanta (SA A)
36   Atlanta (SA A1)
37   Atlanta (SA A1)
38   Atlanta (SA A1)
39   Milwaukee (AA AA)
      Boston (National League)
40   Indianapolis (AA AA)
      Atlanta (SA A1)
41   Toronto (IL AA)
42   San Diego (PCL AAA)
46   San Diego (PCL AAA)
      Tallassee (Ga-Ala D)
47   Tallassee (Ga-Ala D)
      Newnan (Ga-Ala D)
48   Carrollton (Ga-Ala D)

*HOLCOMB, HOT
30   Carrollton (Ga-Ala D)

*HOLSOMBACK, SQUIRT

28	Lindale (Ga-Ala D)
29	Carrollton (Ga-Ala D)
30	Carrollton (Ga-Ala D)
	Atlanta (SA A)

*HOLTZ, RED

20	Carrollton (Georgia St D)

*HOWELL, RED

28	Carrollton (Ga-Ala D)
29	Birmingham (SA A)
30	Greenville (South Atl B)
31	Hartford (Eastern A)
32	Hartford (Eastern A)
	Toronto (IL AA)
33	Toronto (IL AA)
34	Toronto (IL AA)
35	Ft Worth (Texas A)
	Tulsa (Texas A)
36	Tulsa (Texas A1)
37	Los Angeles (PCL AA)
	Birmingham (SA A1)
38	Birmingham (SA A1)
39	Baltimore (IL AA)
40	Baltimore (IL AA)
41	Cleveland (American League)
	Baltimore (IL AA)
42	Milwaukee (AA AA)
	Knoxville (SA A1)
	Jersey City (IL AA)
43	Jersey City (IL AA)
44	Portsmouth (Piedmont B)
	Atlanta (SA A1)

HUDSON, BILL

48	Brewton (Alabama St D)
	Thibodaux (Evangeline D)
49	Carrollton (Ga-Ala D)

*HUGGINS, MILLER

28	Carrollton (Ga-Ala D)
	Gadsden (Ga-Ala D)
29	Cedartown (Ga-Ala D)

*HUMPHRIES, -------

30	Carrollton (Ga-Ala D)

HURLEY, -------

46	Carrollton (Ga-Ala D)

HUTCHINS, BOB

49	Carrollton (Ga-Ala D)
50	Carrollton (Ga-Ala D)
	Rome (Ga-Ala D)
51	Rome (Ga-Ala D)

*INGRAM, JIMMY

20	Carrollton (Georgia St D)

ISRAEL, BILL

40	Brewton (Alabama St D)
	Greenville (Alabama St D)
41	Tallassee (Alabama St D)
46	Carrollton (Ga-Ala D)
	Troy (Alabama St D)
47	Troy (Alabama St D)

*JAMES, FOB

28	Carrollton (Ga-Ala D)
29	Lindale (Ga-Ala D)

JEFTS, VIRGIL

48	Carrollton (Ga-Ala D)
49	Carrollton (Ga-Ala D)
51	Jesup (Georgia St D)

*JESMER, W.H.

20	Rome (Georgia St D)
21	Carrollton (Georgia St D)

JONES, BILL

45	Roanoke (Piedmont B)
	Birmingham (SA A1)
46	Tallassee (Ga-Ala D)
	Newnan (Ga-Ala D)
47	Newnan (Ga-Ala D)
	Carrollton (Ga-Ala D)
	Vicksburg (Southeastern B)
48	El Paso (Arizona-Texas C)
	Statesville (N Carolina St D)
50	Natchez (Cotton St C)
51	Natchez (Cotton St C)
53	Norton (Mountain St D)
54	Meridian (Cotton St D)

JONES, CASEY

49	Carrollton (Ga-Ala D)
50	Carrollton (Ga-Ala D)
	Newnan (Ga-Ala D)
51	Douglas (Georgia St D)

*JUSTISS, RED

29	Carrollton (Ga-Ala D)

30	Carrollton (Ga-Ala D)
	Anniston (Ga-Ala D)

KELLY, DICK

46	Kingsport (Appalachian D)
	Lakeland (Florida Int C)
47	Carrollton (Ga-Ala D)
48	Jackson (Southeastern B)
	Gadsden (Southeastern B)
49	Bristol (Colonial B)
50	Bristol (Colonial B)
	West Palm Beach (Florida Int B)

KELLY, MASON

50	Carrollton (Ga-Ala D)
	Palatka (Florida St D)

KIRSCHNER, GEORGE

46	Carrollton (Ga-Ala D)
	Montgomery (Southeastern B)

*KITTS, CLAUDE

20	Columbia (South Atl C)
21	Columbia (South Atl C)
	Carrollton (Georgia St D)
27	Asheville (South Atl B)
29	Asheville (South Atl B)
31	Asheville (Piedmont B)

KURAS, WALT

49	Natchez (Cotton St C)
	Carrollton (Ga-Ala D)
50	Enid (West Assoc C)
51	Hot Springs (Cotton St C)

*LACEY, -------

28	Carrollton (Ga-Ala D)
29	Carrollton (Ga-Ala D)
	Talladega (Ga-Ala D)
30	Carrollton (Ga-Ala D)

*LAIRD, RED

23	Americus (So Georgia Ind)
28	Carrollton (Ga-Ala D)

LANGEMEIER, PAUL

47	Moultrie (Ga-Fla D)
48	Moultrie (Ga-Fla D)
	Ft Lauderdale (Florida Int C)
49	Carrollton (Ga-Ala D)
50	Ft Lauderdale (Florida Int B)

LANGLEY, JIM

43	Erwin (Appalachian D)
	Montgomery (SA A1)
44	Williamsport (Eastern A)
	Chattanooga (SA A1)
45	Chattanooga (SA A1)
46	Carrollton (Ga-Ala D)
47	Carrollton (Ga-Ala D)
50	Alexander City (Ga-Ala D)

*LASSETTER, ROY

19	Chattanooga (SA A)
20	Carrollton (Georgia St D)
	Lindale (Georgia St D)
21	Lindale (Georgia St D)

LEE, FRED

50	Carrollton (Ga-Ala D)
51	Gainesville (Florida St D)
	Douglas (Georgia St D)
	Eastman (Georgia St D)
52	Graceville (Ala-Fla D)
	Headland (Ala-Fla D)

*LEHMAN, OTTO

21	Carrollton (Georgia St D)
	Cedartown (Georgia St D)

*LITTLE, ------

21	Carrollton (Georgia St D)

LITTLE, WALT

46	Carrollton (Ga-Ala D)
47	Carrollton (Ga-Ala D)
48	Carrollton (Ga-Ala D)
49	Carrollton (Ga-Ala D)
	Alexander City (Ga-Ala D)

*LONG, H.L.

20	Carrollton (Georgia St D)
21	Carrollton (Georgia St D)

*LOPEZ, ------

29	Carrollton (Ga-Ala D)

LOVELADY, WILLARD

48	Carrollton (Ga-Ala D)
49	Chattanooga (SA AA)
	Charlotte (Tri-St B)
50	Charlotte (Tri-St B)

MALOOF, JOE

46	Daytona Beach (Florida St D)
49	Carrollton (Ga-Ala D)

*MANNING, ------

30	Carrollton (Ga-Ala D)
	High Point (Piedmont C)
35	Richmond (Piedmont B)
38	Moultrie (Ga-Fla D)

*MARKS, MAX

28	Cedartown (Ga-Ala D)
	Talladega (Ga-Ala D)
29	Carrollton (Ga-Ala D)
	Anniston (Ga-Ala D)

MARSHALL, SHORTY

46	Carrollton (Ga-Ala D)
47	Carrollton (Ga-Ala D)
48	Carrollton (Ga-Ala D)
49	Stockton (California C)
	West Palm Beach (Florida Int B)
50	Carrollton (Ga-Ala D)
51	Headland (Ala-Fla D)
52	Graceville (Ala-Fla D)
	Jesup (Georgia St D)

*MARTIN, S.R.

20	LaGrange (Georgia St D)
21	Carrollton (Georgia St D)

*MARTIN, AMOS

30	Carrollton (Ga-Ala D)
	Atlanta (SA A)
	Evansville (I.I.I. B)
	Springfield (I.I.I. B)

*MATHEWSON, ------

28	Carrollton (Ga-Ala D)

MATTHEWS, BOB

45	Columbus (AA AA)
	Allentown (Inter-St B)
46	Carrollton (Ga-Ala D)
47	Vicksburg (Southeastern B)
	Carrollton (Ga-Ala D)
	Newnan (Ga-Ala D)

MATTHEWS, LUTHER

49	Carrollton (Ga-Ala D)
50	New Bern (Coastal Plain D)
51	New Bern (Coastal Plain D)
52	Rock Hill (Tri-St B)
53	Rock Hill (Tri-St B)

MAZAK, LEO

50	Carrollton (Ga-Ala D)

*MCGHEE, BILL

29	Carrollton (Ga-Ala D)
30	Carrollton (Ga-Ala D)
	Anniston (Ga-Ala D)
31	Augusta (Palmetto D)
	Galveston (Texas A)
32	Galveston (Texas A)
	Shreveport (Texas A)
	Tyler (Texas A)
35	Galveston (Texas A)
36	Clarksdale (Cotton St D)
	Albany (IL AA)
	Nashville (SA A1)
	Galveston (Texas A1)
37	Winston-Salem (Piedmont B)
	Jackson (Southeastern B)
38	Elmira (Eastern A)
	Winston-Salem (Piedmont B)
39	Winston-Salem (Piedmont B)
	Meridian (Southeastern B)
40	Meridian (Southeastern B)
	Pensacola (Southeastern B)
41	Pensacola (Southeastern B)
42	Little Rock (SA A1)
	Pensacola (Southeastern B)
43	Little Rock (SA A1)
44	Little Rock (SA A1)
	Philadelphia (American League)
45	Philadelphia (American League)
46	Pensacola (Southeastern B)
47	Gadsden (Southeastern B)
48	Gadsden (Southeastern B)
	Brewton (Alabama St D)
49	Pensacola (Southeastern B)
50	Columbia (South Atl A)
	Gadsden (Southeastern B)
51	El Dorado (Cotton St C)
57	Pensacola (Ala-Fla D)

*MCKINNEY, ------

28	Carrollton (Ga-Ala D)
	Lindale (Ga-Ala D)

*MCKINNON, BILL

20	Carrollton (Georgia St D)

*MILNER, HOLT

20	LaGrange (Georgia St D)
21	Spartanburg (South Atl B)
23	Birmingham (SA A)
27	Augusta (South Atl B)
29	Chattanooga (SA A)
30	Carrollton (Ga-Ala D)
31	Beckley (Mid-Atl C)

Augusta (Palmetto D)
32   Beckley (Mid-Atl C)
33   Beckley (Mid-Atl C)
       Dayton (Mid-Atl C)
34   Dayton (Mid-Atl C)
       Zanesville (Mid-Atl C)
       Scranton (NY-P A)
39   Troy (Ala-Fla D)
40   Dothan (Alabama St D)
41   Dothan (Alabama St D)
42   Dothan (Alabama St D)

MILO, ------
46   Carrollton (Ga-Ala D)
       Smithfield (Tobacco St D)

MONARCHI, GENE

48   Carrollton (Ga-Ala D)

MONARCHI, PETE

47   Tampa (Florida Int C)
       Carrollton (Ga-Ala D)
48   Carrollton (Ga-Ala D)
       Vidalia-Lyons (Georgia St D)
49   Hazleton (North Atl D)
50   Bangor (North Atl D)

*MOORE, CLEM
20   Griffin (Georgia St D)
21   Carrollton (Georgia St D)
       Charleston (South Atl B)

*MOORE, J.
28   Carrollton (Ga-Ala D)

MORELLI, JIM

49   Carrollton (Ga-Ala D)
50   Carrollton (Ga-Ala D)
51   Douglas (Georgia St D)
53   Hagerstown (Piedmont B)

MURPHEE, BILL
47   Carrollton (Ga-Ala D)

NAGLE, BOB
47   St Cloud (Northern C)
       Grand Forks (Northern C)
48   Carrollton (Ga-Ala D)
       Enterprise (Alabama St D)
49   Enterprise (Alabama St D)
       Brewton (Alabama St D)
       Bridgeport (Colonial B)
50   St Cloud (Northern C)

NASWORTHY, LUTHER
48   Carrollton (Ga-Ala D)

49   Carrollton (Ga-Ala D)

NELSON, BUREL

46   Tallassee (Ga-Ala D)
47   Tallassee (Ga-Ala D)
49   Carrollton (Ga-Ala D)

NELSON, DICK
46   Palatka (Florida St D)
       St Augustine (Florida St D)
48   Eastman (Georgia St D)
       Carrollton (Ga-Ala D)

*NETTLES, HOKE
29   Carrollton (Ga-Ala D)

OGLESBY, HUGH
46   Carrollton (Ga-Ala D)

PADGETT, CHARLES
46   Newnan (Ga-Ala D)
       LaGrange (Ga-Ala D)
47   Carrollton (Ga-Ala D)
49   New Iberia (Evangeline C)
50   Rome (Ga-Ala D)
       Jesup (Georgia St D)

PATTERSON, BILL

46   Carrollton (Ga-Ala D)
47   Carrollton (Ga-Ala D)
48   DeLand (Florida St D)
       Vidalia-Lyons (Georgia St D)
50   Carrollton (Ga-Ala D)
       Griffin (Ga-Ala D)
       Valley (Ga-Ala D)
       Alexander City (Ga-Ala D)

*PATTON, HENRY

29   Carrollton (Ga-Ala D)
30   Cedartown (Ga-Fla D)
       Bloomington (I.I.I. B)

PITTMAN, AL

42   Decature (I.I.I. B)
       Williamson (Mountain St C)
45   Winston-Salem (Carolina C)
       Rochester (IL AA)
46   Carrollton (Ga-Ala D)

POOLE, BUDDY
48   Duncan (Sooner St D)
       Leavenworth (West Assoc C)
49   Carrollton (Ga-Ala D)

*POWERS, ------
21   Carrollton (Georgia St D)

*PRATT, FRANK

20   Carrollton (Georgia St D)
21   Chicago (American League)

*PRESSLEY, BABE
15   Fitchburg (New England B)
20   Carrollton (Georgia St D)
21   Spartanburg (South Atl B)
23   Fulton (Kitty D)

PRZEWORSKI, TED
48   Carrollton (Ga-Ala D)
       LaGrange (Ga-Fla D)

*PULLIAM, J.C.
20   Carrollton (Georgia St D)
23   Greenville (Appalachian D)

REACH, CLIFTON

48   Alexander City (Ga-Ala D)
49   Alexander City (Ga-Ala D)
       Johnson City (Appalachian D)
50   Carrollton (Ga-Ala D)
       Opelika (Ga-Ala D)

REED, JIM
41   Greenville (Alabama St D)
       Ft Pierce (Florida East Coast D)
       Amarillo (W Texas-NM D)
46   Greenville (Alabama St D)
       Carrollton (Ga-Ala D)
       LaGrange (Ga-Ala D)

*REESE, EDDIE

29   Carrollton (Ga-Ala D)
30   Carrollton (Ga-Ala D)
       Huntsville (Ga-Ala D)
31   Beckley (Mid-Atl C)

*REESE, RED

20   Carrollton (Georgia St D)

*REGISTER, -------
20   Sanford (Florida St D)
     Carrollton (Georgia St D)
21   LaGrange (Georgia St D)

*REIS, -------
21   Carrollton (Georgia St D)

REVELS, BILL
45   Greensboro (Carolina C)
47   Terre Haute (I.I.I. B)
48   St Petersburg (Florida Int C)
     Carrollton (Ga-Ala D)
49   West Palm Beach (Florida Int B)
     Anniston (Southeastern B)
50   Anniston (Southeastern B)
     Florence (Tri-St B)

*RICHARDS, BABE
15   Rome (Ga-Ala D)
21   Carrollton (Georgia St D)
23   Morristown (Appalachian D)

RIDENOUR, ROY
48   Miami Beach (Florida Int C)
     Palatka (Florida St D)
49   Carrollton (Ga-Ala D)
     Middlesboro (Mountain St D)
50   Middlesboro (Mountain St D)
51   Middlesboro (Mountain St D)
     Big Stone Gap (Mountain St D)

ROBERTS, RED

35   Carrollton (Ga-Ala Ind)
40   Sanford (Florida St D)
41   Charlotte (Piedmont B)
42   Charlotte (Piedmont B)
43   Montgomery (SA A1)
     Washington (American League)
45   Louisville (AA AA)
46   Carrollton (Ga-Ala D)
47   Charleston (South Atl A)
     Carrollton (Ga-Ala D)
48   Carrollton (Ga-Ala D)
49   Alexander City (Ga-Ala D)
50   Alexander City (Ga-Ala D)

*ROBERTSON, -------
20   Carrollton (Georgia St D)

ROBISON, ROY
46   Carrollton (Ga-Ala D)

ROEDEL, BOB

48   Carrollton (Ga-Ala D)
49   Lawrenceville (Virginia D)
50   Whiteville (Tobacco St D)
51   Kinston (Coastal Plain D)
53   Superior (Northern C)

ROMAN, CARL

48   Carrollton (Ga-Ala D)
49   Bristol (Appalachian D)

*ROWE, BOB

28   Carrollton (Ga-Ala D)
     Gadsden (Ga-Ala D)

RUCKER, BILL
36   Fargo-Moorhead (Northern D)
37   Fargo-Moorhead (Northern D)
38   Bloomington (I.I.I. B)
     Springfield (Mid-Atl C)
39   Wilkes-Barre (Eastern A)
     Bloomington (I.I.I. B)
     Cedar Rapids (I.I.I. B)
40   Brewton (Alabama St D)
     New Bern (Coastal Plain D)
     Waycross (Ga-Fla D)
49   Carrollton (Ga-Ala D)
50   Alexander City (Ga-Ala D)

RUSSELL, BING

48   Carrollton (Ga-Ala D)
49   Carrollton (Ga-Ala D)

*SAPPENFIELD, COLON

29   Carrollton (Ga-Ala D)
30   Anniston (Ga-Ala D)

*SCHULTE, J.
21   Carrollton (Georgia St D)

SEAL, BILL

38   Fayetteville (Ark-Mo D)
39   Bowling Green (Kitty D)
     Greenville (Cotton St C)
40   Greenville (Cotton St C)
41   Vicksburg (Cotton St C)
46   Memphis (SA AA)
     Anniston (Southeastern B)
47   Vicksburg (Southeastern B)
48   Vicksburg (Southeastern B)
49   Carrollton (Ga-Ala D)
     Anniston (Southeastern B)
50   Dublin (Georgia St D)
     Gadsden (Southeastern B)
51   St Petersburg (Florida Int B)
52   St Petersburg (Florida Int B)
53   St Petersburg (Florida Int B)

SEIGLER, BILL
42   Hickory (N Carolina St D)
46   Carrollton (Ga-Ala D)

*SESSIONS, PETE
21   High Point (Piedmont C)
     Carrollton (Georgia St D)
     Griffin (Georgia St D)
23   Raleigh (Piedmont C)
27   Winston-Salem (Piedmont C)
29   Winston-Salem (Piedmont C)
31   Winston-Salem (Piedmont B)
32   Winston-Salem (Piedmont B)

*SHAW, POP

20   Carrollton (Georgia St D)
21   Cedartown (Georgia St D)

SHIRLEY, JIM

40   Gainesville (Florida St D)
46   Selma (Southeastern B)
     Spartanburg (Southeastern B)
47   Lynn (New England B)
48   Binghampton (Eastern A)
49   Carrollton (Ga-Ala D)
50   Carrollton (Ga-Ala D)
52   Binghampton (Eastern A)
     Three Rivers (Provincial C)
55   Sanford (Florida St D)
     Orlando (Florida St D)

SHIVERS, -------
46   Carrollton (Ga-Ala D)

SHOEMAKE, CLAUDE
39   Danville-Schoolfield (Bi-St D)
40   Danville-Schoolfield (Bi-St D)
46   Newnan (Ga-Ala D)

47   Newnan (Ga-Ala D)
49   St Augustine (Florida St D)
50   St Augustine (Florida St D)
     Carrollton (Ga-Ala D)
51   Rome (Ga-Ala D)
52   St Augustine (Florida St D)

SILVERMAN, JEROME
46   Sanford (Florida St D)
47   Sanford (Florida St D)
48   Carrollton (Ga-Ala D)
     Vidalia-Lyons (Georgia St D)
49   Vidalia (Georgia St D)
50   Vidalia-Lyons (Georgia St D)

SINGLEY, HULEN
47   Carrollton (Ga-Ala D)

*SMITH, ------
47   Carrollton (Ga-Ala D)

*SMITH, J.
21   Carrollton (Georgia St D)

*SMITH, REUBEN
30   Carrollton (Ga-Ala D)
36   Jacksonville (South Atl B)
     Columbia (South Atl B)
37   Columbia (South Atl B)
38   Columbia (South Atl B)

SNIDER, FLOYD

42   Dothan (Ga-Fla D)
46   Newnan (Ga-Ala D)
     Carrollton (Ga-Ala D)
47   Carrollton (Ga-Ala D)
48   Carrollton (Ga-Ala D)
     Vidalia-Lyons (Georgia St D)
49   Vidalia (Georgia St D)

SOLT, GENE

48   Vidalia-Lyons (Georgia St D)
     West Palm Beach (Florida Int C)
49   West Palm Beach (Florida Int B)
50   West Palm Beach (Florida Int B)
     Carrollton (Ga-Ala D)
51   Hagerstown (Inter-St B)
52   Atlanta (SA AA)
53   Toledo (AA AAA)
54   Atlanta (SA AA)
55   Atlanta (SA AA)
     Beaumont (Texas AA)
56   Austin (Texas AA)
     Amarillo (Western A)
57   Austin (Texas AA)
58   Austin (Texas AA)
     Atlanta (SA AA)

SOUTER, GEORGE

38   Johnson City (Appalachian D)
39   Sanford (Florida St D)
44   Jersey City (IL AA)
45   Toronto (IL AA)
     New Orleans (SA A1)
46   Carrollton (Ga-Ala D)
     New Orleans (SA A1)
47   Miami (Florida Int C)
     Lakeland (Florida Int C)
48   Pine Bluff (Cotton St C)
     Lakeland (Florida Int C)
49   Reidsville (Carolina B)
50   Reidsville (Carolina B)
51   Reidsville (Carolina B)
52   Reidsville (Carolina B)
53   Reidsville (Carolina B)
54   Reidsville (Carolina B)

*SOWARD, JIM
29   Pensacola (Southeastern B)
     Gadsden (Ga-Ala D)
30   Carrollton (Ga-Ala D)
     Talladega (Ga-Ala D)
     Pensacola (Southeastern B)
34   El Dorado (East Dixie C)

SPENCER, BILL
42   Hutchinson (West Assoc C)
46   Carrollton (Ga-Ala D)
53   Albany (Eastern A)
56   New Iberia (Evangeline C)

SPRAYBERRY, JIM
46   Carrollton (Ga-Ala D)
     Valley (Ga-Ala D)
49   Alexander City (Ga-Ala D)

*STANFIELD, RALPH

29   Lindale (Ga-Ala D)
     Carrollton (Ga-Ala D)
30   Carrollton (Ga-Ala D)
     Anniston (Ga-Ala D)
37   Cambridge (Eastern Shore D)
     New Iberia (Evangeline D)

STEEL, ------
46   Carrollton (Ga-Ala D)

STOYLE, JIM
46   Carrollton (Ga-Ala D)
     Montgomery (Southeastern C)
47   Newnan (Ga-Ala D)
48   St Petersburg (Florida Int B)
49   Sparta (Georgia St D)
50   Griffin (Ga-Ala D)
51   Jesup (Georgia St D)
52   Jesup (Georgia St D)
53   Fitzgerald (Ga-Fla D)

*STRICKLAND, ------
29   Carrollton (Ga-Ala D)

*SUMMERLIN, FRITZ
15   New Orleans (SA A)

20   Carrollton (Georgia St D)
23   Hopkinsville (Kitty D)

*SURATT, CLYDE
21   Carrollton (Georgia St D)
     Greenville (South Atl B)
23   Greenville (South Atl B)
27   Greenville (South Atl B)
29   Greenville (South Atl B)

*SUTTON, LEFTY

20   Carrollton (Georgia St D)

*SWANN, P.P.

20   Carrollton (Georgia St D)
21   LaGrange (Georgia St D)
     Meridian (Cotton St D)
23   Orlando (Florida St D)

*TALIAFERRO, DICK

28   Carrollton (Ga-Ala D)
29   Shawnee (West Assoc C)
30   Shawnee (West Assoc C)
33   Winston-Salem (Piedmont B)
     Charlotte (Piedmont B)

*TATE, J.R.
29   Carrollton (Ga-Ala D)
     Cedartown (Ga-Ala D)

*TAYLOR, ZACHERY
30   Carrollton (Ga-Ala D)
     Scottsdale (Mid-Atl C)
     Greenville (South Atl B)
31   Bartlesville (West Assoc C)
32   Quincy (I.I.I. B)
     Ft Smith (West Assoc C)
33   Zanesville (Mid-Atl C)
34   Rayne (Evangeline D)
35   Rayne (Evangeline D)
38   Texarkana (East Texas C)

*TAYLOR, BILL
18   Chattanooga (SA A)
19   Charlotte (South Atl C)
21   Carrollton (Georgia St D)

TERRY, HORACE
46   Brewton (Alabama St D)
     Carrollton (Ga-Ala D)

THOMAS, DALLAS

40	Beaver Falls (Penn ST D)
44	Buffalo (IL AA)
	Hagerstown (Inter-St B)
46	Carrollton (Ga-Ala D)
47	Carrollton (Ga-Ala D)
48	New Castle (Mid-Atl C)
	Greenville (Cotton St C)

*THOMPSON, ERSKINE

30	Carrollton (Ga-Ala D)
	Huntsville (Ga-Ala D)

THOMPSON, JIM

47	Rocky Mount (Coastal Plain D)
48	Geneva (Alabama St D)
49	Leesburg (Florida St D)
	Carrollton (Ga-Ala D)
50	Valley (Ga-Ala D)
51	Valley (Ga-Ala D)
52	Bradford (PONY D)
54	Gainesville (Sooner ST D)

TIDWELL, JOHN

48	Clarksdale (Cotton St C)
	Thibodaux (Evangeline D)
49	Thibodaux (Evangeline D)
	Alexandria (Evangeline D)
	Carrollton (Ga-Ala D)
50	Dublin (Georgia St D)
51	Dublin (Georgia St D)
	Tifton (Ga-Fla D)
52	Greenwood (Cotton St C)

TILLEY, TRAVIS

47	Carrollton (Ga-Ala D)
	LaGrange (Ga-Ala D)

*TURK, ------

30	Carrollton (Ga-Ala D)

*TURNER, ------

30	Carrollton (Ga-Ala D)

UMSCHEID, DON

48	Sanford (Florida St D)
49	Carrollton (Ga-Ala D)
	Griffin (Ga-Ala D)

VARNER, BUCK

48	Carrollton (Ga-Ala D)
	Emporia (Virginia D)
49	Orlando (Florida St D)
50	Chattanooga (SA AA)
52	Chattanooga (SA AA)
	Washington (American League)

53	Chattanooga (SA AA)
54	Charlotte (South Atl A)

VICTOR, ERNIE

50	Carrollton (Ga-Ala D)
	DeLand (Florida St D)

WADEWITZ, OSWIN

47	Grand Forks (Northern C)
48	Grand Forks (Northern C)
	Duluth (Northern C)
49	Graceville (Cotton St C)
	Carrollton (Ga-Ala D)

*WALTON, BATTLEAXE

21	Carrollton (Georgia St D)

*WATSON, JULES

20	Carrollton (Georgia St D)
21	Carrollton (Georgia St D)

WEBB, BILL

41	Mobile (Southeastern B)
42	Macon (South Atl B)
43	Philadelphia (National League)
	Montreal (IL AA)
44	St Paul (AA AA)
45	St Paul (AA AA)
	Minneapolis (AA AA)
46	Minneapolis (AA AAA)
47	Carrollton (Ga-Ala D)
48	Lakeland (Florida Int C)
50	Gadsden (Southeastern B)

WELDON, BILL

49	Dublin (Georgia St D)
50	Carrollton (Ga-Ala D)

*WESLEY, ------

30	Carrollton (Ga-Ala D)
	Huntsville (Ga-Ala D)

WESTBROOK, JOHN

40	Tallassee (Alabama St D)
46	Tallassee (Ga-Ala D)
	Carrollton (Ga-Ala D)

*WHITE, ABE

28	Carrollton (Ga-Ala D)
29	Carrollton (Ga-Ala D)
30	Carrollton (Ga-Ala D)
	Lindale (Ga-Ala D)
31	Monroe (Cotton St D)
32	Birmingham (SA A)
33	Birmingham (SA A)
34	Birmingham (SA A)
35	Birmingham (SA A)
37	Rochester (IL AA)
	St Louis (National League)
41	Mobile (Southeastern B)
42	Mobile (Southeastern B)
44	Mobile (SA A1)
45	Mobile (SA A1)
46	New Bern (Coastal Plain D)
47	Griffin (Ga-Ala D)

WHITE, CURTIS

50	Carrollton (Ga-Ala D)
51	Cocoa (Florida St D)
	Valley (Ga-Ala D)
	Alexander City (Ga-Ala D)
52	Statesboro (Georgia St D)
53	Statesboro (Georgia St D)
54	Statesboro (Georgia St D)

*WHITE, H.

30	Carrollton (Ga-Ala D)

WHITE, JO-JO

28	Carrollton (Ga-Ala D)
29	Evansville (I.I.I. B)
30	Ft Smith (West Assoc C)
31	Beaumont (Texas A)
32	Detroit (American League)
33	Detroit (American League)
34	Detroit (American League)
35	Detroit (American League)
36	Detroit (American League)
37	Detroit (American League)
38	Detroit (American League)
39	Seattle (PCL AA)
40	Seattle (PCL AA)
41	Seattle (PCL AA)
42	Seattle (PCL AA)
43	Philadelphia (American League)
44	Philadelphia (American League)
	Cincinnati (National League)
45	Sacramento (PCL AA)
46	Sacramento (PCL AAA)
	Seattle (PCL AAA)
47	Seattle (PCL AAA)
48	Seattle (PCL AAA)
49	Hollywood (PCL AAA)

WHITED, GERALD
49　New Iberia (Evangeline C)
　　Carrollton (Ga-Ala D)

*WICKER, KEMP

28　Carrollton (Ga-Ala D)
29　Goldsboro (Eastern Carolina D)
　　Jeannette (Mid-Atl C)
30　Jeannette (Mid-Atl C)
31　Charleroi (Mid-Atl C)
　　Bechley (Mid-Atl C)
32　Cumberland (Mid-Atl C)
33　Wheeling (Mid-Atl C)
34　Binghamton (NY-P A)
35　Newark (IL AA)
36　New York (American League)
　　Newark (IL AA)
37　New York (American League)
　　Newark (IL AA)
38　Kansas City (AA AA)
　　New York (American League)
39　Montreal (IL AA)
40　Montreal (IL AA)
41　Montreal (IL AA)
　　Brooklyn (National League)
42　Sacramento (PCL AA)
43　Rochester (IL AA)
44　Rochester (IL AA)
45　Rochester (IL AA)
46　Columbus (South Atl A)
47　Columbus (South Atl A)
48　Columbus (South Atl A)

WILLIAMS, BOB

48　San Jose (California C)
　　Carrollton (Ga-Ala D)

*WILLIAMS, LUKE
20　Carrollton (Georgia St D)
21　Birmingham (SA A)
27　Augusta (South Atl B)
29　Augusta (South Atl B)
31　Raleigh (Piedmont B)

WILLIAMS, PAUL
41　Dothan (Alabama St D)
　　Natchez (Evangeline D)
46　Carrollton (Ga-Ala D)

*WILSON, JACK
20　Carrollton (Georgia St D)
21　Clarksdale (Cotton St D)
27　St Augustine (Southeastern B)
29　Pensacola (Southeastern B)

*WINN, BREEZY
29　Carrollton (Ga-Ala D)
30　Huntsville (Ga-Ala D)

YARBOROUGH, MACK

48　West Palm Beach (Florida Int B)
　　Daytona Beach (Florida St D)
49　Carrollton (Ga-Ala D)
50　Cordele (Ga-Fla D)

YEARTY, SAM
46　Carrollton (Ga-Ala D)
53　Sandersville (Georgia St D)

YORK, LEW

46　Carrollton (Ga-Ala D)
47　Vancouver (West Int B)

League Abbreviations:
AA = American Association
Ala-Fla = Alabama-Florida League
Ala-Tenn = Alabama-Tennessee League
Alabama St = Alabama State League
Appalachian = Appalachian League
Arizona St = Arizona State League
Arizona-Mexico = Arizona-Mexico League
Arizona-Texas = Arizona-Texas League
Ark-Mo = Arkansas-Missouri League
Ark-Tex = Arkansas-Texas League
Arkansas St = Arkansas State League
Atlantic = Atlantic League
Big State = Big State League
Bi-St = Bi-State League
Blue Grass = Blue Grass League
Blue Ridge = Blue Ridge League
Border = Border League
Buckeye = Buckeye League
Cal St = California State League
California = California League
Canad-Amer = Canadian-American League
Canadian = Canadian League
Cape Breton = Cape Breton Colliery League
Carolina = Carolina League
Carolina Assoc = Carolina Association
Central = Central League
Central Assoc = Central Assoc
Coastal Plain = Coastal Plain League
Colonial = Colonial League
Cotton St = Cotton States League
Dakota = Dakota League
Dixie = Dixie League
East Dixie = East Dixie League
East Texas = East Texas League
Eastern = Eastern League
Eastern Assoc = Eastern Association
Eastern Carolina = Eastern Carolina League
Eastern Shore = Eastern Shore League
Empire St = Empire State League
Evangeline = Evangeline League
FLAG = Florida-Alabama-Georgia League
Far West = Far West League
Florida East Coast = Florida East Coast League
Florida Int = Florida International League
Florida St = Florida State League
Ga-Ala = Georgia-Alabama League
Ga-Fla = Georgia-Florida League
Georgia St = Georgia State League
Gulf Coast = Gulf Coast League
I.I.I. = Illinois-Iowa-Indiana League
IL = International League
Ill-Mo = Illinois-Missouri League
Illinois St = Illinois State League
Inter-St = Interstate League
Kitty = Kentucky-Illinois-Tennessee League
KOM = Kansas-Oklahoma-Missouri League
Lone Star = Lone Star League
Longhorn = Longhorn League
Louisiana St = Louisiana State League
Mich-Ont = Michigan-Ontario League
Michigan St = Michigan State League

Mid-Atl = Middle Atlantic League
Midwest = Midwest League
Miss Valley = Mississippi Valley League
Miss-Ohio Valley = Mississippi-Ohio Valley League
Mountain St = Mountain State League
N Carolina St = North Carolina State League
NE Arkansas = Northeast Arkansas League
Nebraska St = Nebraska State League
New England = New England League
North Atl = North Atlantic League
North Dakota = North Dakota League
Northeastern = Northeastern League
Northern = Northern League
Northwest = Northwest League
NY-P = New York-Pennsylvania League
Ohio St = Ohio State League
Ohio-Ind = Ohio-Indiana League
Oklahoma St = Oklahoma State League
Ontario = Ontario League
Palmetto = Palmetto League
Panhandle-Pecos = Panhandle-Pecos Valley League
PC Int = Pacific Coast International League
PCL = Pacific Coast League
Penn St = Pennsylvania State Association
Piedmont = Piedmont League
Pioneer = Pioneer League
PONY = Pennsylvania-Ontario-New York League
Provincial = Provincial League
Que-Ont-Ver = Quebec-Ontario-Vermont League
Quebec Prov = Quebec Provincial League
Rio Grande Valley – Rio Grande Valley League
SA = Southern Association
Sooner St = Sooner State League
Sophomore = Sophomore League
South Atl = South Atlantic League
South Dakota = South Dakota League
Southeastern = Southeastern League
Southern = Southern League
Southwest Int = Southwest International League
Southwestern = Southwestern League
Sunset = Sunset League
Tar Heel = Tar Heel League
Tex-Ok = Texas-Oklahoma League
Texas = Texas League
Texas Assoc = Texas Association
Texas Valley = Texas Valley League
Tobacco St = Tobacco State League
Tri-St = Tri-State League
Twin Ports = Twin Ports League
Ut-Idaho = Utah-Idaho League
Virginia = Virginia League
W Carolina = Western Carolina League
W Carolinas = Western Carolinas League
W Texas-NM = West Texas-New Mexico League
West Dixie = West Dixie League
West Texas = West Texas League
West Assoc = Western Association
West Int = Western International League
Western = Western League
Wisconsin St = Wisconsin State League

Opponent Rosters

The following are rosters for teams that played against Carrollton in the Georgia State League in 1920-21 and in the Georgia-Alabama League in 1928-30, 46-50.

1920

Cedartown:

Boone, Ike	
Carter, ---	OF
Craddock, ---	SS
Durham, J.C.	
Hughes, ---	P
Hunter, H.C.	3B
Johnson, ---	P
Jones, D.	M, C
Kelton, Wiley	1B
Schroeder, A.L.	P
Sells, Albert	
Skinner, ---	OF
Suggs, Eugene	2B
Tattler, Henry	C, OF
Tolbert, C.	OF
Vardeman, F.C.	P

Griffin:

Bowden, L.H.	2B
Burgess, ---	2B
Dillon, J.T.R.	
Ellington, ---	P
Garrett, Tige	M, 1B
Gilbert, Lewis	OF
Hawkins, G.B.	P
Johansen, ---	3B
Johnson, ---	P
Livingston, ---	C
Manush, ---	2B
McLaughlin, Edward	SS
Moore, Clem	OF
Osborne, E.P.	P, OF
Proctor, ---	P
Roberts, C.J.	OF
Stanley, Bill	SS, 3B
Watters, Lark	
Wheat, B.C.	C
Wheat, Lafe	P

LaGrange:

Bedingfield, J.R.	P
Bonifay, Albert	P
Chipman, A.B.	C
Culpepper, J.E.	M, P
Foster, R.A.	P
Gould, ---	P
Konneman, W.H.	P
Marbet, Otto	1B
Martin, S.R.	
Miller, C.	SS
Miller, Dan	2B
Milner, Holt	
Moon, Eulas	
Nitram, ---	SS
Sikes, E.B.	OF
Smith, Red	M, P, OF
Thrasher, Ike	3B, OF
Thrasher, George	OF, 2B
Williams, ---	

Lindale:

Brenner, Herbert	1B
Cornelius, Rusty	P

Donaldson, ---	SS
Driscoll, ---	OF
Ennis, ---	2B
Herndon, Hardin	M, OF
Flohr, ---	3B
Lassetter, Roy	
Mittewede, Walter	3B
Nunn, ---	C
Parilla, ---	
Rich, ---	OF
Schmidt, ---	
Summit, ---	

Rome:

Bachelor, Harry	OF
Bowden, Tim	M, OF
Gross, ---	OF
Hall, ---	
Hawkins, Cy	C
Jesmer, W.H.	1B
Kane, ---	3B
Lowery, D.D.	P, OF
Lucus, ---	P
Overton, H.A.	2B
Palmantier, A.B.	OF
Prince, ---	SS
Walker, Flem	

1921

Cedartown:

Bradley, Eugene	OF
Carter, ---	C
Chambers, ---	P
Cook, ---	OF, P
Culp, ---	P
DeBosky, Edward	
Dumas, ---	SS
Ellis, ---	2B
Hawkins, E.J.	P
Kelton, Wiley	OF, 1B
Lehman, Otto	P
McAuliffe, ---	2B
Munford, ---	SS
Sargent, ---	2B
Schwartz, Bill	M, 1B
Sells, ---	P
Shaw, Pop	OF
Simon, Dewey	3B
Tatler, Henry	C, OF
Tucker, Ollie	OF
Vardeman, F.C.	P
Whitfield, ---	OF
Yost, ---	SS

Griffin:

Bates, ---	P
Brewer, Henry	
Carlisle, Roy	
Davenport, ---	2B
Dillon, J.T.R.	
Duval, ---	OF
Fish, Hamilton	1B

Gaines, R.H.	1B
Gibson, ---	OF
Hawkins, Cy	OF, C
Hicks, R.E.	1B
Hunter, Bob	
Marion, ---	2B
Matthews, Harry	M
McLaughlin, Edward	SS
Mosley, C.S.	SS
Osborn, E.P.	
Parks, James	OF
Pounds, J.P.	OF
Purcell, E.E.	
Sessions, Pete	
Stanley, Bill	3B
Thrasher, Loren	OF
Townsend, Arnold	C
Vandergriff, H.L.	C
Wheat, Lafe	P
Wheeler, Buck	

LaGrange:

Barnhart, ---	C
Chancey, ---	
Chestnut, H.C.	C
Green, ---	SS, 2B
Hager, Fred	M, C
Fortner, ---	SS
Konneman, W.H.	P, OF
Krankie, ---	
McAuliffe, ---	SS, 2B
Milner, Dan	3B
Register, ---	OF
Ricks, Lloyd	1B
Sells, ---	P
Sargent, ---	2B
Schroeder, ---	P
Schwartz, ---	P
Sikes, ---	OF
Swann, P.P.	OF, P
Thrasher, George	OF
Williamson, ---	P
Workman, ---	P

Lindale:

Black, ---	P
Bolt, ---	P
Brenner, ---	1B
Cornelius, Rusty	P
Donaldson, ---	SS
Driscoll, ---	OF
Earp, Whitfield	C
Herndon, Hardin	M, 1B, OF
Humphries, ---	P
Lassetter, Roy	
Mittewede, Walter	3B
Overton, H.A.	2B
Powell, ---	C
Rich, ---	OF
Smith, J.	OF
Suggs, Eugene	
Veazie, ---	OF

Rome:

Fortner, ---	2B

Fox, Jim	M, 1B
Gross, J.F.	P
Hanson, C.W.	
Hodgin, W.H.	OF
Hunter, ---	2B
James, R.E.	OF, P
Kane, ---	3B
Lowery, D.D.	P
McAuliffe, ---	2B
Morrow, ---	C
Nunnally, ---	OF
Parnell, M.R.	
Ramsey, ---	OF
Schmidt, ---	SS
Veazie, ---	OF
Weaver, C.B.	

1928

Anniston:

Ammons, Bud	M, 1B
Atchley, Loy	OF, P
Bailey, ---	P
Bruner, Ben	M, SS
Camp, ---	OF
Case, ---	C
Craft, ---	1B
Floyd, ---	P
Fuqua, Roger	SS
Gray, ---	OF, P
Hamner, ---	OF
Harris, ---	P
Lamineck, ---	3B
Oldfield, ---	3B
Parks, ---	P
Sanders, ---	2B
Sharpe, ---	P
Stroecker, ---	OF
Thompson, R.L.	OF
Walker, Tom	P
Washington, ---	P
Williams, ---	P
Wilson, ---	OF

Cedartown:

Atchley, Loy	OF, P
Bains, ---	SS
Beck, ---	1B, OF
Clark, ---	2B, OF, C
Davis, ---	1B, P
DeArman, ---	1B, P
Glass, ---	P
Hydringer, ---	P
Kelton, W.F.	M, OF
Knowles, Charles	OF, C
Marks, ---	P
Mason, S.	OF
Parks, ---	P
Rainwater, ---	P
Selley, ---	P
Shipley, Jack	2B
Smith, Sherrod	M, P
Thompson, Bill	2B, OF
Tredaway, ---	3B, SS

Gadsden:

Abell, ---	1B
Allen, ---	OF, P
Almon, ---	OF
Carter, Homer	P
Donahue, ---	OF
Floyd, ---	P
Frakes, Ben	P
Garner, ---	OF, C
Gentry, W.E.	2B, 3B, SS
Green, R.C.	C
Greene, Ray	C
Hockett, ---	OF, P
Howell, C.	OF
Huggins, Miller	3B
Hunter, ---	OF
Lowry, ---	2B, 3B, SS
Martz, ---	SS
Moore, H.H.	2B, SS

Mulkin, ---	OF
Newton, Doc	M, P
Rowe, Bob	OF
Schepner, Joe	M, 1B
Stine, ---	OF
Swift, ---	P

Lindale:

Abell, ---	1B
Alexander, Bill	3B, SS, OF
Burton, ---	
Cartwright, ---	1B, OF
Cash, ---	SS
Cosby, ---	SS
Craft, ---	1B
Crowe, Hoyt	OF, P
Dodson, ---	P
Donaldson, Earl	M, 2B
Duff, ---	OF
Early, ---	OF, C
Gray, ---	OF, P
Greene, Ray	C
Grimes, ---	SS
Hawkins, Earl	P
Holsomback, Squirt	3B
Howell, C.	OF
Mason, J.	
McCollum, ---	P
McKinney, ---	C
Perryman, ---	OF
Stanfield, ---	OF, P
Waldrip, ---	P
White, E.	1B
Wilkie, ---	P
Williams, ---	P

Talladega:

Beck, ---	1B, OF
Bruner, Ben	SS
Carroll, ---	OF
Finney, Lou	C
Gallagher, ---	1B, OF, P
Hawkins, Earl	M, P
Laminack, ---	3B
Lane, ---	OF, P
Lewis, Bernard	OF
Marks, ---	3B, P
McCarthy, ---	C
McLaughlin, ---	P
Rowe, H.J.	P
Swift, ---	P
Vernon, ---	OF
Vincent, A.	2B, SS
Vincent, C.E.	SS
Walker, L.G.	M
Waller, Jack	3B, P
Wheeler, ---	1B
Wilson, ---	OF

1929

Anniston:

Ammons, Bud	M, 1B
Bassett, Grady	P
Burbank, ---	OF
Caldwell, ---	OF
Carroll, ---	OF
DeArman, H.P.	1B
Elmore, Verdo	M, 1B
Fanning, Rip	C
Feeley, ---	OF
Fuqua, Roger	SS
Holloran, ---	2B
Kelly, Harold	P
Landgon, Joe	OF
Long, ---	P
Marks, Max	P
Oldfield, Pat	3B
Pellicier, ---	OF
Posey, ---	OF
Ramsey, ---	P
Ray, ---	OF
Reed, ---	P
Smith, P.	OF

Valdez, ---	P
Walker, ---	OF
Ward, ---	P
Washington, ---	P

Cedartown:

Adams, Marvin	P
Chitwood, K.E.	P
Christiansen, ---	OF
Clark, R.H.	OF
Davis, W.C.	P
Fowler, ---	P
Gault, Pat	P
Gentry, W.E.	3B
Harris, C.	2B
Huggins, Miller	3B
Joyner, ---	P
Kelly, George	1B
Knowles, Charles	C
Lessley, John	OF
McDonald, ---	P
Nobles, ---	P
Rainwater, Dewey	P
Robinson, ---	P
Shipley, Jack	2B
Smith, Sherrod	M, P
Tate, J.R.	SS
Thompson, Bill	OF
Thrasher, Frank	M
Truitt, D.E.	
White, ---	P

Gadsden:

Allen, ---	P
Costa, F.	2B
Costa, T.	SS
Crowder, H.F.	P
Freeman, ---	OF, P
Land, ---	OF
Finney, Lou	C
Heidlebach, ---	P
Hockette, George	P
King, ---	P
McDonough, ---	2B
McLaughlin, ---	P
Persons, ---	OF
Ray, ---	C
Senn, Yancy	1B
Sorrell, Jesse	3B
Soward, Jim	P
Stroecker, ---	OF
Walker, Louis	M

Lindale:

Alexander, Bill	OF
Baker, James	P
Currie, Frank	3B
Dobbins, Howard	OF
Griffith, Ralph	P
Hardwick, George	P
Harris, Joe	P
James, Fob	1B
Lott, Edgar	OF
Moulton, Jack	M, 1B, P
Ogle, Hugh	P
Poindexter, R.C.	C
Pugh, Gordon	OF
Sanford, ---	2B
Smith, C.H.	SS
Smith, Howard	3B
Stanfield, Ralph	P
Stevens, J.E.	C
Stoutenboro, Y.C.	P
Walker, Louis	OF
White, H.	SS
Wood, Norman	P

Talladega:

Beagle, H.E.	3B
Boling, Edward	1B
Butler, C.L.	2B
Camp, Howard	M, OF
Coker, E.R.	
Gray, ---	SS
Green, ---	P

Harris, Jack	2B
Holbrooke, ---	C
Hunnicut, ---	3B
Lacey, ---	P
Lane, ---	P
Laminack, ---	3B
Lewis, Bernard	OF
Lott, F.O.	P
McKay, F.S.	P
McLaughlin, ---	P
Query, Wray	P
Verner, Cliff	OF
White, E.R.	SS

1930

Anniston:

Bassett, Grady	P
Carter, ---	P
Crowder, H.F.	P
DeArman, ---	1B
Dixon, ---	3B
East, Carl	OF
Fittery, Paul	M, P
Fuqua, Roger	2B, SS
Goggans, G.E.	C
Hand, D.E.	P
Higginbotham, ---	OF
Hill, ---	P
Hockette, George	P
Hurst, ---	C
Justiss, Red	P
Kelly, ---	P
Langdon, ---	2B, OF
Ledbetter, Robert	P
Lott, E.D.	OF
Lott, F.O.	P
McGhee, Bill	1B
Ray, ---	C
Sappenfield, Colon	SS
Sidwell, ---	
Stanfield, Ralph	OF, P
Turner, ---	P
Urquhart, ---	P
Verner, Cliff	OF
Walker, Dixie	M
Watson, ---	2B
Williamson, ---	P
Wright, ---	3B

Cedartown:

Adams, ---	P
Chitwood, K.E.	P
Clark, ---	OF, C
Cleveland, ---	SS
Crowder, H.F.	P
Gault, ---	P
Gentry, W.E.	3B
Glass, ---	P
Glazner, ---	P
Fuller, ---	P
Kelly, George	1B
Knowles, Charles	OF, C
Lessley, John	OF
Oldfield, ---	2B, 3B, C
Ozburn, ---	2B
Patton, Henry	OF
Pruitt, ---	P
Seagraves, ---	P
Shipley, Jack	OF
Smith, Sherrod	M, P
Washington, ---	P

Huntsville:

Barnes, ---	3B
Carroll, Dixie	M
Carter, ---	P
Collier, ---	P
Crosslin, ---	SS
Curry, ---	P
Denton, Malcolm	P
Dickson, ---	P
Frazee, ---	P
Frey, ---	SS

Gray, ---	1B, 2B, OF, P
Green, ---	OF, C
Hahn, ---	2B
Hammond, J.H.	1B, OF
Harris, ---	2B, P
Hart, Clarence	M
Hoellman, ---	P
Holcomb, E.	P
Lambert, ---	P
McSwain, Cliff	OF
Parker, ---	1B
Patterson, ---	C
Pierre, Bill	M, P
Reese, Eddie	2B, 3B, SS
Thomas, ---	P
Thompson, Erskine	M
Walker, ---	OF
Walton, Tubby	M
Warren, ---	P
Watson, ---	P
Wesley, ---	
Wilson, ---	2B, 3B
Winn, Breezy	P
Wolfe, Tom	3B, SS, OF

Lindale:

Anderson, ---	P
Baker, J.G.	P
Bassett, Grady	P
Costa, Frank	SS
Granger, George	P
Holloran, ---	1B, 2B
Fanning, ---	C
Granger, George	P
Holloran, ---	
Land, Doc	1B, OF
Lewis, Bernard	OF
Moulton, Jack	M, 1B, OF, P
Pugh, Gordon	OF
Sanders, Red	
Smith, Howard	2B, 3B
Stoutenboro, Y.C.	P
Wall, ---	OF, P
Wesley, ---	OF
West, ---	3B
White, Abe	P
Wood, ---	P
Wright, ---	P

Talladega:

Allen, ---	1B
Amadee, Joe	P
Barbare, P.	2B, OF
Barbare, Walt	M
Boling, ---	1B
Brannon, ---	C
Chadwick, ---	OF
Davis, ---	P
Deal, ---	2B
Giglio, Joe	P
Lane, ---	P
McDonald, ---	P
McKay, F.S.	P
Newsome, Skeeter	SS
Picklesimer, ---	3B, OF
Query, Wray	OF, P
Reeves, ---	P
Sidwell, ---	P
Soward, James	OF, P
Thompson, ---	OF
Thorpe, ---	3B
Tice, ---	P
Verner, Cliff	M, P
Warner, ---	P

1946

LaGrange:

Allen, Johnny	P, 2B, 3B, OF
Bennett, ---	P
Bridges, Harold	P
Camp, Loy	P
Carter, Emil	
Copeland, Elmer	P

Cox, Max	P
Daniel, Jake	M, P, 1B
Davis, ---	P
Deal, Nip	
Dean, ---	P
Dean, Charles	3B, OF
Dickerson, ---	P
Gilson, John	P
Green, ---	P
Griggs, ---	P
Harper, Bill	3B
Hoflac, Joe	OF
Holmes, Jim	P
Hubbard, Carl	P
Humberson, Roxie	
Jeter, Cleo	P, OF
Johnson, Joe	P, OF
Kilgore, Bill	
Kirksey, Calvin	P
Lyons, Ray	
Malcolm, Lew	
Mashburn, Ernest	P, OF
McRae, Bill	3B
Melton, Ray	
Minor, Howard	
Murray, Tom	P, 3B
Padgett, Charles	SS
Parker, Gashouse	M, 1B
Pratt, Tom	OF
Pritchett, Doug	SS
Putnam, Basil	OF
Reed, Jim	P
Reese, Ed	2B
Rucker, ---	
Satterfield, Cicero	C
Scobbins, ---	
Smith, Reuben	P
Spitzer, Lloyd	OF
Standard, ---	P
Stephens, T.W.	
Stowe, John	P, OF
Sweatt, Bill	P
Towns, Jim	SS
Walls, Howard	C
Ware, Dan	
White, Bill	3B
Whitley, Tom	
Woodruff, Ridley	

Newnan:

Astin, Bob	P
Ball, John	P, 2B
Borders, Aubrey	P
Bottoms, Woodrow	3B, SS
Brown, Hubert	P, OF
Brown, Lloyd	M, P
Browning, Ted	OF
Bucek, John	3B, OF
Carpenter, John	P
Childs, Frank	P, OF
Collum, Ambrose	P
Daugherty, Mike	OF
Denny, Horace	
Dickinson, John	P
Dye, Hoyle	
Evans, Millard	P
Faucette, Lew	
Gallart, Armando	3B, SS
George, Milt	
Grimes, Dave	
Harris, ---	P
Hitt, Ray	P
Hunt, Ray	C
Johnson, John	P
Jones, Bill	P
Jones, Jim	P
Jones, Ward	2B
Lutes, Jim	
McCravy, Charles	P
McGee, Wilson	P
McRae, Bill	3B
Najour, George	3B
Nix, George	M
O'Connell, Tom	
Padgett, Charles	SS

123

Satterfield, Ralph — 1B
Shoemake, Claude — P, 1B, OF
Sinnott, John
Snider, Floyd — OF
Stanley, Bob — P, C
Whiteside, Bright
Willingham, Coney

Opelika:
Bailey, Don — P, 1B, OF
Boyer, Milt — P
Brogden, Otis — 2B
Bryson, Jesse
Bryson, Joe
Burnett, Ed — P, 1B, 3B
Condit, --- — P
Davis, Jim — P
Day, --- — P
Dennis, C.T. — P
Finney, Lou — 1B, OF
Frederick, Bill — P
Gill, Audis — 3B, OF
Godwin, Bill — 3B
Harrell, Ben — P
Hayes, Frank — P
Hitchcock, Jimmy — M, 2B, SS
Hitson, John — SS
Humbracht, Hal — 1B
Jackson, --- — P
Jeter, Cleo — P, OF
Kenmore, ---
Kent, Otis — P
Kreamcheck, Ed — P, 1B, OF
Kritsky, Walt — P
McConnell, Ed
McGarrity, Les — P, C
Medlock, ---
Moore, Jewell
Morris, Ray — P
Nelson, Jim — C
Hewhall, Bob — P, 2B, C
Noto, Phil — SS
O'Kelley, Clyde — C
Peacock, Cecil — P
Peake, --- — P
Plyn, Percy — SS
Pope, C. — P
Quick, John — OF
Rollo, Charles — 2B
Schuessler, Zach — P
Scott, Jim — P
Sensussler, Zack — M
Smeltzer, Charles — C
Talbert, --- — P
Tarvin, Art — P
Thompson, Jack — P, OF
Vickers, Jim — P
Wallin, Carl — P

Tallassee:
Buck, Joe
Bundrick, Clinton — SS
Chandler, Jack — OF
Dabbs, Chester — 3B
Davis, Clarence
Downs, Wilburn — 2B
Duncan, John — P
Hammock, Bill — C
Hall, Carl — P
Hathcock, Marlin — 2B, SS
Heving, John — M
Higginbotham, Morris
Hill, Oliver — 3B
Hornsby, Leonard — P
Jones, Bill — 1B
Knowles, Earl — P, OF
Lamb, --- — P
Land, Dick — P
Lantrip, Bill — P
Latta, John
Leitz, Al
Lohr, Larry — P
Lowell, --- — P
Mahoney, --- — P
Manheim, Francis — P

McGarrity, Les — P, C
Mihalik, Mickey — P
Muti, Nick
Nelson, Burl — P
Parks, Jack — P, C
Parks, Woodford — P
Poole, Ralph — P
Porterfield, Lee — P
Posey, Walt — OF
Schivone, Ralph
Smeraglia, Anthony
Smithley, ---
Spitzer, Lloyd — OF
Wallin, Carl — P
Wellman, Bob — OF
Westbrook, John — P
Wilson, Nesby — OF
Wright, Maurice — SS

Valley:
Bartula, Matthew — P
Benezue, --- — P
Blackstock, Hal — 3B
Blaze, Frank — P
Bosarge, Vince — SS
Bridges, Harold — P
Casey, Charles — C
Chambers, Joe — 2B
Colley, Owen — 3B
Crow, Paul — OF
Daniel, Jake — P, 1B
Ellington, Paul
Ferguson, ---
Finney, Bob — C
Finney, Lou — 1B, OF
Folson, ---
Frazier, Lance — OF, C
Frazier, Ralph — 1B
Gilbert, Art — P
Hall, Floyd — OF
Herring, Bill
Hornsberg, Art — P
Johnson, Joe — P, OF
Kent, Otis — P
Kirksey, Calvin — P
Lewis, Jim — 1B
Marshall, --- — P
Milner, Holt — M, P
Montalvo, Jose — OF, C
Morgan, Malvern — P, 3B, OF
Morrison, Dean — P
Newsome, Art — P
Peters, Charles — P
Place, Paul — C
Ray, Stan
Robinson, Tom — OF
Satterfield, Cicero — C
Sharp, Bill — P, OF
Shaw, Floyd — P
Siegfield, --- — P
Smith, Luther — P
Sprayberry, Jim
Tillery, Tom
Tomlin, Ed
Whitten, Norm
Wiggins, LeRoy — P
Williams, Ed — P

1947
Alexander City:
Adkinson, Bill — C
Alexander, Bill — 1B
Boatman, Jim — SS, OF
Boos, Wendell — OF
Carmichael, Ed — OF
Carter, Steve — 3B, OF
Chappell, Marv — P, OF
Chitwood, Ed — P
Collins, Lee — OF
Culpepper, Bill — 3B, OF
Davis, Fred — P
Davis, Max — 1B, OF
Davis, Ralph — 2B, 3B

Doerflinger, Gene — P
Driskell, Roy — OF
Ellison, Lee — P
Harrell, Joe — SS
Hebert, Walter — 3B
Huesman, Jack — 2B
Huffman, Bob — C
Mann, Elbert
McKinney, Bill — C
Mitchell, Joe — P
Nichols, Fred — OF
Osteen, Bill
Osteen, Frank — OF
Patterson, Derwood
Persons, Jim — 3B, C
Reed, Bob — OF
Rizzetta, Anthony — OF
Spencer, Dave — 2B
Stephens, Frank — P
Taitt, Doug — M, 1B
Teyema, Dave — SS, OF
Wenclewicz, Walt — P
Williams, Bill
Yawn, Sid — C

Griffin:
Alexander, Bill — P
Anderson, Dick — C
Ayers, Lonzo — P
Blackstock, Hal — 3B, SS
Blackwell, Tom — 3B
Brodzinski, Jim — P
Brooks, Warren — 2B
Childs, Frank — P, OF
Ello, Jim — C
Forrester, Frank — OF
Guettler, Ken — OF
Harrelson, John — P
Hartman, Earl — 1B
Jones, Roser — OF
King, Claude — P
Kirkland, Bill
Lohr, Larry — P
McWhorter, Marcus — P
Murphy, Jim — OF
Swanson, Dale — 2B
Swanson, Ralph — SS
White, Abe — M, P
Wiggins, LeRoy — P
Witzke, Howard — 2B

LaGrange:
Adams, Bob — SS
Allen, John — 2B, OF
Balais, Alex — P
Briggs, Harold — P
Camp, Loy — P
Chandler, Dave — P
Copeland, Elmer — P
Daniel, Jake — 1B
Danish, Chris — C
East, Carl — M
Ermisch, Howard — M, 3B, SS
Ford, Don — C
Glaze, Hugh — SS
Griffin, Edsel — 3B, OF, C
Hall, Bob — 1B, OF
Hammack, Shurley — 2B
Hamrick, Charles — OF
Hamrick, Roy — 1B
Hoflack, Dan — OF
Jones, Roser — OF
Lomberger, John — OF
Melton, Ray — 3B
Murray, Tom — P
Murray, Walt — P
Regan, Bill — P
Sloan, George — 2B
Tilley, Travis — P
Travers, Tom — P
Walls, Boyd — OF
Watson, Ed — P
Williams, Curtis — P
Wilson, Walt — P

Newnan:

Abreu, Joe	M, 2B
Astin, Bob	OF
Ayers, Lonzo	P
Bottoms, Woodrow	3B, SS
Brock, Paul	P, OF
Browning, Ted	OF
Collins, Lee	OF
Daniel, Jake	1B
DePillo, George	2B
Edison, Lewis	
Hamrick, Charles	OF
Harrell, Ben	
Hill, John	3B
Jones, Bill	P, OF
Krohn, Duane	P
Lohr, Larry	P
Mason, George	OF
Matthews, Bob	
McFarland, Bill	1B
McGravy, Charles	P
Morris, Dave	OF
Powers, Tom	SS
Shoemake, Claude	OF
Skalski, Chester	SS
Stanley, Bob	C
Stoyle, Jim	1B
Swanson, Dale	SS
Swygert, Alan	OF
Westbrook, Ed	M, P
Whitney, Jim	C

Opelika:

Bailey, Don	OF
Ball, Jim	OF
Burnette, Etheridge	P, 3B
Cole, Ken	C
Dennany, Bob	P
Flemming, Wheeler	1B
Glaze, Claude	P
Gunnells, Luther	M, SS
Hicks, Elroy	P
Jeter, Cleo	P
Jones, Tom	P
Kallaher, Bill	P
Nelson, Jim	C
Noto, Phil	2B
Reed, Bob	OF
Riddle, Jim	P
Schuessler, Zach	P
Sinquefield, Roy	P
Vinson, Earl	2B

Tallassee:

Aurelio, Ed	1B
Beavers, Jim	P
Brawner, Ralph	OF
Brodzinski, Jim	P
Campo, Ray	C
Carmichael, Ed	OF
Carter, Steve	3B, OF
Collins, Lee	OF
Corley, Art	P
Edwards, Ray	3B, OF
Ford, Don	C
Hill, John	M, 3B
Knowles, Earl	OF
Lohr, Larry	P
Mason, George	OF
Medlock, Frank	C
Nelson, Burl	P
Noto, Phil	2B
Powers, Tom	SS
Rhyne, Marvel	
Rizzetta, Anthony	OF
Robertson, Preston	P
Ryan, Jim	1B
Schwab, Bob	OF
Smith, Joe	OF
Urso, Joe	2B
Ward, Milt	1B, OF
Westbrook, Ed	
Wollitz, Herman	P
Wright, Tyre	SS

Valley:

Anderson, Martin	P
Blackburn, Tom	3B, OF
Blackstock, Hal	3B, SS
Bosarge, Vince	SS
Chambers, Joe	2B
Crain, Paul	P
Danna, Charles	C
Danna, Jesse	P, OF
Edwards, Earl	OF
Frazier, Lance	C
Frazier, Ralph	
Giglio, Joe	P
Hartlein, Bill	OF
Jones, Barry	SS
Lewis, Jim	1B
Luce, Arthur	M, OF
Martini, ---	OF
McGravy, Charles	P
Milner, Bruce	OF
Minarck, Bill	SS
Morgan, Malvern	1B, 3B
White, John	OF
Wiggins, Bob	P
Wiggins, LeRoy	P
Williams, Ed	P
Wiseman, Bob	P

1948

Alexander City:

Booker, John	SS
Brodzinski, Jim	P
Brown, Bill Jr.	1B
Catchings, Ben	M, 3B, SS
Chappell, Marvin	M, P, OF
Coker, Jim	C
Culpepper, Bill	OF
Davis, Fred	P
Davis, Max	OF
Dorsky, Mike	OF
Ello, Jim	C
Eustice, Willis	P
Farrar, Bill	OF
Glaze, Claude	P
Glover, Omer	C
Gunnells, Luther	M, SS
Haynes, Willard	P
Huesman, Jack	2B
Johnson, George	3B
Keller, George	
Lindsey, John	P
Linsley, Paul	P
McTaggert, Charles	P
Miller, Charles	C
Powell, John	SS
Reach, Clifton	3B, OF
Ross, Jerome	3B
Wooley, Jim	OF

Griffin:

Allen, John	3B
Blackwell, Tom	2B, 3B
Brinkman, Frank	OF
Campbell, Paul	M, P, SS, C
Carroll, Bill	1B
Creamer, Brice	P
Ellis, Gerhart	P
Ello, Jim	C
Evins, John	OF
Hale, Don	P
Hammett, Miles	P
Kane, Henry	OF
Knoke, John	P
Knopp, Mel	2B
Kulig, Al	P
Lovett, Bill	2B, OF
Mlynarek, Anthony	C
Noga, George	3B
O'Donnell, John	P, OF
Porco, Frank	
Rettie, Joe	
Rolfs, Frank	1B
Sanders, Lou	OF

Savage, Bill	OF
Stock, Lloyd	2B, SS
Votaw, Jim	P
White, Abe	M

LaGrange:

Acton, James	M, 1B, OF, C
Adams, Bob	2B, SS
Bobowski, Ed	P
Cohen, Hy	P
Dan, Virgil	1B
Dyser, Bill	P
Federow, Emil	P
Franson, Carl	3B
Garone, Mike	OF
Griffin, Edsel	
Guido, Ed	3B, OF
Hall, Bob	1B
Heisig, Bill	P
Kramer, Bob	3B, OF, C
Liddy, George	OF
Magnatta, Jim	P
McLeod, Jim	P
Muse, Don	3B, C
Nazzaro, Carmen	OF
Pheister, Paul	1B, 3B, OF
Poulas, Nick	
Przeworski, Ted	3B, OF
Raehse, Bill	1B
Roth, Jac	2B
Striffler, Charles	OF
Travers, Tom	P
Trotter, Bill	2B, 3B
Watson, Ed	P
Webb, Marion	3B, SS
Zazzera, Ben	OF

Newnan:

Barger, John	P
Campbell, Ben	OF, C
Chaptman, Devon	P
Devaney, Bob	P
Dunn, ---	P
Fisher, Ron	C
Joyce, Arnold	P, OF
Lassiter, Bob	P
Lewis, Bill	C
McAfee, Alton	1B
McBride, Tom	
McLeod, Pete	OF
Mihalik, Mickey	P
Millard, John	SS
Ortiz, Otoniel	2B
Reid, Russ	3B
Rettie, Joe	
Turner, McDonald	OF
Veazey, Norm	M, OF
Wiacek, Ray	OF

Opelika:

Bailey, George	OF
Ball, James	M, OF
Beavers, Jim	P
Collins, Charlie	P
Conovan, Mike	P
Dennany, Bob	P
Diffly, Peter	SS
Dorsky, Mike	OF
Flemming, Wheeler	1B
Gilmore, John	2B
Glaze, Claude	P
Gunnells, Luther	M, SS
Hudson, Bill	OF
Irvin, John	C
Jackson, Claude	P
Jarvis, Bob	3B
Kallaher, Bill	P, 1B
Keller, George	
Kilgore, Bill	P
Olayko, Alex	C
Philpott, Carey	C
Yancey, Charles	SS

Tallassee:

Adams, Bob	2B, 3B, SS, OF

Berg, Ed	2B
Betz, Bob	OF
Boyer, Milt	P, OF
Brunson, Marion	P
Childs, Delton	OF
Comiskey, Robert	M, C
Conovan, Mike	P
Coss, Royden	P
Deibler, Mason	P
Duke, Willie	
Duncan, Charles	P
East, Hugh	M
Edwards, Ray	3B
Galloway, Oliver	C
Gregory, Bob	P
Hathcock, Marlin	2B
Martini, Fernando	OF
Mellinger, Jim	P
Monaco, Frank	SS
Popovich, Charles	
Pruett, John	SS
Rikard, Denver	OF
Sutton, Jim	OF
Taylor, John	P
Tefft, Al	3B
Tiefenauer, Bob	P
Zich, Henry	1B

Valley:

Chambers, Joe	2B
Clark, Ray	SS
Danna, Charles	C
Danna, Jesse	M, P, OF
Edge, Harvey	P
Edmondson, Lee	C
Edwards, Bob	OF
Embry, Joel	P
Eustice, Willis	P
Frazier, John	1B, OF
Gustavson, Carl	P
Hall, Jesse	OF
Hammons, Herb	
Lee, Frank	OF
Lewis, Jim	1B
Martini, Fernando	OF
McCraney, Wayne	P
McWhorter, Marcus	P
Ray, Tom	SS, OF
Spruill, Jack	3B
Still, Jim	OF
Swigler, Norm	OF

1949

Alexander City:

Alonso, John	OF
Bozzuto, Bert	P
Brown, Bill Jr.	1B
Chappell, Marv	P, OF
Coker, Jim	1B
Diebler, Mason	P
Edwards, Ray	3B
Ello, Jim	C
Hartman, Dick	C
Hovell, Bob	OF
Huesman, Jack	2B, SS
Kittrell, Ed	
Little, Walt	
McBride, Delton	
McCraney, Wayne	P
McTaggert, Charles	P
Mink, Joe	OF
Reach, Clifton	2B, OF
Rinaldi, Charles	P
Roberts, Red	M, SS
Sprayberry, Jim	P
Thompson, Dick	P
Wooley, Jim	OF

Griffin:

Adcock, Bob	OF
Battistelli, Angelo	SS
Bianchi, Frank	P
Chafin, Bob	P

Chechile, Bill	OF
DeFeo, Bob	3B
Ebetino, John	P
Etchison, Buck	M, 1B
Fleisch, Don	SS
Forrester, Frank	OF
Gibson, Sam	M, P
Green, Paul	SS
Hargis, Jim	OF
Hart, Norm	
Jackson, Frank	OF
Kemmerer, Nathaniel	P
Laney, Floyd	3B, C
Lopez, Carlos	P
McAndrew, Bob	2B
Noga, George	3B, SS
Pollard, Gene	1B, OF
Rinker, Bob	C
Sanders, Lew	M, SS, OF
Sewell, Bill	OF
Tomasic, George	P
Umscheid, Don	P
Wassel, Bill	OF
York, Rudy	M, 1B

LaGrange:

Beaird, Dick	
Bobowski, Ed	P
Braganca, Joe	C
Burk, Ron	2B
Charles, Jim	P
Cohen, Hy	P
Cooper, Bill	M, 1B, OF
Dembinski, Dan	C
Feinstein, Joe	P
Ferra, Joe	OF
Flaherty, Chris	1B, 3B
Goff, Jim	OF
Gounaris, Alex	P
Hammack, Shurley	2B, SS
Hayden, John	P
Katalinic, John	P
Krings, Dave	SS
Krochina, John	OF
Lawson, Leroy	1B, OF
Lyons, Pat	OF
Mancini, Herb	3B
Morrongiello, Mike	2B
Muse, Don	SS, C
Stevenson, Fred	P, OF
Thrift, Syd	P, 1B
Wallace, Jim	P
Wallis, Gerald	P
Woodruff, Ernest	OF

Newnan:

Chechile, Bill	OF
Dickson, Ed	OF
Franson, Carl	3B
Fulton, Bob	OF, C
Garner, Homer	P
Hardegree, Bill	OF
Hargis, Jim	OF
Konek, Pete	P
Lazzari, Jim	OF
McAfee, Alton	1B
McCulloch, Bob	C
McFadden, John	P
Millard, John	SS
Mink, Joe	OF
Nierpoetter, Bill	P
Powers, Fred	
Rees, Ernest	OF
Schmidt, Bob	M, 2B
Shoemake, Benton	1B, OF
Taylor, Spafford	OF
Tenney, Jim	P
Thomas, Parks	P
Wagner, Dick	P
Wallace, Elmer	P
Wassel, Bill	OF

Opelika:

Ball, James	M, OF
Bottorff, Tom	1B

Flemming, Wheeler	1B
Flores, Paul	SS
Howton, Frank	P
Hudson, Bill	OF
Jackson, Claude	P
Jarvis, Bob	3B
Julian, Al	OF
Julian, Bob	2B
Kilgore, Bill	P
Kittrell, Ed	P
Martin, Bill	P
Noto, Phil	C
Perdue, Glenn	P
Powers, Fred	
Steadman, Bob	P
Vanatistein, Herb	C

Tallassee:

Adams, Bob	SS
Berg, Ed	2B
Blackwell, William	M, OF
Ciani, Nick	OF
Clements, Ralph	P
Comiskey, Robert	M, C
Davis, Jim	P
DeFeo, Bob	3B
Deibler, Mason	P
Dickerman, Ed	3B
Herdt, Don	3B, C
Hinkle, Leon	P
Jacobs, Ottis	P
Joyner, Julian	P
Mathey, Bud	
Owen, Maurice	P
Pinson, Harold	1B
Reinagle, Ed	P
Rikard, Denver	OF
Teater, Rollie	C
Tiefenauer, Bob	P

Valley:

Beach, Ed	P
Blackburn, Tom	OF
Bottoms, Woodrow	M, 3B
Carey, Charles	C
Chapman, Herb	1B, OF
Clark, Ray	SS
Colson, Rod	OF
Danna, Jesse	M, P
Davenport, Nevil	2B
Edge, Harvey	P
Frazier, Lance	C
Galloway, Oliver	C
Griggs, Bill	P
Harrison, Bill	2B
Haynes, Hoover	P
Henegar, Russ	P
Johnson, George	2B
Langdon, Joe	P
Mason, John	OF, C
Morgan, Malvern	M, 1B, 2B
Nance, Hoover	OF
Pappas, Nick	P
Powers, John	OF
Ray, Tom	SS
Shoemake, Benton	1B, OF
Spruill, Jack	2B, 3B
Steckel, Bob	2B
Stuckey, Rex	C

1950

Alexander City:

Adams, Bob	2B, 3B, SS
Barker, Norb	2B
Bastion, Marv	P
Berman, Norm	2B
Brown, Bill Jr.	1B
Chappell, Marv	P, OF
Collins, Charles	P, OF
Falcigno, Harry	OF
Hanson, J.W.	3B, SS
Harrelson, Cleveland	2B
Hartman, Dick	C

Hovell, Bob	OF
Krohn, Layton	P
Langley, Jim	
Lindsley, John	P
Lopez, Carlos	P, OF
Moss, Joe	OF
Nierpoertter, Bill	P
Patterson, W.E.	C
Roberts, Red	M, SS
Rucker, Bill	3B, OF
Savarese, Al	SS
Steave, John	C
Venditto, Al	3B
Wooley, Jim	OF

Griffin:

Battistelli, Angelo	3B
Bearden, Jack	M, OF
Busch, George	P
Byrd, Walt	OF
Collins, Bob	P
Columbano, Aldo	3B
Corley, Earl	C
Ebetino, John	P
Hudson, Bill	OF
Jarvis, Bob	3B, SS
Jones, Lou	3B, OF, C
Kelecava, Clem	P
Kemmerer, Nathaniel	P
Kulesa, John	P
Lopez, Carlos	P, OF
McAndrew, Bob	2B
Noga, George	SS
Padgett, Bill	P
Patterson, W.E.	C
Schmitt, Fred	OF
Sowell, Bill	3B
Stoyle, Jim	1B
Upshaw, Charles	P
Utley, Ewell	P
White, Abe	M
Winters, Bill	P

LaGrange:

Bessent, Don	P
Braganca, Joe	C
Cacciola, Jim	OF
Carter, Leon	3B
Chappell, Marv	P, OF
Cooper, Bill	M, OF
Dawkins, Bob	P
DeGourscey, Joe	P
Durkin, Jim	C
Gaillard, Ted	P
Goff, Jim	1B, OF
Jeakle, Ed	OF
Johengen, George	P, 1B
Krings, Dave	OF
Marshall, Dick	P
Pescitelli, Pasquale	2B
Russell, Dick	OF
Taussig, Don	
Troy, Jim	
Umbach, Ken	1B
Wallis, Gerald	P
Walls, Boyd	C
Webster, Ed	P
Wingard, Ernie Jr.	2B
Winkelspecht, Bob	SS

Newnan:

Bradshaw, Hugh	C
Bustle, Bill	P, 1B, OF
Chechile, Bill	OF
Cuedemo, Mike	C
Diehl, Leonard	SS
Franson, Carl	3B
Heath, Norm	SS
Hobbs, ---	P
Hooks, Dave	OF
Jones, Roy	
Kozubal, Alex	OF
Laney, Lee	1B

McAfee, Alton	1B
Punyko, Art	OF
Saffer, Les	P
Schmidt, Bob	M, 2B
Seaman, Al	P
Simmons, Jack	2B, C
Spamer, Bill	
Subbiondo, Joe	
Sweatt, Bill	P
Tenney, Jim	P
Terrell, Thurman	P
Thomas, Parks	P

Opelika:

Anthony, Stan	2B
Azzarello, Frank	1B
Baker, Allen	C
Bailey, Don	M
Booker, John	SS
Bottoms, Woodrow	M
Bryant, Irwin	OF
Chandler, Ray	
Creel, Jim	P, OF
Creel, Scobie	P, 2B, OF
DeFeo, Bob	3B
Dorsky, Mike	OF
Flemming, Wheeler	M, 1B
Ellis, George	P
Hamilton, George	2B
Harris, Bob	
Irons, Ed	3B, C
Jackson, Claude	P
Jones, Tom	P
Julian, Al	OF
Julian, Bob	3B, SS
Letlow, Lou	OF
Liedtke, Clyde	P
Maddox, Delma	P
Martin, Bill	P
Meads, Charles	2B
Michael, J.E.	OF
Moss, Joe	2B, OF
Riddle, Jim	OF
Ridgon, Bill	SS
Schultz, Otto	OF
Sims, Dewey	OF
Smith, Ken	1B
Stevens, Bill	
Tisdale, Bill	OF
Zaden, Lou	OF, C

Rome:

Beasley, John	SS
Brown, Al	P, OF
Bryant, Jim	C
Busch, George	P
Caruso, Enrico	P
Clements, Mason	3B
Cole, Harold	OF
Columbano, Aldo	3B
Crawford, Wayne	OF, C
Crowl, Ernest	P
DeMatteis, John	OF
DaMatteis, Sal	
Frady, Herb	3B
Hoag, Myril	M, P
Hutchins, Bob	P
Joyce, Arnold	P
Knowles, Lowe	1B
Padgett, Bill	P
Padgett, Charles	SS
Patterson, Derward	
Pinson, John	2B
Reeves, Herb	P
Roig, Tony	2B, 3B, SS, OF
Savarese, Al	SS
Sommer, Bill	3B
Sparks, Jim	P
Stowe, John	M, P, 1B, 3B, OF
Talley, Sam	2B
Veazey, Norman	M, OF

Valley:

Albritton, Ervin	
Ard, Tom	P
Cook, Hugh	P, 1B, 3B, OF
Daniel, Jake	M, 1B
Dragotto, Ralph	OF
Hanson, J.W.	3B, SS
Haynes, Willard	P
Hoag, Myril	M, P
Hughes, George	OF
Jarvis, Bob	3B, SS
Jones, Lou	3B, OF, C
Kemmerer, Nathaniel	P
Lazicky, Dick	P
Maririch, Eli	2B, SS
Nierpoetter, Bill	P
Patterson, Derward	
Patterson, W.E.	C
Perry, Bob	3B
Philpott, Carey	C
Puffer, Gerald	P
Rogers, Marion	P
Roth, Jac	2B
Savarese, Al	SS
Smith, Ken	1B
Socha, George	P
Sommer, Bill	3B
Thompson, Jim	OF
Wachtman, Dave	P
Walker, Milt	1B, 2B, OF

Notable Players

The following players played for Carrollton during the established minor league years. Each player listed below is noted for as a standout in the history of Carrollton baseball, played major league baseball, or an accomplishment outside of baseball. Many of the players from the Carrollton teams through the years made their names known for various reasons. Every attempt has been made to compile this listing as completely and accurately as possible.

Ed Bobowski

During the 1950 season Carrollton pitcher Ed "Bobo" Bobowski pulled two "Iron Man" stunts within two weeks of each other by pitching and winning both games of double headers. The first one occurred on July 24 in a twin bill against Newnan in which Carrollton won the games 7 to 5 and 9 to 1. Twelve days later, on August 2, in a pair of games against Valley, Bobo shutdown the opposing team twice again. The final scores this time were 5 to 0 and 14 to 4.

Major League Information and Statistics
Melvin Edward Bosser
Born: February 8, 1914 in Johnstown, Pennsylvania
Died: March 26, 1986 in Crossville, Tennessee
Threw: Right   Batted: Left
Height: 6' 0"   Weight: 173 lbs.

Major League Debut: April 29, 1945

Pitching Statistics
Year	Tm	Lg	W	L	G	IP	H	ER	BB	SO	ERA
1945	CIN	NL	2	0	7	16	9	6	17	3	3.38
TOTALS			2	0	7	16	9	6	17	3	3.38

Batting Statistics
Year	Tm	Lg	G	AB	R	H	2B	3B	HR	RBI	BB	SO	BA
1945	CIN	NL	7	4	1	0	0	0	0	0	0	1	.000
TOTALS			7	4	1	0	0	0	0	0	0	1	.000

Fielding Statistics
Year	Tm	Lg	POS	G	PO	A	E	DP	FA
1945	CIN	NL	P	7	0	2	0	0	1.000
TOTALS				7	0	2	0	0	1.000

Mel Bosser

Mel Bosser broke into baseball in 1938 at Dover of the class-D Eastern Shore League. He advanced through the ranks until he got to the major league level for a short stay early in 1945 with the Cincinnati Reds. The following season, Bosser pitched for Carrollton briefly for four games before moving on to Memphis of the class-AA Southern Association. He played in the minor leagues until 1952 when he finished his career with Augusta of the class-A South Atlantic League.

Sugar Cain

Merritt "Sugar" Cain played for Carrollton on the 1930 team before quickly advancing to the major league level. He spent 1931 in Harrisburg of the class-B New York-Pennsylvania League and was in a Philadelphia Athletics uniform by opening day of 1932. After pitching at baseball's top level until 1938 with the St. Louis Browns and the Chicago White Sox, Cain played on with several advanced class-A teams until 1943. He finished his playing career with

Birmingham of the class-A1 Southern Association.

Cain worked as an umpire for several years after his playing days were over including 1946 and 1949 in the Georgia-Alabama League.

Cain's son, Pat, also played baseball in the minor leagues and for the Carrollton Lakers semi-pro team, and he still lives in the Carrollton area.

Major League Information and Statistics
Merritt Patrick Cain
Born: April 5, 1907 in Macon, Georgia
Died: April 3, 1975 in Atlanta, Georgia
Threw: Right   Batted: Left
Height: 5' 11"   Weight: 190 lbs.

Major League Debut: April 15, 1932

Pitching Statistics

Year	Tm	Lg	W	L	G	IP	H	ER	BB	SO	ERA
1932	PHI	AL	3	4	10	45	42	25	28	24	5.00
1933	PHI	AL	13	12	38	218	244	103	137	43	4.25
1934	PHI	AL	9	17	36	231	235	113	128	66	4.41
1935	PHI	AL	0	5	6	26	39	19	19	5	4.54
	STL	AL	9	8	31	168	198	98	104	68	5.26
1936	STL	AL	1	1	4	16	20	12	9	8	6.61
	CHI	AL	14	10	30	195	228	103	75	42	4.75
1937	CHI	AL	4	2	18	69	88	47	51	17	6.16
1938	CHI	AL	0	1	5	20	26	10	18	6	4.58
TOTALS			**53**	**60**	**178**	**987**	**1119**	**530**	**569**	**279**	**4.83**

Batting Statistics

Year	Tm	Lg	G	AB	R	H	2B	3B	HR	RBI	BB	SO	BA
1932	PHI	AL	10	12	0	3	0	0	0	0	2	3	.250
1933	PHI	AL	39	80	3	16	2	0	0	4	2	17	.200
1934	PHI	AL	36	82	4	13	1	0	0	6	1	23	.169
1935	PHI	AL	6	8	0	0	0	0	0	0	0	1	.000
	STL	AL	31	57	3	11	1	0	0	5	1	15	.193
1936	STL	AL	4	7	1	2	0	0	0	0	0	1	.286
	CHI	AL	31	68	5	7	0	0	0	4	7	14	.103
1937	CHI	AL	18	22	2	4	0	0	0	2	0	4	.182
1938	CHI	AL	5	8	0	0	0	0	0	0	0	5	.000
TOTALS			**180**	**344**	**18**	**56**	**4**	**0**	**0**	**21**	**13**	**83**	**.163**

Fielding Statistics

Year	Tm	Lg	POS	G	PO	A	E	DP	FA
1932	PHI	AL	P	10	1	8	0	0	1.000
1933	PHI	AL	P	38	6	45	2	5	.962
1934	PHI	AL	P	36	4	47	5	2	.911
1935	PHI	AL	P	6	0	7	1	1	.875
	STL	AL	P	31	2	19	2	3	.913
1936	STL	AL	P	4	1	1	0	0	1.000

	CHI	AL	P	30	2	27	3	3	.906
1937	CHI	AL	P	18	0	14	0	1	1.000
1938	CHI	AL	P	5	1	0	1	0	.500
TOTALS				**178**	**17**	**168**	**14**	**15**	**.930**

Appearances on Leaderboards:
Complete Games:
    7th place in 1933 with 16
Home Runs Allowed:
    4th place in 1933 with 18
    9th place in 1936 with 18
Base on Balls Allowed:
    2nd place in 1933 with 137
    3rd place in 1934 with 128
    1st place in 1935 with 123
Hits Allowed:
    8th place in 1933 with 244
Losses:
    4th place in 1934 with 17
    8th place in 1935 with 13

Ed Chaplin

Ed Chaplin played catcher and outfield on the pennant winning 1920 Carrollton team and contributed greatly to that effort. He left the team a few days before the season came to an end and played in four games for the Boston Red Sox as a backup catcher. Chaplin returned to the Red Sox briefly in 1921 and 1922 between minor league assignments. He finished out his professional baseball career in 1929 with the class-B Pensacola, Florida club of the Southeastern League.

Major League Information and Statistics
Bert Edgar Chaplin (born Bert Edgar Chapman)
Born: September 25, 1893 in Pelzer, South Carolina
Died: August 15, 1978 in Sanford, Florida
Threw: Right   Batted: Left
Height: 5' 7"   Weight: 158 lbs.

Major League Debut: September 4, 1920

Batting Statistics

Year	Tm	Lg	G	AB	R	H	2B	3B	HR	RBI	BB	SO	BA
1920	BOS	AL	4	5	2	1	1	0	0	1	4	1	.200
1921	BOS	AL	3	2	0	0	0	0	0	0	0	1	.000
1922	BOS	AL	28	69	8	13	1	1	0	6	9	9	.188
TOTALS			**35**	**76**	**10**	**14**	**2**	**1**	**0**	**7**	**13**	**11**	**.184**

Fielding Statistics

Year	Tm	Lg	POS	G	PO	A	E	DP	FA
1920	BOS	AL	C	2	8	1	1	1	.900
1921	BOS	AL	C	1	0	1	0	0	1.000
1922	BOS	AL	C	21	56	16	3	2	.960
TOTALS				**24**	**64**	**18**	**4**	**3**	**.953**

Stan Coulling

Stanley H. Coulling pitched in Carrollton late in the 1950 season. He was also briefly the interim manager of the club after Herb "Shorty" Marshall was suspended indefinitely from the Georgia-Alabama League that year.

In 1999, Coulling was inducted into the State of Maine Baseball Hall of Fame for his achievements as a high school pitcher and his professional playing career. At Belgrade High School, Coulling accumulated 31 wins and lost only 6 as a pitcher, and he had an 86 and 82 record in eight seasons in minor league baseball. He joined the ranks at the Maine Baseball Hall of Fame along side former President George Bush.

Harry Dean

Harry Dean started his professional baseball career at Sanford, Florida of the class-D Florida State League in 1939. He moved up to class-B baseball by 1940,

and in 1941 started the season with the Washington Senators of the American League. After pitching in relief for only two games, Dean went to pitch for Greenville of the class-B South Atlantic League. Following World War II, Dean finished his baseball playing career pitching two games for the Carrollton Hornets.

Major League Information and Statistics

James Harry Dean
Born: May 12, 1915 in Rockmart, Georgia
Died: June 1, 1960 in Rockmart, Georgia
Threw: Right   Batted: Right
Height: 6' 4"   Weight: 185 lbs.

Major League Debut: April 16, 1941

Pitching Statistics

Year	Tm	Lg	W	L	G	IP	H	ER	BB	SO	ERA
1941	WSH	AL	0	0	2	2	2	1	3	0	4.50
TOTALS			**0**	**0**	**2**	**2**	**2**	**1**	**3**	**0**	**4.50**

Fielding Statistics

Year	Tm	Lg	POS	G	PO	A	E	DP	FA
1941	WSH	AL	P	2	0	0	1	0	.000
TOTALS				**2**	**0**	**0**	**1**	**0**	**.000**

Fred DeSouza

In 1950, Fred DeSouza set Georgia-Alabama League single season records for the most runs with 149 and the most walks drawn by a batter with 165. Both of these records remain the highest of all time for the league as neither one was ever bettered.

Gene Doerflinger

Carrollton ace pitcher, from the 1948 season, Gene Doerflinger set Georgia-Alabama League single season records for the most wins with 23 and the most strikeouts issued with 233. Both of these records still stand as the all time highest for the league. Doerflinger's 233 strikeouts compared to his 253 innings pitched that season equates to just under one strikeout per inning pitched.

Carl East

Carl East played for and managed the 1930 Carrollton baseball team of the Georgia-Alabama League. The league disbanded after this season but was revived in 1946 following World War II. East was appointed to the position of president of the newly remodeled league. He did not return as president of the league the next year, but he remained active in baseball at all levels in the Carrollton area for many years.

East began his professional baseball career with the Independent Lindale club in 1912. This club had the distinction of having a female manager name Lillian Duke. He worked his way through the ranks of baseball and had two separate stints at the major league level nine years apart between 1915 and 1924 with the St. Louis Browns and the Washington Senators respectively. He left organized baseball after 1924 and played in semi-pro and industrial leagues throughout the south. In 1928, he returned to the established minor league realm and played until 1931 when he finished his career

with Florence of the class-D Palmetto League.

A lifetime batting average of .364 in the minor leagues still holds Carl East as fifth on the all time minor league batting average list.

East lived in the Carrollton area until his death in 1953. His grave is located in Clem, Georgia, five miles from Carrollton.

Major League Information and Statistics

Carlton William East
Born: August 27, 1894 in Marietta, Georgia
Died: January 15, 1953 in Whitesburg, Georgia
Threw: Right   Batted: Left
Height: 6' 2"   Weight: 178 lbs.

Major League Debut: August 24, 1915

Pitching Statistics

Year	Tm	Lg	W	L	G	IP	H	ER	BB	SO	ERA
1915	STL	AL	0	0	1	3	6	6	2	1	16.20
TOTALS			**0**	**0**	**1**	**3**	**6**	**6**	**2**	**1**	**16.20**

Batting Statistics

Year	Tm	Lg	G	AB	R	H	2B	3B	HR	RBI	BB	SO	BA
1915	STL	AL	1	1	0	0	0	0	0	0	0	0	.000
1924	WSH	AL	2	6	1	2	1	0	0	2	2	1	.333
TOTALS			**3**	**7**	**1**	**2**	**1**	**0**	**0**	**2**	**2**	**1**	**.286**

Fielding Statistics

Year	Tm	Lg	POS	G	PO	A	E	DP	FA
1915	STL	AL	P	1	0	0	0	0	.000
1924	WSH	AL	OF	2	4	0	1	0	.800
TOTALS				**3**	**4**	**0**	**1**	**0**	**.800**

Bob Ezzell

Bob Ezzell played first base for Carrollton in 1929 and 1930. It was Ezzell's incredible batting performance in the 1929 league championship series that makes him stand out. During the six games of the series against Lindale, Ezzell hit five home runs. More impressive are his 33 total bases in 26 at bats during the series equating to an astounding slugging percentage of 1.269.

Lou Finney

Lou Finney played in the Georgia-Alabama League for three different teams in three different years to begin his long and productive baseball career. He played with Talladega in 1928, with Gadsden in 1929, and with Carrollton in 1930. Following stays in Harrisburg and York of the class-B New York-Pennsylvania League that took up most of the 1931 season, Finney took the outfield for eight games at the end of the season with the Philadelphia Athletics. He went back to AA baseball, the next highest level under major league at the time, in 1932 and 1933. Toward the end of the 1933 season, Finney came back to the Athletics and stayed until 1939 when he went to Boston to play for the Red Sox. He was with

Boston until the St. Louis Browns hired him in 1945 and stayed there until 1946. After playing in 16 games in 1946 for the Browns, Finney returned to his roots in the Georgia-Alabama League to play for Opelika and Valley. In 1947, Finney returned to Philadelphia, this time in the National League, to play for the Phillies. But after only four games with the Phillies, he hung up his cap in the majors. Finney played in the minor leagues until 1950 when he finished his career with Temple of the class-B Big State League.

1936 Goudey card   *1941 Playball card*

1930's Ken-Wel brand Lou Finney model glove.

Major League Information and Statistics
Louis Klopsche Finney
Born: August 13, 1910 in Buffalo, Alabama
Died: April 22, 1966 in Lafayette, Alabama
Threw: Right   Batted: Left
Height: 6' 0"   Weight: 180 lbs.

Major League Debut: September 12, 1931

Batting Statistics

Year	Tm	Lg	G	AB	R	H	2B	3B	HR	RBI	BB	SO	BA
1931	PHI	AL	9	24	7	9	0	1	0	3	6	1	.375
1933	PHI	AL	74	240	26	64	12	2	3	32	13	17	.267
1934	PHI	AL	92	272	32	76	11	4	1	28	14	17	.279
1935	PHI	AL	109	410	45	112	11	6	0	31	18	18	.273
1936	PHI	AL	151	653	100	197	26	10	1	41	47	22	.302
1937	PHI	AL	92	379	53	95	14	9	1	20	20	16	.251
1938	PHI	AL	122	454	61	125	21	12	10	48	39	25	.275
1939	PHI	AL	9	22	1	3	0	0	0	1	2	0	.136
	BOS	AL	95	249	43	81	18	3	1	46	24	11	.325
1940	BOS	AL	130	534	73	171	31	15	5	73	33	13	.320
1941	BOS	AL	127	497	83	143	24	10	4	53	38	17	.288
1942	BOS	AL	113	397	58	113	16	7	3	61	29	11	.285
1944	BOS	AL	68	251	37	72	11	2	0	32	23	7	.287
1945	BOS	AL	2	2	0	0	0	0	0	0	0	1	.000
	STL	AL	57	213	24	59	8	4	2	22	21	6	.277
1946	STL	AL	16	30	0	9	0	0	0	3	2	4	.300
1947	PHI	NL	4	4	0	0	0	0	0	0	0	0	.000
TOTALS			1270	4631	643	1329	203	85	31	494	329	186	.287

Fielding Statistics

Year	Tm	Lg	POS	G	PO	A	E	DP	FA
1931	PHI	AL	OF	8	19	1	0	1	1.000
1933	PHI	AL	OF	63	136	6	8	1	.947
1934	PHI	AL	OF	54	112	3	7	1	.943
			1B	15	120	9	2	16	.985
1935	PHI	AL	OF	76	145	5	9	1	.943
			1B	18	171	10	0	17	1.000
1936	PHI	AL	1B	78	782	34	8	70	.990
			OF	73	179	3	5	1	.973
1937	PHI	AL	1B	50	428	28	5	38	.989
			OF	39	91	2	7	1	.930
			2B	1	0	1	0	1	1.000
1938	PHI	AL	1B	64	574	24	6	35	.990
			OF	46	124	4	3	0	.977
1939	PHI	AL	OF	4	12	0	0	0	1.000
	BOS	AL	1B	32	280	11	4	27	.986
			OF	24	48	1	2	1	.961
1940	BOS	AL	OF	69	148	10	4	0	.975
			1B	51	504	23	3	41	.994
1941	BOS	AL	OF	92	181	7	11	2	.945
			1B	24	214	15	3	8	.987
1942	BOS	AL	OF	95	199	8	5	1	.976
			1B	2	22	0	0	2	1.000
1944	BOS	AL	1B	59	521	23	7	53	.987
			OF	2	7	1	0	0	1.000
1945	STL	AL	OF	36	68	4	1	1	.986
			1B	22	165	14	1	13	.994
			3B	1	1	0	1	0	.500
1946	STL	AL	OF	7	14	1	1	0	.937
TOTALS				1105	5265	248	103	331	.982

Appearances on Leaderboards:
All-Star Team:
    1940
Batting Average:
    9th place in 1940 with .320
At Bats:
    1st place in 1936 with 653
Triples:
    4th place in 1938 with 12
    2nd place in 1940 with 15
    8th place in 1941 with 10

Paul Fittery

Paul Fittery was one of the toughest pitchers to ever take the mound for any of the Carrollton teams. His baseball career of twenty some-odd years included two brief stops in the major leagues for a total of three games. Fittery spent most of his years in baseball playing for class-AA teams, the level just below major league at the time. Although he was over forty years old when he began pitching for Carrollton in 1928, he feasted on the inexperience of the class-D Georgia-Alabama league batters. During the two years on the hill for the Champs, Fittery won thirty-seven games and lost only four. Fittery set a Georgia-Alabama League record for the highest winning percentage by a pitcher in a single season with .913 in 1928 with a 21 and 2 record. In the same season, he also set a league mark for the lowest single season ERA with 1.60. Neither of these records were ever broken through the rest of the existence of the league.

Aside from being the ace pitcher for Carrollton in 1928 and 1929, Fittery managed the club to a pair of pennants and one league championship series flag. He finished his baseball playing career the following year pitching against Carrollton with the Anniston club of the Georgia-Alabama League.

Major League Information and Statistics
Paul Clarence Fittery
Born: October 10, 1887 in Lebanon, Pennsylvania
Died: January 28, 1974 in Cartersville, Georgia
Threw: Left   Batted: Right
Height: 5' 8"   Weight: 156 lbs.

Major League Debut: September 5, 1914

Pitching Statistics

Year	Tm	Lg	W	L	G	IP	H	ER	BB	SO	ERA
1914	CIN	NL	0	2	8	44	41	15	12	21	3.09
1917	PHI	NL	1	1	17	56	69	28	27	13	4.53
TOTALS			**1**	**3**	**25**	**99**	**110**	**43**	**39**	**34**	**3.90**

Batting Statistics

Year	Tm	Lg	G	AB	R	H	2B	3B	HR	RBI	BB	SO	BA
1914	CIN	NL	11	17	1	1	0	0	0	1	0	7	.059
1917	PHI	NL	19	22	3	2	0	0	0	0	4	13	.091
TOTALS			**30**	**39**	**4**	**3**	**0**	**0**	**0**	**1**	**4**	**20**	**.077**

Fielding Statistics

Year	Tm	Lg	POS	G	PO	A	E	DP	FA
1914	CIN	NL	P	8	2	13	3	0	.833
			OF	1	1	0	0	0	1.000
1917	PHI	NL	P	17	2	23	0	2	1.000
			OF	2	4	0	0	0	1.000
TOTALS				**28**	**9**	**36**	**3**	**2**	**.937**

Phil Gallivan

During his assent to the major leagues, Phil Gallivan pitched in seven games for Carrollton in 1930. In 1931, he started the season pitching for the Brooklyn Robins (Dodgers) but lasted only six games with the club. He would come back to the majors in 1932 and 1934 for relatively brief stays both times in between playing for teams one level down in the minors. In 1935, Gallivan finished his professional playing career with class-AA Indianapolis of the American Association.

Major League Information and Statistics
Philip Joseph Gallivan
Born: May 29, 1907 in Seattle, Washington
Died: November 24, 1969 in St. Paul, Minnesota
Threw: Right   Batted: Right
Height: 6' 0"   Weight: 170 lbs.

Major League Debut: April 21, 1931

Pitching Statistics

Year	Tm	Lg	W	L	G	IP	H	ER	BB	SO	ERA
1931	BRO	NL	0	1	6	15	23	9	7	1	5.28
1932	CHI	AL	1	3	13	33	49	28	24	12	7.56
1934	CHI	AL	4	7	35	127	155	79	64	55	5.61
TOTALS			**5**	**11**	**54**	**175**	**227**	**116**	**95**	**68**	**5.95**

Batting Statistics

Year	Tm	Lg	G	AB	R	H	2B	3B	HR	RBI	BB	SO	BA
1931	BRO	NL	6	3	1	0	0	0	0	0	1	3	.000
1932	CHI	AL	13	8	1	3	0	0	0	0	0	2	.375
1934	CHI	AL	35	40	3	9	3	0	0	2	0	5	.225
TOTALS			**54**	**40**	**5**	**12**	**3**	**0**	**0**	**2**	**1**	**10**	**.264**

Fielding Statistics

Year	Tm	Lg	POS	G	PO	A	E	DP	FA
1931	BRO	NL	P	6	3	6	0	1	1.000
1932	CHI	AL	P	13	2	5	0	0	1.000
1934	CHI	AL	P	35	5	20	2	0	.926
TOTALS				**54**	**10**	**31**	**2**	**1**	**.953**

Bob Hasty

Bob Hasty holds the unique distinction of being the only player to play at the major league level before and after he played in Carrollton. His brief stop in Carrollton of less than ten games in 1921 came at the recommendation of a Philadelphia Athletics scout when Carrollton needed better pitching. Hasty was soon recalled to Philadelphia that season and manned the mound there until 1924. He spent four seasons with Birmingham of the class-A Southern Association from 1929 to 1932 and parts of two years with the Atlanta Crackers of the same league in 1932 and 1933. He finished the 1933 season and his baseball career with Jersey City of the class-AA International League.

Major League Information and Statistics
Robert Keller Hasty
Born: May 3, 1896 in Canton, Georgia
Died: May 28, 1972 in Dallas, Georgia
Threw: Right   Batted: Right
Height: 6' 3"   Weight: 210 lbs.

Major League Debut: September 11, 1919

Pitching Statistics

Year	Tm	Lg	W	L	G	IP	H	ER	BB	SO	ERA
1919	PHI	AL	0	2	2	12	15	7	4	5	5.25
1920	PHI	AL	1	3	19	72	91	40	28	12	5.02
1921	PHI	AL	5	16	35	179	238	97	40	46	4.87
1922	PHI	AL	9	14	28	192	225	91	41	33	4.26
1923	PHI	AL	13	15	44	243	274	120	72	56	4.44
1924	PHI	AL	1	3	18	53	57	33	30	15	5.64
TOTALS			**29**	**53**	**146**	**751**	**900**	**388**	**215**	**167**	**4.65**

Batting Statistics

Year	Tm	Lg	G	AB	R	H	2B	3B	HR	RBI	BB	SO	BA
1919	PHI	AL	2	3	0	1	0	0	0	0	0	0	.333
1920	PHI	AL	19	24	2	6	1	0	0	2	1	4	.250
1921	PHI	AL	35	68	5	20	4	0	0	7	2	17	.294
1922	PHI	AL	28	75	3	15	1	0	1	9	1	19	.200
1923	PHI	AL	44	88	5	17	2	1	0	12	1	18	.193
1924	PHI	AL	18	13	1	1	1	0	0	0	0	1	.077
TOTALS			**146**	**271**	**16**	**60**	**9**	**1**	**1**	**30**	**5**	**59**	**.221**

Fielding Statistics

Year	Tm	Lg	POS	G	PO	A	E	DP	FA
1919	PHI	AL	P	2	1	0	1	0	.500
1920	PHI	AL	P	19	3	27	1	0	.968
1921	PHI	AL	P	35	3	53	5	2	.918

1922 PHI AL P	28	8	41	7	1		.875
1923 PHI AL P	44	9	61	6	4		.921
1924 PHI AL P	18	5	19	2	3		.923
TOTALS	**146**	**29**	**201**	**22**	**10**		**.913**

Oliver Hill

Oliver Hill came to Carrollton in 1948 and finished out his professional baseball career as the player/manager of the team replacing the injured Red Roberts. Hill was well known to baseball fans of the area from his days with the Atlanta Crackers between 1935 and 1938. In 1939, Hill started the season with the Boston Bees (Braves) and pinch hit in two games before being sent to class-AA Milwaukee of the American Association. In 1946 and 1947, Hill played for Tallassee in the Georgia-Alabama League, and he also spent part of 1947 with Newnan.

<u>Major League Information and Statistics</u>
John Clinton Hill
Born: October 16, 1909 in Powder Springs, Georgia
Died: September 20, 1970 in Decatur, Georgia
Threw: Right   Batted: Left
Height: 5' 11"   Weight: 178 lbs.

Major League Debut: April 19, 1939

Batting Statistics

Year Tm Lg	G	AB	R	H	2B	3B	HR	RBI	BB	SO	BA
1939 BOS NL	2	2	1	1	1	0	0	0	0	0	.500
TOTALS	**2**	**2**	**1**	**1**	**1**	**0**	**0**	**0**	**0**	**0**	**.500**

Red Howell

Murray "Red" Howell began his professional baseball playing career with Carrollton in 1928. His talent was quickly recognized, and he advanced to the level of class-AA baseball, just below major league, by 1932 with Toronto of the International League. Howell played for several teams at that level and the advanced class-A level until he started the

1941 season with the Cleveland Indians. He played only as a pinch hitter and pinch runner for the Indians and soon found his way back to class-AA Baltimore where he had been the previous season. He finished his long and productive minor league baseball career with the Atlanta Crackers of the class-A1 Southern Association in 1944.

<u>Major League Information and Statistics</u>
Murray Donald Howell
Born: January 29, 1909 in Atlanta, Georgia
Died: October 1, 1950 in Greenville, South Carolina
Threw: Right   Batted: Right
Height: 6' 0"   Weight: 215 lbs.

Major League Debut: April 24, 1941

Batting Statistics

Year Tm Lg	G	AB	R	H	2B	3B	HR	RBI	BB	SO	BA
1941 CLE AL	11	7	0	2	0	0	0	2	4	2	.286
TOTALS	**11**	**7**	**0**	**2**	**0**	**0**	**0**	**2**	**4**	**2**	**.286**

Herb Marshall

Herb "Shorty" Marshall remains to be one of the best-known, most-remembered Carrollton baseball players. During his four years in a Carrollton uniform, 1946-48 and 1950, Marshall played in a total of 450 games, the most of any Carrollton player. Marshall also served as manager of the 1950 and led this last team to represent the city in organized minor league baseball to the post-season playoffs.

the A's until the end of that season and for all of the next. In 1946, he returned to the minor leagues where he played regularly until 1951. In 1957, McGhee returned to baseball and finished his extensive career as he briefly played for Pensacola of the class-D Alabama-Florida League at the age of fifty-one.

Contract disposition assigning Herb Marshall to West Palm Beach of the class-C Florida International League on November 24, 1949.

Major League Information and Statistics

William Mac McGhee
Born: September 5, 1905 in Shawmut, Alabama
Died: March 10, 1984 in Decatur, Georgia
Threw: Left   Batted: Left
Height: 5' 10"   Weight: 185 lbs.

Major League Debut: July 5, 1944

Batting Statistics

Year	Tm	Lg	G	AB	R	H	2B	3B	HR	RBI	BB	SO	BA
1944	PHI	AL	77	287	27	83	12	0	1	19	21	20	.289
1945	PHI	AL	93	250	24	63	6	1	0	19	24	16	.252
TOTALS			170	537	51	146	18	1	1	38	45	36	.272

Fielding Statistics

Year	Tm	Lg	POS	G	PO	A	E	DP	FA
1944	PHI	AL	1B	75	701	46	8	51	.989
1945	PHI	AL	OF	48	84	2	1	0	.989
			1B	8	59	7	0	7	1.000
TOTALS				131	844	55	9	58	.990

Bill McGhee

After playing in Carrollton in 1929 and 1930, Bill McGhee played for almost twenty different minor league teams, several of them more than once, and the majority of them were at the class-A or class-B level. At the age of thirty-eight, McGhee made his major league debut in the middle of the 1944 season with the Philadelphia Athletics. He played first for

Gene and Pete Monarchi, and Eddie Giombetti

In 1948, Gene and Pete Monarchi and Eddie Giombetti turned the Carrollton baseball team into a family affair. Gene and Pete are brothers, and Eddie is their uncle. Pete played on the team in 1947, so early in the 1948 season, he was traded to Vidalia-Lyons of the Georgia State

League to keep the team from violating the class-man rules. Eddie, a pitcher, did not stay with the club for long and made only one appearance in a game. Gene played with the club for the rest of the 1948 season, but did not return in 1949. But for a short, special time, the Carrollton team was all in the family for the Monarchi-Giombetti clan.

Left to right: Gene Monarchi, Pete Monarchi, Eddie Giombetti

Frank Pratt

Frank Pratt played for Carrollton in 1920 as a pitcher and utility player. In 1921, Pratt had one at bat in one game in the major leagues with the Chicago White Sox of the American League. His only time at the plate in the big league was on May 13, 1921, and he grounded out.

<u>Major League Information and Statistics</u>
Francis Bruce Pratt
Born: August 24, 1897 in Blocton, Alabama
Died: March 8, 1974 in Centreville, Alabama
Threw: Right   Batted: Left
Height: 5' 10"   Weight: 155 lbs.

Major League Debut: May 13, 1921

Batting Statistics

Year	Tm	Lg	G	AB	R	H	2B	3B	HR	RBI	BB	SO	BA
1921	CHI	AL	1	1	0	0	0	0	0	0	0	0	.000
TOTALS			1	1	0	0	0	0	0	0	0	0	**.000**

Red Roberts

Charles Emory "Red" Roberts played in Carrollton from 1946 through 1948 managing the team the last two years. His time spent playing for the Washington Senators of the American League at the end of the 1943 season put him in the record book as the first and only player born in Carrollton, Georgia to play at the major league level. During Roberts' nine-game stint with the Senators, he hit an inside-the-park home run in a game against the New York Yankees. This was Red's only major league home run, and he batted .261 across 23 at-bats at baseball's highest level.

Roberts made a name for himself on the diamond in 1935 when he played on the national championship Junior American Legion Carrollton Farmers team. He spent a brief period of time playing for the Carrollton Hornets of the independent Georgia-Alabama League, no relation to the league of the same name from 1928-30 and 1946-51, that same summer. He began playing in organized baseball in 1940 with Sanford of the class-D Florida State League. Roberts worked his way up in baseball until he had a short stay in the major leagues. He returned to Carrollton to play for the home team in 1946 and was an integral part of the pennant-winning team of that year. He led the way to a repeat performance for the league flag as manager of the Hornets in 1947. After coming up only two games short of a third pennant in 1948 with Carrollton, Roberts went to work for

Alexander City of the same league and continued to manage and play well there through the 1950 season.

On December 2, 1918, Carrollton's lone major-leaguer passed away in Atlanta at the age of 80.

Charles E Roberts

Major League Information and Statistics
Charles Emory Roberts
Born: August 8, 1918 in Carrollton, Georgia
Died: December 2, 1998 in Atlanta, Georgia
Threw: Right   Batted: Right
Height: 6' 0"   Weight: 170 lbs.

Major League Debut: September 3, 1943

Batting Statistics

Year	Tm	Lg	G	AB	R	H	2B	3B	HR	RBI	BB	SO	BA
1943	WSH	AL	9	23	1	6	1	0	1	3	4	2	.261
TOTALS			9	23	1	6	1	0	1	3	4	2	.261

Fielding Statistics

Year	Tm	Lg	POS	G	PO	A	E	DP	FA
1943	WSH	AL	SS	6	7	7	4	1	.778
			3B	1	1	2	1	0	.750
TOTALS				7	8	9	5	1	.773

Bing Russell

Neil "Bing" Russell played in Carrollton in 1948 and 1949. He went on to Hollywood to become an actor starting his career in the 1951 "The Living Christ Series". Having been a professional baseball player, Russell appeared in a baseball movie in 1953 called "Big Leaguer" starring Edward G. Robinson. He also had a part in another baseball movie in "Fear Strikes Out" in 1957 with Anthony Perkins and Karl Malden.

In 1963, Russell gained fame when he landed the role of "Deputy Clem Foster" on the hit TV show "Bonanza." He stayed with the show until its end in 1973.

During Russell's acting career of nearly forty years, he had more than seventy guest appearances on hit television shows such as "Emergency", "The Rockford Files", "Gunsmoke", "The Big Valley", "I Dream of Jeannie", "The Fugitive", and "The Twilight Zone." He also had roles in over forty motion pictures and television movies, mainly westerns, such as "Gunfight at the O.K. Corral", "Rio Bravo", "The Apple Dumpling Gang", "Tango and Cash", "The Magnificent Seven" (probably his most remembered movie role), and "Dick Tracy," the last movie appeared in before he retired from acting.

Bing Russell is also the father of well-known actor Kurt Russell and grandfather of major league baseball player Matt Franco.

Bing Russell photo from "Bonanza"

1977 Portland Mavericks team photo. The team owned by Bing Russell, his son, Kurt, played for the club, and his grandson, Matt Franco, was the ball boy.

Gene Solt

Gene Solt set the single season home run record for the Georgia-Alabama League while playing for Carrollton in 1950. Solt's 38 homers that season remains to be the all-time record in the league for home runs in one season. Solt also set single season league marks that year in RBI's with 151 and total bases with 311. Neither of these records were ever broken as well.

Buck Varner

Buck Varner began his professional baseball career with Carrollton in 1948. In 1950, he had advanced to class-AA

with the Chattanooga club of the Southern Association. At the end of the 1952 season, Varner played in two games for the Washington Senators. He played the 1953 season back in Chattanooga, and in 1954, he retired from playing after being with Charlotte of the class-A South Atlantic League.

Major League Information and Statistics

Glen Gann Varner
Born: August 17, 1930 in Hixson, Tennessee
Threw: Right   Batted: Left
Height: 5' 10"   Weight: 170 lbs.

Major League Debut: September 19, 1952

Batting Statistics

Year	Tm	Lg	G	AB	R	H	2B	3B	HR	RBI	BB	SO	BA
1952	WSH	AL	2	4	0	0	0	0	0	0	0	1	1	.000
TOTALS			**2**	**4**	**0**	**0**	**0**	**0**	**0**	**0**	**1**	**1**	**.000**

Fielding Statistics

Year	Tm	Lg	POS	G	PO	A	E	DP	FA
1952	WSH	AL	OF	1	1	0	0	0	1.000
TOTALS				**1**	**1**	**0**	**0**	**0**	**1.000**

Bill Webb

In 1941, Bill Webb entered minor league baseball with Mobile of the class-B Southeastern League. His strong arm enabled him to start the 1943 season with the Philadelphia Phillies where he got the break to pitch one inning of one game on May 15. Webb finished the season with Montreal of the class-AA International League and spent the next three seasons with St. Paul and Minneapolis of the class-AA American Association. In 1947, Webb was hired to pitch for Carrollton and was the ace of the staff as he won twenty-two games. He pitched for two more seasons before calling it quits with Gadsden of the class-B Southeastern League in 1950.

William Frederick Webb

Major League Information and Statistics
William Franklin Webb
Born: December 12, 1913 in Atlanta, Georgia
Died: June 1, 1994 in Austell, Georgia
Threw: Right   Batted: Right
Height: 6' 2"   Weight: 180 lbs.

Major League Debut: May 15, 1943

Pitching Statistics

Year	Tm	Lg	W	L	G	IP	H	ER	BB	SO	ERA
1943	PHI	NL	0	0	1	1	1	1	1	0	9.00
TOTALS			**0**	**0**	**1**	**1**	**1**	**1**	**1**	**0**	**9.00**

Fielding Statistics

Year	Tm	Lg	POS	G	PO	A	E	DP	FA
1943	PHI	NL	P	1	0	0	0	0	.000
TOTALS				**1**	**0**	**0**	**0**	**0**	**.000**

Abe White

Abe White was a mainstay of the Carrollton club in its first two years in the Georgia-Alabama League in 1928 and 1929. He also started the 1930 season with Carrollton before going to pitch for Lindale and playing a large role on that championship team.   In 1932, White landed a job on the Birmingham team of the class-A Southern Association and pitched well there through 1935.   He joined the St. Louis Cardinals in the middle of the 1937 season for five ball games as a relief pitcher. In White's only at bat in the majors, he got a base hit making his career major league batting average 1.000. In 1947, White played his

last season in the familiar Georgia-Alabama League as the player/manager of the Griffin team.

Major League Information and Statistics
Adel White
Born: May 16, 1904 in Winder, Georgia
Died: October 1, 1978 in Atlanta, Georgia
Threw: Left   Batted: Right
Height: 6' 0"   Weight: 185 lbs.

Major League Debut: July 10, 1937

Pitching Statistics

Year	Tm	Lg	W	L	G	IP	H	ER	BB	SO	ERA
1937	STL	NL	0	1	5	9	14	7	3	2	6.75
TOTALS			**0**	**1**	**5**	**9**	**14**	**7**	**3**	**2**	**6.75**

Batting Statistics

Year	Tm	Lg	G	AB	R	H	2B	3B	HR	RBI	BB	SO	BA
1937	STL	NL	5	1	0	1	0	0	0	0	0	0	1.000
TOTALS			**5**	**1**	**0**	**1**	**0**	**0**	**0**	**0**	**0**	**0**	**1.000**

Fielding Statistics

Year	Tm	Lg	POS	G	PO	A	E	DP	FA
1937	STL	NL	P	5	0	2	0	0	1.000
TOTALS				**5**	**0**	**2**	**0**	**0**	**1.000**

Jo-Jo White

Jo-Jo White burst onto the professional baseball scene in 1928 with Carrollton and hit twenty-seven home runs contributing greatly the pennant-winning team of his rookie season.   He quickly advanced through the ranks of the minor leagues and was playing in the major leagues by the beginning of the 1932 season with the Detroit Tigers.   Jo-Jo stayed with the Tigers through 1938, and played for Seattle of the class-AA Pacific Coast League from 1939 to 1942.   He returned   to   the   majors   with   the

Philadelphia Athletics in 1943 and 1944, and he played briefly for the Cincinnati Reds at the end of the 1944 season. The following season, Jo-Jo went back to the Pacific Coast League and played with Sacramento, Seattle, and Hollywood until his last season in 1949. Following his playing days, White found a career in coaching baseball in the major leagues. He was a long time coach for the Braves in Milwaukee and Atlanta and he managed the Cleveland Indians for one game in 1960.

1935 Diamond Stars card   *1930's Hutch Model F54 Jo-Jo White model buckle-back glove.*

Major League Information and Statistics
Joyner Clifford White
Born: June 1, 1909 in Red Oak, Georgia
Died: October 9, 1986 in Tacoma, Washington
Threw: Right   Batted: Left
Height: 5' 11"   Weight: 165 lbs.

Major League Debut: April 15, 1932

Batting Statistics

Year	Tm	Lg	G	AB	R	H	2B	3B	HR	RBI	BB	SO	BA
1932	DET	AL	80	208	25	54	6	3	2	21	22	19	.260
1933	DET	AL	91	234	43	59	9	5	2	34	27	26	.252
1934	DET	AL	115	384	97	120	18	5	0	44	69	39	.312
1935	DET	AL	114	412	82	99	13	12	2	32	68	42	.240
1936	DET	AL	58	51	11	14	3	0	0	6	9	10	.275
1937	DET	AL	94	305	50	75	5	7	0	21	50	40	.246
1938	DET	AL	78	206	40	54	6	1	0	15	30	15	.262
1943	PHI	AL	139	500	69	124	17	7	1	30	61	51	.248
1944	PHI	AL	85	267	30	59	4	2	1	21	40	27	.221
	CIN	NL	24	85	9	20	2	0	0	5	10	7	.235
TOTALS			**878**	**2652**	**456**	**678**	**83**	**42**	**8**	**229**	**386**	**276**	**.256**

Fielding Statistics

Year	Tm	Lg	POS	G	PO	A	E	DP	FA
1932	DET	AL	OF	48	96	6	4	2	.962
1933	DET	AL	OF	54	122	4	3	1	.977
1934	DET	AL	OF	100	225	9	10	2	.959
1935	DET	AL	OF	98	247	7	10	1	.962
1936	DET	AL	OF	18	14	1	1	0	.937
1937	DET	AL	OF	82	216	4	6	0	.973
1938	DET	AL	OF	55	141	4	5	0	.967
1943	PHI	AL	OF	133	335	8	12	2	.966
1944	PHI	AL	OF	74	162	5	9	2	.949
			SS	1	0	0	0	0	.000
	CIN	NL	OF	23	55	4	0	0	1.000
TOTALS				**686**	**1613**	**52**	**60**	**10**	**.965**

Post-Season Batting Statistics

Year	Tm	Rd	G	AB	R	H	2B	3B	HR	RBI	BB	SO	BA
1934	DET	WS	7	23	6	3	0	0	0	0	8	4	.130
1935	DET	WS	5	19	3	5	0	0	0	1	5	7	.263
TOTALS			**12**	**42**	**9**	**8**	**0**	**0**	**0**	**1**	**13**	**11**	**.190**

Appearances on Leaderboards:
On-Base Percentage:
    7th place in 1934 with .418
Triples:
    6th place in 1935 with 12
Stolen Bases:
    2nd place in 1934 with 28
    4th place in 1935 with 19
    10th place in 1937 with 12

Kemp Wicker

Kemp Wicker pitched seven games of the 1928 Carrollton team contributing to the pennant winning season. His advancement to the major leagues was not a quick one as he spent much of the next seven years in the class-C Mid-Atlantic League. Toward the end of the 1936 season, Wicker worked as a relief pitcher for the New York Yankees. He would continue to pitch on again off again for New York until 1938. He made one more appearance at baseball's highest level with the Brooklyn Dodgers of the National League in 1941. In 1946, Wicker came back to Georgia to play for Columbus of the class-A South Atlantic League where he stayed until retirement in 1948.

Major League Information and Statistics

Kemp Caswell Wicker
Born: August 13, 1906 in Kernersville, North Carolina
Died: June 11, 1973 in Kernersville, North Carolina
Threw: Left   Batted: Right
Height: 5' 11"   Weight: 182 lbs.

Major League Debut: August 14, 1936

Pitching Statistics

Year	Tm	Lg	W	L	G	IP	H	ER	BB	SO	ERA
1936	NY	AL	1	2	7	20	31	17	11	5	7.65
1937	NY	AL	7	3	16	88	107	43	26	14	4.40
1938	NY	AL	1	0	1	1	0	0	1	0	0.00
1941	BRO	NL	1	2	16	32	30	13	14	8	3.66
TOTALS			**10**	**7**	**40**	**141**	**168**	**73**	**52**	**27**	**4.66**

Batting Statistics

Year	Tm	Lg	G	AB	R	H	2B	3B	HR	RBI	BB	SO	BA
1936	NY	AL	7	7	0	1	1	0	0	0	0	1	.143
1937	NY	AL	16	35	4	4	0	0	0	7	1	6	.114
1941	BRO	NL	16	4	0	1	0	0	0	1	1	1	.250
TOTALS			**40**	**46**	**4**	**6**	**1**	**0**	**0**	**8**	**2**	**8**	**.130**

Fielding Statistics

Year	Tm	Lg	POS	G	PO	A	E	DP	FA
1936	NY	AL	P	7	0	5	0	0	1.000
1937	NY	AL	P	16	0	9	1	0	.900
1938	NY	AL	P	1	0	0	0	0	.000
1941	BRO	NL	P	16	0	7	0	0	1.000
TOTALS				**40**	**0**	**21**	**1**	**0**	**.955**

Carrollton Team and League Records

Batting

Single Season Highest Batting Average
(100 at bat minimum)
1. Carl East .453 1930
2. Red Howell .392 1928
   Dick Taliaferro .392 1928
4. Lou Finney .388 1930
5. Red Roberts .385 1947

Single Season Most Total Hits
1. Shorty Marshall 171 1947
2. Gene Solt 168 1950
3. Jim Hill 163 1946
4. Dick Kelly 159 1947
5. Ray Clark 155 1950

Single Season Most Total Runs
1. Fred DeSouza 149 1950
2. Jim Morelli 112 1950
3. Gene Solt 106 1950
4. Shorty Marshall 99 1947
5. Shorty Marshall 99 1948

*Single Season Most Total Doubles
1. Ray Clark 38 1950
2. Fred DeSouza 33 1950
3. Bob Ezzell 32 1929
   Shorty Marshall 32 1948
5. Henry Patton 30 1929

*Single Season Most Total Triples
1. Floyd Snider 9 1947
   Frank Cichon 9 1948
3. Dick Taliaferro 8 1928
   Jo-Jo White 8 1928
   John Allen 8 1947

*Single Season Most Total Home Runs
1. Gene Solt 38 1950
2. Jo-Jo White 27 1928
3. Luther Gunnells 24 1946
   Fred DeSouza 24 1950
5. Bill Seal 23 1949

**Single Season Most Total Runs Batted In
1. Gene Solt 151 1950
2. Floyd Snider 102 1947
3. Bill Seal 97 1949
4. Luther Gunnells 96 1946
5. Fred DeSouza 92 1950

Fielding

*Single Season Most Total Put-Outs
1. Bob Ezzell – 1B 961 1929
2. Jim Stoyle – 1B 947 1946
3. Bob Ezzell – 1B 835 1930
4. Jim Langley – 1B 771 1947
5. Fob James – 1B 733 1928

*Single Season Most Total Put-Outs by Position
P   Paul Fittery 85 1928
C   Jim Hill 553 1946
1B Bob Ezzell 961 1929
2B Shorty Marshall 360 1948
3B Red Roberts 169 1947
SS Luther Gunnells 180 1946
OF Jim Morrelli 257 1949
OF Floyd Snider 228 1947
OF Jim Morrelli 228 1950

*Single Season Most Total Assists
1. Shorty Marshall – 2B 334 1948
2. Luther Gunnells – SS 326 1946

3. Shorty Marshall – 2B   316   1946
4. Shorty Marshall – 2B   305   1947
5. Red Roberts – 3B   297   1947

*Single Season Most Total Assists by Position

P	Paul Fittery	73	1928
C	Virgil Jefts	71	1949
1B	Jim Shirley	44	1950
2B	Shorty Marshall	334	1948
3B	Red Roberts	297	1947
SS	Luther Gunnells	326	1946
OF	Jo-Jo White	21	1928
OF	Jim Morelli	15	1950
OF	Bill McGhee	12	1929
	Frank Cichon	12	1948 & 1949

*Single Season Most Total Errors

1. Dick Kelly – 3B   53   1947
2. Gene Monarchi – SS   44   1948
3. Luther Gunnells – SS   40   1946
4. Shorty Marshall – 2B   38   1948
     Ray Clark – SS   38   1950

*Single Season Most Total Errors by Position

P	Blas Arroyo	16	1948
C	Virgil Jefts	26	1949
1B	Jim Stoyle	23	1946
2B	Shorty Marshall	38	1948
3B	Dick Kelly	53	1947
SS	Gene Monarchi	44	1948
OF	Frank Cichon	28	1948
OF	Dallas Thomas	18	1947
OF	Jim Morelli	14	1949

Pitching

*Single Season Most Total Wins

1. Gene Doerflinger 23   1948
2. Bill Webb   22   1947
3. Paul Fittery   21   1928
4. Paul Crain   19   1947
5. Ed Bobowski   17   1950

*Single Season Most Total Losses

1. Paul Crain   14   1947
     Bert Bozzuto   14   1949
3. Bob Mathews   13   1946
     Ed Bobowski   13   1949
5. Red Justiss   12   1929

*Single Season Highest Winning Percentage
(20 game minimum)

1. Paul Fittery   .913   21-2   1928
2. Paul Fittery   .889   16-2   1929
3. Bill Webb   .815   22-5   1947
4. Bob Hutchins   .750   9-3   1950
5. Ed Bobowski   .708   17-7   1950

*Single Season Lowest Earned Run Average
(100 inning minimum)

1. Paul Fittery   1.60   225 in.   1928
2. Paul Fittery   1.81   174 in.   1929
3. Gene Doerflinger 2.13   253 in.   1948
4. Bill Webb   2.40   229 in.   1947
5. John Westbrook   2.51   104 in.   1946

*Single Season Most Total Strikeouts Issued

1. Gene Doerflinger 233   1948
2. Abe White   141   1928
3. Paul Fittery   137   1928
4. Bill Webb   131   1947
5. Bob Mathews   111   1946

*Single Season Most Base on Balls Issued

1. Gene Doerflinger 123   1948
2. Ed Bobowski   118   1950
3. Ed Bobowski   112   1949
4. Walt Kuras   92   1949
5. Walt Little   85   1948

*Single Season Most Hits Allowed

1. Bob Mathews   227   1946
2. Paul Crain   225   1947
3. Abe White   217   1928
4. Abe White   214   1929
5. Red Justiss   211   1929

* = this stat not kept in 1920-21 seasons.
** = this stat not kept in 1920-21, 28-30 seasons.

Carrollton Season League Leaders

1920   None

1921   None

1928   BA: Dick Taliaferro, Red Howell   .392
          Runs: Jo-Jo White   92
          Hits: Red Howell   152
          HRs: Jo-Jo White   27

Wins: Paul Fittery   21
SOs: Abe White   141
ERA: Paul Fittery 1.60
Pct: Paul Fittery .913   21-2

1929 SOs: Abe White   101
         ERA: Paul Fittery 1.81
         Pct: Paul Fittery .889   16-2

1930 None

1946 BA: Luther Gunnells   .381

1947 BA: Red Roberts .385

1948 Wins: Gene Doerflinger 23
            (tied with William Kallaher of Opelika)
        SOs: Gene Doerflinger 233

1949 None

1950 BA: Gene Solt .365
        Runs: Fred DeSouza 149
        Hits: Gene Solt   168
        RBIs: Gene Solt   151
        HRs: Gene Solt   38
        TBs: Gene Solt   311
        BBs: Fred DeSouza 165

All-Time Georgia-Alabama League Records Held by Carrollton Players

Batting
  Runs: 149 by Fred DeSouza in 1950
  RBIs: 151 by Gene Solt in 1950
  HRs: 38 by Gene Solt in 1950
  TBs: 311 by Gene Solt in 1950
  BBs: 165 by Fred DeSouza in 1950
  SO's: 118 by Ted Przeworski in 1948 (stats split
        between play in LaGrange and Carrollton)

Pitching
  Wins: 23 by Gene Doerflinger in 1948
  Pct: .913 (21-2) by Paul Fittery in 1928
  ERA: 1.60 by Paul Fittery in 1928
  SO's: 233 by Gene Doerflinger in 1948

Carrollton All-Star Team Players

1920 No All-Star Team selected

1921 No All-Star Team selected

1928 No All-Star Team selected

1929 No All-Star Team selected

1930 Bill Alexander - UT

1946 Luther Gunnells – SS
        Jim Hill – C
        Buck Matthews – P
        Lew York – LF

1947 Red Roberts – SS
        Jim Hill – C
        Shorty Marshall – UT
        Bill Webb – P
        Buck Mathews – P

1948 Gene Doerflinger – P
        Shorty Marshall – 2B
        Frank Cichon – LF

1949 Bill Seal – 3B
        Jim Morelli – UT
        Walt Kuras – P
        Frank Cichon – RF

1950 Gene Solt – C
        Bob Hutchins – P
        Bill Weldon – P
        Ed Bobowski – P
        Jim Morelli – OF
        Fred DeSouza – 3B

Bibliography

Atlanta Journal-Constitution, Atlanta, Georgia, July 1921 through July 1948.

Bell, John. *Shoeless Summer: The summer of 1923 when Shoeless Joe Jackson played baseball in Americus, Georgia.* Carrollton, Georgia: Vabella Publishing, 2001.

Carrollton County Georgian, Carrollton, Georgia, August 1947 through August 1965.

Carroll County Times, Carrollton, Georgia, June 1914 through September 1947.

Carroll Free Press, Carrollton, Georgia, June 1914 through August 1929.

Johnson, Lloyd and Miles Wolff. *The Encyclopedia of Minor League Baseball.* Durham, North Carolina: Baseball America, Inc., 1997.

Obojski, Robert. *Bush League, A Colorful, Factual Account of Minor League Baseball from 1877 to the Present.* New York: Macmillan, 1975.

Reach Official American League Base Ball Guide 1928. Philadelphia: A.J. Reach Company, 1929.

Reach Official American League Base Ball Guide 1929. Philadelphia: A.J. Reach Company, 1930.

Reach Official American League Base Ball Guide 1930. Philadelphia: A.J. Reach Company, 1931.

Spalding's OfficialBase Ball Guide 1946. New York: American Sports Publishing Company, 1947.

Spalding's OfficialBase Ball Guide 1947. New York: American Sports Publishing Company, 1948.

Spalding's OfficialBase Ball Guide 1948. New York: American Sports Publishing Company, 1949.

Spalding's OfficialBase Ball Guide 1949. New York: American Sports Publishing Company, 1950.

Spalding's OfficialBase Ball Guide 1950. New York: American Sports Publishing Company, 1951.

The Professional Baseball Player Database, Old-Time Data, Inc.: Shawnee Mission. Version 4.00.

Times-Free Press, Carrollton, Georgia, August 1948 Through August 1965.

www.baseball-reference.com, website.

Photo and Graphic Sources

"Carrollton's New Base…" – June 11, 1914 edition of Carroll County Times.
1920 Georgia State League Map – Vabella Publishing original artwork.
"Carrollton Takes First…" – May 20, 1920 edition of Carroll County Times.
South Street Ballpark Map – Vabella Publishing original artwork.
"Cedartown's Steam Roller…" – June 3, 1920 edition of Carroll County Times.
"Rome's Fans Make…" – June 22, 1920 edition of Carroll Free Press.
"Shake-up Needed On…" – July 8, 1920 edition of Carroll County Times.
"Georgia State League…" – July 15, 1920 edition of Carroll County Times.
"Carrollton Wins Two…" – July 22, 1920 edition of Carroll County Times.
"Carrollton Takes Three…" – July 29, 1920 edition of Carroll County Times.
"Crucial Series Between…" – August 19, 1920 edition of Carroll County Times.
"Georgia State League…" – September 2, 1920 edition of Carroll County Times.
"Carrollton Cops Georgia…" – September 7, 1920 edition Carroll Free Press.
1921 Georgia State League Map – Vabella Publishing original artwork.
"Carrollton Can't Win…" – May 19, 1921 edition of Carroll County Times.
"If you think…" – May 26, 1921 edition of Carroll County Times.
"Baseball Meeting…" – June 16, 1921 edition of Carroll County Times.
"Carrollton Drops Four…" – June 23, 1921 edition of Carroll County Times.
"Carrollton Will Present…" – June 30, 1921 edition of Carroll County Times.
"Georgia State League…" – July 6, 1921 edition of Atlanta Journal-Constitution.
"Carrollton Club Playing…" – July 21, 1921 edition of Carroll County Times.
"Booster Day For…" – August 4, 1921 edition of Carroll County Times.
1928 Georgia-Alabama League Map – Vabella Publishing original artwork.
"New Class 'D'…" – May 24, 1928 edition of Atlanta Journal-Constitution.
City Athletic Field Map – Vabella Publishing original artwork.
"Carrollton Takes Six…" – June 14, 1928 edition of Carroll County Times.
"Carrollton Wins Four…" – June 21, 1928 edition of Carroll County Times.
"Howell Leads League…" – June 28, 1928 edition of Carroll County Times.
"Can You Suggest…" – July 12, 1928 edition of Carroll County Times.
"Carrollton Club Is…" – July 19, 1928 edition of Carroll County Times.
"Taking Three From…" – August 2, 1928 edition of Carroll County Times.
"Carrollton Again Leading…" – August 9, 1928 edition of Carroll County Times.
"Playoff For Pennant…" – August 30, 1928 edition of Carroll County Times.
"Talladega Is Almost…" – August 30, 1928 edition of Carroll County Times.
"Official League…" – September 6, 1928 edition of Carroll County Times.
"Indians Lose…" – September 11, 1928 edition of Atlanta Journal-Constitution.
"Indians Win 3rd…" – September 13, 1928 edition of Atlanta Journal-Constitution.
"Carrollton Defeats…" – September 20, 1928 edition of Carroll County Times.
"Takes Four Out…" – September 20, 1928 edition of Carroll County Times.
1929 Georgia-Alabama League Map – Vabella Publishing original artwork.
"Talk of the…" – July 4, 1929 edition of Carroll Free Press.
"Georgia-Alabama League…" – May 9, 1929 edition of Carroll County Times.
"League Standing…" – May 30, 1929 edition of Carroll County Times.
"Georgia-Alabama…" – June 6, 1929 edition of Atlanta Journal-Constitution.
"Carrollton Defeats Cedartown…" – June 13, 1929 edition of Carroll Free Press.
"Georgia-Alabama…" – July 6, 1929 edition of Atlanta Journal-Constitution.
"Ten Homers Hit…" – August 13, 1929 edition of Atlanta Journal-Constitution.
"League Standing…" – August 15, 1929 edition of Carroll Free Press.
"Schedule of Little…" – August 29, 1929 edition of Carroll Free Press.
"League Standing…" – September 5, 1929 edition of Carroll County Times.
"Entire Team Played…" – September 12, 1929 edition of Carroll County Times.
"Carrollton Wins…" – September 12, 1929 edition of Carroll County Times.
1930 Georgia-Alabama League Map – Vabella Publishing original artwork.
"Rounding Up A…" – April 17, 1930 edition of Carroll County Times.
"Georgia-Alabama League…" – May 1, 1930 edition of Carroll County Times.
"Mayor Luck's Proclamation…" – May 8, 1930 edition of Carroll County Times.
"Carrollton Wins…" – May 15, 1930 edition of Carroll County Times.
"Monday Will Be…" – May 29, 1930 edition of Carroll County Times.
"Cedars Victors In…" – July 4, 1930 edition of Atlanta Journal-Constitution.
"Talladega Opens Second…" – July 3, 1930 edition of Carroll County Times.
"League Standing…" – August 7, 1930 edition of Carroll County Times.
"Carrollton May Withdraw…" – August 14, 1930 edition of Carroll County Times.
1946 Georgia-Alabama League Map – Vabella Publishing original artwork.
"The Opening Game…" – April 25, 1946 edition of Carroll County Times.
"Charley Roberts Signs…" – May 9, 1946 edition of Carroll County Times.
"Shorty Marshall And…" – May 16, 1946 edition of Carroll County Times.
"Buck Mathews Does…" – May 23, 1946 edition of Carroll County Times.
"Marriage on Field…" – June 6, 1946 edition of Carroll County Times.
"Three Hornets Are…" – July 11, 1946 edition of Carroll County Times.
"League President Gives…" – July 18, 1946 edition of Carroll County Times.
"Standings Including Games…" – August 15, 1946 edition of Carroll County Times.
"Gunnells And Hill…" – August 22, 1946 edition of Carroll County Times.
"Carrollton Wins Flag…" – August 29, 1946 edition of Carroll County Times.
"Final Standings of…" – September 5, 1946 edition of Carroll County Times.
"Carrollton Wins First…" – September 5, 1946 edition of Carroll County Times.
"Hornets Lose Final…" – September 12, 1946 edition of Carroll County Times.
1947 Georgia-Alabama League Map – Vabella Publishing original artwork.
"Dispute on Sunday…" – March 27, 1947 edition of Carroll County Times.
"Ga.-Ala. League…" – April 17, 1947 edition of Carroll County Times.
"Hornets Show Old-Time…" – May 15, 1947 edition of Carroll County Times.
"Standings Includes…" – May 29, 1947 edition of Carroll County Times.

"Charley Roberts Captures..." – June 12, 1947 edition of Carroll County Times.
"Roberts, Mathews, And..." – July 3, 1947 edition of Carroll County Times.
"Standings Does Not..." – July 10, 1947 edition of Carroll County Times.
"Newnan Et Al..." – August 21, 1947 edition of Carrollton County Georgian.
"Roberts Hits .404..." – August 14, 1947 edition of Carroll County Times.
"Hornets Hold Even..." – August 21, 1947 edition of Carroll County Times.
"Those Hornets Do..." – September 4, 1947 edition of Carroll County Georgian.
"Valley Wallops Hornets..." – September 4, 1947 edition of Carroll County Times.
"Hornets Out Rebels..." – September 11, 1947 edition of Carroll County Georgian.
1948 Georgia-Alabama League Map – Vabella Publishing original artwork.
"Hornets Swamp Newnan..." – April 22, 1948 edition of Carroll County Georgian.
"Win Opening Day..." – April 22, 1948 edition of Carroll County Georgian.
"Gunnells Leads Hitters..." – May 27, 1948 edition of Carroll County Georgian.
"Ga.-Alabama League..." – July 1, 1948 edition of Atlanta Journal-Constitution.
"Revels Hurls No-Hitter..." – August 17, 1948 edition of Times-Free Press.
"Doerflinger Wins 20th..." – August 24, 1948 edition of Times-Free Press.
"Valley Trips Hornets..." – September 2, 1948 edition of Times-Free Press.
"Alex City Draws..." – September 7, 1948 edition of Times-Free Press.
"Revels Gives Alex..." – September 7, 1948 edition of Times-Free Press.
"Crucial Game Ends..." – September 9, 1948 edition of Times-Free Press.
"Revels Cinches Play-Off..." – September 9, 1948 edition of Times-Free Press.
"Errors Cost Hornets..." – September 14, 1948 edition of Times-Free Press.
"Valley Takes Play-Off..." – September 14, 1948 edition of Times-Free Press.
1949 Georgia-Alabama League Map – Vabella Publishing original artwork.
"Browns Smother Hornets..." – April 28, 1949 edition of Times-Free Press.
"Back The 1949..." – April 26, 1949 edition of Times-Free Press.
"Hornets Drop 4-1..." – May 3, 1949 edition of Times-Free Press.
"Hornets Protest Saturday..." – May 31, 1949 edition of Times-Free Press.
"LaGrange Manager Suspended..." – June 7, 1949 edition of Times-Free Press.
"Seal, Chichon, Kuras,..." – July 5, 1949 edition of Times-Free Press.
"Seal Is Sold..." – August 2, 1949 edition of Times-Free Press.
"Hornets Play .533..." – August 23, 1949 edition of Times-Free Press.
"Hornets Drop Final..." – September 6, 1949 edition of Times-Free Press.
1950 Georgia-Alabama League Map – Vabella Publishing original artwork.
"Back Those Hornets..." – April 25, 1950 edition of Times-Free Press.
"Hornets Average 12..." – May 18, 1950 edition of Times-Free Press.
"Decatur Resigns; New..." – May 25, 1950 edition of Times-Free Press.
"Alex City Millers..." – June 6, 1950 edition of Times-Free Press.
"Marshall's .423 Batting..." – June 20, 1950 edition of Times-Free Press.
"Weds Hornets Pitcher" – June 27, 1950 edition of Times-Free Press.
"Five Hornets On..." – July 6, 1950 edition of Times-Free Press.
"Gene Solt Ties..." – July 18, 1950 edition of Times-Free Press.
"Browns Drop Pair..." – July 25, 1950 edition of Times-Free Press.
"Boston Braves Get..." – August 1, 1950 edition of Times-Free Press.
"Pitcher's Second Iron..." – August 3, 1950 edition of Times-Free Press.
"1,100 Greet Old..." – August 15, 1950 edition of Times-Free Press.
"Marshall Suspended And..." – August 29, 1950 edition of Times-Free Press.
"Fernandez Tosses 2-Hitter..." – September 5, 1950 edition of Times-Free Press.
"Bessant's No-Hitter..." – September 5, 1950 edition of Times-Free Press.
"Troupers Bump Hornets..." – September 7, 1950 edition of Times-Free Press.
"Solt, Bowski Make..." – September 7, 1950 edition of Times-Free Press.
"Hornets In League..." – August 31, 1950 edition of Times-Free Press.
Present day City Athletic Field photograph by Vabella Publishing.
1920 Carrollton baseball team photograph number one courtesy of the Annie Belle Weaver Special Collections of the Ingram Library of the State University of West Georgia.
1920 Carrollton baseball team photograph number two courtesy of the Annie Belle Weaver Special Collections of the Ingram Library of the State University of West Georgia.
Charlie Bell photograph courtesy of Annie Belle Weaver Special Collections of the Ingram Library of the State University of West Georgia.
Jess Craven photograph courtesy of the Annie Belle Weaver Special Collections of the Ingram Library of the State University of West Georgia.
Visiting team batting photograph courtesy of the Annie Belle Weaver Special Collections of the Ingram Library of the State University of West Georgia.
Pop Shaw, Goat Brandon, and Ed Chaplin photograph courtesy of the Annie Belle Weaver Special Collections of the Ingram Library of the State University of West Georgia.
Jules Watson stops at third photograph courtesy of the Annie Belle Weaver Special Collections of the Ingram Library of the State University of West Georgia.
Ed Chaplin slides into second photograph courtesy of the Annie Belle Weaver Special Collections of the Ingram Library of the State University of West Georgia.
Red Reese and Albert Bonifay photograph courtesy of the Annie Belle Weaver Special Collections of the Ingram Library of the State University of West Georgia.
Red Reese photograph courtesy of the Annie Belle Weaver Special Collections of the Ingram Library of the State University of West Georgia.
Visiting team photo batting photograph courtesy of the Annie Belle Weaver Special Collections of the Ingram Library of the State University of West Georgia.
South Street Ballpark bleachers photograph courtesy of the Annie Belle Weaver Special Collections of the Ingram Library of the State University of West Georgia.
Ed Chaplin and Red Reese photograph courtesy of the Annie Belle Weaver Special Collections of the Ingram Library of the State University of West Georgia.

South Street Ballpark game action photographs courtesy of the Annie Belle Weaver Special Collections of the Ingram Library of the State University of West Georgia.
Lefty Sutton, Goat Brandon, and Bill McKinnon photograph courtesy of the Annie Belle Weaver Special Collections of the Ingram Library of the State University of West Georgia.
Charlie Bell photograph courtesy of Annie Belle Weaver Special Collections of the Ingram Library of the State University of West Georgia.
1928 Carrollton Frogs baseball team photograph courtesy of the Annie Belle Weaver Special Collections of the Ingram Library of the State University of West Georgia.
Paul Fittery photograph courtesy of the Annie Belle Weaver Special Collections of the Ingram Library of the State University of West Georgia.
Jo-Jo White rounding third photograph courtesy of the Annie Belle Weaver Special Collections of the Ingram Library of the State University of West Georgia.
Red Howell photograph courtesy of the Annie Belle Weaver Special Collections of the Ingram Library of the State University of West Georgia.
Paul Fittery and Jo-Jo White photograph courtesy of the Annie Belle Weaver Special Collections of the Ingram Library of the State University of West Georgia.
Red Howell, Cheese Goggans, and Jo-Jo White photograph courtesy of the Annie Belle Weaver Special Collections of the Ingram Library of the State University of West Georgia.
Kemp Wicker photograph courtesy of the Annie Belle Weaver Special Collections of the Ingram Library of the State University of West Georgia.
Bob Rowe photograph courtesy of the Annie Belle Weaver Special Collections of the Ingram Library of the State University of West Georgia.
Game action at City Athletic Field photograph courtesy of the Annie Belle Weaver Special Collections of the Ingram Library of the State University of West Georgia.
Dick Taliaferro photograph courtesy of the Annie Belle Weaver Special Collections of the Ingram Library of the State University of West Georgia.
1929 Carrollton Champs baseball team photograph courtesy of the Annie Belle Weaver Special Collections of the Ingram Library of the State University of West Georgia.
Five 1929 Carrollton players photograph courtesy of the Annie Belle Weaver Special Collections of the Ingram Library of the State University of West Georgia.
1946 Carrollton Hornets baseball team photograph courtesy of the Herb Marshall collection.
1946 Carrollton baseball team bus photograph courtesy of the Edwin Roberts collection.
Luther Gunnells and Harvey Copeland photograph courtesy of the Herb Marshall collection.
Red Roberts, Luther Gunnells, Shorty Marshall, and Lew York photograph courtesy of the Herb Marshall collection.
Bert Bozzuto photograph courtesy of the Bert Bozzuto collection.
1947 Carrollton Hornets baseball team photograph courtesy of the Bert Bozzuto collection.
John Allen photograph courtesy of the Pete Monarchi collection.
Pete Monarchi photograph courtesy of the Pete Monarchi collection.
Bill Patterson photograph courtesy of the Pete Monarchi collection.
Five 1947 Carrollton players photograph courtesy of the Bert Bozzuto collection.
Dallas Thomas photograph courtesy of the Pete Monarchi collection.
Elmer Bertha, Bob Bess, Bert Bozzuto, Eddie Giombetti, Pete Kurowski, Shorty Marshall, Gene Monarchi, Pete Monarchi, Corbet Newton, Bernie Povanda, Red Roberts, Bob Roedel, and Harvey Copeland photographs from the April 15, 1948 edition of the Carroll County Times courtesy of the Gene Monarchi collection.
1947 Georgia-Alabama League pennant presentation ceremonies photograph number one courtesy of the Blas Arroyo collection.
1947 Georgia-Alabama League pennant presentation ceremonies photograph number two courtesy of the Blas Arroyo collection.
1948 Carrollton Opening Day ticket courtesy of the Herb Marshall collection.
1948 Carrollton Pocket Schedule courtesy of the Herb Marshall collection.
F.M. Kline letter courtesy of Gene Monarchi collection.
Eddie Giombetti and Gilbert Sanchez photograph courtesy of the Eddie Giombetti collection.
William O. Cobb, William Seal, Walt Little, J.C. Thompson, Walt Kuras, Frank Cichon, Dick Cervino, Carl Laubach, Marvin Freeman, Mack Yarborough, Burel Nelson, Bing Russell, Buddy Berman, Bert Bozzuto, Jack Meeks, and Don Umscheid photographs from the April 26, 1949 edition of the Times-Free Press courtesy of the Red Roberts collection.
"Back The 1949..." – April 26, 1949 edition of Times-Free Press.
1950 Carrollton Hornets baseball team photograph number one courtesy of the Annie Belle Weaver Special Collections of the Ingram Library of the State University of West Georgia.
1950 Carrollton Hornets baseball team photograph number two courtesy of the Annie Belle Weaver Special Collections of the Ingram Library of the State University of West Georgia.
1950 Carrollton crowd at home opener photograph from the April 28, 1950 edition of the Times-Free Press newspaper courtesy of the Herb Marshall collection.
Blas Arroyo photograph courtesy of the Blas Arroyo collection.
Blas Arroyo, Reggie Corrales, and Fred DeSouza photograph courtesy of the Blas Arroyo collection.
City Athletic Field scoreboard photograph courtesy of the Blas Arroyo collection.
1961 Carrollton Lakers baseball team photograph courtesy of the Jelp Robinson collection.

1962-63 Carrollton Lakers baseball team banquet photograph courtesy of the Jelp Robinson collection.
1961 West Georgia Association championship trophy from Vabella photograph collection.
Harry Allen photograph courtesy of the Annie Belle Weaver Special Collections of the Ingram Library of the State University of West Georgia.
John Allen photograph courtesy of the Pete Monarchi collection.
Marion Anderson photograph courtesy of the Annie Belle Weaver Special Collections of the Ingram Library of the State University of West Georgia.
Blas Arroyo photograph courtesy of the Annie Belle Weaver Special Collections of the Ingram Library of the State University of West Georgia.
Charlie Bell photograph courtesy of Annie Belle Weaver Special Collections of the Ingram Library of the State University of West Georgia.
Buddy Berman photograph courtesy of the Annie Belle Weaver Special Collections of the Ingram Library of the State University of West Georgia.
Elmer Bertha photograph from the April 15, 1948 edition of the Carroll County Times courtesy of the Gene Monarchi collection.
Fred Bieser photograph courtesy of the Herb Marshall collection.
Albert Bonifay photograph courtesy of the Annie Belle Weaver Special Collections of the Ingram Library of the State University of West Georgia.
Aubrey Borders photograph courtesy of the Herb Marshall collection.
Brant Boswell photograph courtesy of the Annie Belle Weaver Special Collections of the Ingram Library of the State University of West Georgia.
Bert Bozzuto photograph courtesy of the Bert Bozzuto collection.
Goat Brandon photograph courtesy of the Annie Belle Weaver Special Collections of the Ingram Library of the State University of West Georgia.
Paul Brock photograph courtesy of the Herb Marshall collection.
Sugar Cain photograph courtesy of the Pat Cain collection.
Ed Chaplin photograph courtesy of the Annie Belle Weaver Special Collections of the Ingram Library of the State University of West Georgia.
Frank Cichon photograph from the April 26, 1949 edition of the Times-Free Press courtesy of the Red Roberts collection.
Ray Clark photograph courtesy of the Annie Belle Weaver Special Collections of the Ingram Library of the State University of West Georgia.
Condit photograph courtesy of the Herb Marshall collection.
Reinaldo Corrales photograph courtesy of the Annie Belle Weaver Special Collections of the Ingram Library of the State University of West Georgia.
Stan Coulling photograph courtesy of the Stan Coulling collection.
Jess Craven photograph courtesy of the Annie Belle Weaver Special Collections of the Ingram Library of the State University of West Georgia.
Hoyt Crowe photograph courtesy of the Annie Belle Weaver Special Collections of the Ingram Library of the State University of West Georgia.
Jacob Dendinger photograph courtesy of the Bert Bozzuto collection.
Jack Dennis photograph courtesy of the Annie Belle Weaver Special Collections of the Ingram Library of the State University of West Georgia.
Fred DeSouza photograph courtesy of the Annie Belle Weaver Special Collections of the Ingram Library of the State University of West Georgia.
Carl East photograph courtesy of the Jodi Lane collection.
Bob Ezzell photograph courtesy of the Annie Belle Weaver Special Collections of the Ingram Library of the State University of West Georgia.
Lou Finney photograph from the 1936 Goudey baseball card set.
Paul Fittery photograph courtesy of the Annie Belle Weaver Special Collections of the Ingram Library of the State University of West Georgia.
Dick Fraker photograph courtesy of the Herb Marshall collection.
Benny Freedman photograph courtesy of the Annie Belle Weaver Special Collections of the Ingram Library of the State University of West Georgia.
Eddie Giombetti photograph courtesy of the Eddie Giombetti collection.
G.E. Goggans photograph courtesy of the Annie Belle Weaver Special Collections of the Ingram Library of the State University of West Georgia.
Leo Goicoechea photograph courtesy of the Bert Bozzuto collection.
Cotayo Gonzalez photograph courtesy of the Annie Belle Weaver Special Collections of the Ingram Library of the State University of West Georgia.
Grimes photograph courtesy of the Annie Belle Weaver Special Collections of the Ingram Library of the State University of West Georgia.
Luther Gunnells photograph courtesy of the Herb Marshall collection.
Jim Hill photograph courtesy of the Herb Marshall collection.
Squirt Holsomback photograph courtesy of the Annie Belle Weaver Special Collections of the Ingram Library of the State University of West Georgia.
Red Howell photograph courtesy of the Annie Belle Weaver Special Collections of the Ingram Library of the State University of West Georgia.
Miller Huggins photograph courtesy of the Annie Belle Weaver Special Collections of the Ingram Library of the State University of West Georgia.
Bill Israel photograph courtesy of the Herb Marshall collection.
Fob James photograph courtesy of the Annie Belle Weaver Special Collections of the Ingram Library of the State University of West Georgia.
Bill Jones photograph courtesy of the Bert Bozzuto collection.
Red Justiss photograph courtesy of the Annie Belle Weaver Special Collections of the Ingram Library of the State University of West Georgia.
Dick Kelly photograph courtesy of the Bert Bozzuto collection.
Mason Kelly photograph courtesy of the Annie Belle Weaver Special Collections of the Ingram Library of the State University of West Georgia.
Walt Kuras photograph from the April 26, 1949 edition of the Times-Free Press courtesy of the Red Roberts collection.
Lacey photograph courtesy of the Annie Belle Weaver Special Collections of the Ingram Library of the State University of West Georgia.

Red Laird photograph courtesy of the Davidson College Archives, Davidson College, Davidson, North Carolina.
Free Lee photograph courtesy of the Annie Belle Weaver Special Collections of the Ingram Library of the State University of West Georgia.
Walt Little photograph courtesy of the Bert Bozzuto collection.
Shorty Marshall photograph courtesy of the Herb Marshall collection.
Bob Mathews photograph courtesy of the Herb Marshall collection.
Leo Mazak photograph courtesy of the Annie Belle Weaver Special Collections of the Ingram Library of the State University of West Georgia.
Bill McGhee photograph courtesy of the Annie Belle Weaver Special Collections of the Ingram Library of the State University of West Georgia.
Bill McKinnon photograph courtesy of the Annie Belle Weaver Special Collections of the Ingram Library of the State University of West Georgia.
Gene Monarchi photograph from the April 15, 1948 edition of the Carroll County Times courtesy of the Gene Monarchi collection.
Pete Monarchi photograph from the April 15, 1948 edition of the Carroll County Times courtesy of the Gene Monarchi collection.
Jim Morelli photograph courtesy of the Annie Belle Weaver Special Collections of the Ingram Library of the State University of West Georgia.
Burel Nelson photograph from the April 26, 1949 edition of the Times-Free Press courtesy of the Red Roberts collection.
Bill Patterson photograph courtesy of the Herb Marshall collection.
Henry Patton photograph courtesy of the Annie Belle Weaver Special Collections of the Ingram Library of the State University of West Georgia.
Al Pittman photograph courtesy of the Herb Marshall collection.
Frank Pratt photograph courtesy of the Annie Belle Weaver Special Collections of the Ingram Library of the State University of West Georgia.
Clifton Reach photograph courtesy of the Annie Belle Weaver Special Collections of the Ingram Library of the State University of West Georgia.
Eddie Reese photograph courtesy of the Annie Belle Weaver Special Collections of the Ingram Library of the State University of West Georgia.
Red Reese photograph courtesy of the Annie Belle Weaver Special Collections of the Ingram Library of the State University of West Georgia.
Red Roberts photograph courtesy of the Herb Marshall collection.
Bob Roedel photograph from the April 15, 1948 edition of the Carroll County Times courtesy of the Gene Monarchi collection.
Carl Roman photograph from the April 15, 1948 edition of the Carroll County Times courtesy of the Gene Monarchi collection.
Bob Rowe photograph courtesy of the Annie Belle Weaver Special Collections of the Ingram Library of the State University of West Georgia.
Bing Russell photograph from the April 26, 1949 edition of the Times-Free Press courtesy of the Red Roberts collection.
Colon Sappenfield photograph courtesy of the Annie Belle Weaver Special Collections of the Ingram Library of the State University of West Georgia.
Bill Seal photograph from the April 26, 1949 edition of the Times-Free Press courtesy of the Red Roberts collection.
Pop Shaw photograph courtesy of the Annie Belle Weaver Special Collections of the Ingram Library of the State University of West Georgia.
Jim Shirley photograph courtesy of the Annie Belle Weaver Special Collections of the Ingram Library of the State University of West Georgia.
Floyd Snider photograph courtesy of the Herb Marshall collection.
Gene Solt photograph courtesy of the Annie Belle Weaver Special Collections of the Ingram Library of the State University of West Georgia.
George Souter photograph courtesy of the Herb Marshall collection.
Ralph Stanfield photograph courtesy of the Annie Belle Weaver Special Collections of the Ingram Library of the State University of West Georgia.
Lefty Sutton photograph courtesy of the Annie Belle Weaver Special Collections of the Ingram Library of the State University of West Georgia.
P.P. Swann photograph courtesy of the Annie Belle Weaver Special Collections of the Ingram Library of the State University of West Georgia.
Dick Taliaferro photograph courtesy of the Annie Belle Weaver Special Collections of the Ingram Library of the State University of West Georgia.
Dallas Thomas photograph courtesy of the Herb Marshall collection.
Jim Thompson photograph from the April 26, 1949 edition of the Times-Free Press courtesy of the Red Roberts collection.
Don Umscheid photograph from the April 26, 1949 edition of the Times-Free Press courtesy of the Red Roberts collection.
Ernie Victor photograph courtesy of the Annie Belle Weaver Special Collections of the Ingram Library of the State University of West Georgia.
Jules Watson photograph courtesy of the Annie Belle Weaver Special Collections of the Ingram Library of the State University of West Georgia.
Bill Webb photograph courtesy of the Bert Bozzuto collection.
Bill Weldon photograph courtesy of the Annie Belle Weaver Special Collections of the Ingram Library of the State University of West Georgia.
Abe White photograph courtesy of the Annie Belle Weaver Special Collections of the Ingram Library of the State University of West Georgia.
Curtis Whtie photograph courtesy of the Annie Belle Weaver Special Collections of the Ingram Library of the State University of West Georgia.
Jo-Jo White photograph courtesy of the Annie Belle Weaver Special Collections of the Ingram Library of the State University of West Georgia.
Kemp Wicker photograph courtesy of the Annie Belle Weaver Special Collections of the Ingram Library of the State University of West Georgia.
Bob Williams photograph from the April 15, 1948 edition of the Carroll County Times courtesy of the Gene Monarchi collection.
Mack Yarborough photograph from the April 26, 1949 edition of the Times-Free

Press courtesy of the Red Roberts collection.
Lew York photograph courtesy of the Herb Marshall collection.
Sugar Cain photograph courtesy of the Pat Cain collection.
Ed Chaplin photograph courtesy of the Annie Belle Weaver Special Collections of the Ingram Library of the State University of West Georgia.
Stan Coulling photograph courtesy of the Stan Coulling collection.
Fred DeSouza photograph courtesy of the Annie Belle Weaver Special Collections of the Ingram Library of the State University of West Georgia.
Carl East photograph courtesy of the Jodi Lane collection.
Carl East signature courtesy of the Jodi Lane collection.
Bob Ezzell photograph courtesy of the Annie Belle Weaver Special Collections of the Ingram Library of the State University of West Georgia.
Lou Finney 1936 Goudey card from the Goudey baseball card set.
Lou Finney 1941 Playball card from the Playball baseball card set.
Lou Finney model baseball glove photo from Vabella collection.
Lou Finney signature photo from the Vabella collection.
Paul Fittery photograph courtesy of the Annie Belle Weaver Special Collections of the Ingram Library of the State University of West Georgia.
Red Howell photograph courtesy of the Annie Belle Weaver Special Collections of the Ingram Library of the State University of West Georgia.
Herb Marshall photograph courtesy of the Annie Belle Weaver Special Collections of the Ingram Library of the State University of West Georgia.
Herb Marshall contract courtesy of the Herb Marshall collection.
Bill McGhee photograph courtesy of the Annie Belle Weaver Special Collections of the Ingram Library of the State University of West Georgia.
Gene Monarchi photograph from the April 15, 1948 edition of the Carroll County Times courtesy of the Gene Monarchi collection.
Pete Monarchi photograph from the April 15, 1948 edition of the Carroll County Times courtesy of the Gene Monarchi collection.
Eddie Giombetti photograph courtesy of the Eddie Giombetti collection.
Frank Pratt photograph courtesy of the Annie Belle Weaver Special Collections of the Ingram Library of the State University of West Georgia.
Red Roberts photograph courtesy of the Herb Marshall collection.
Red Roberts signature from Vabella collection.
Bing Russell Bonanza photo courtesy of the Bing Russell collection.
1977 Portland Mavericks team photo from Vabella collection.
Gene Solt photograph courtesy of the Annie Belle Weaver Special Collections of the Ingram Library of the State University of West Georgia.
Bill Webb photograph courtesy of the Bert Bozzuto collection.
Bill Webb signature from Vabella collection.
Abe White photograph courtesy of the Annie Belle Weaver Special Collections of the Ingram Library of the State University of West Georgia.
Jo-Jo White 1935 Diamond Stars card from the Diamond Stars baseball card set.
Jo-Jo White model glove photo from Vabella collection.
Jo-Jo White signature from Vabella collection.
Kemp Wicker photograph courtesy of the Annie Belle Weaver Special Collections of the Ingram Library of the State University of West Georgia.
John Bell photograph by Vabella Publishing.

Acknowledgments

Special thanks to the following for making this book possible:
Blas Arroyo
Elmer Bertha
Bert and Dolores Bozzuto
Hiram Bray
Bruce Browning
Pat Cain
Louis Cardillo
Clint Chafin
Stan Coulling
Steve Densa at Minor League Baseball
Charles East
Eddie Giombetti
Myron House at the State University of West Georgia
Jodi Lane
Neva Lomason Library staff
Herb "Shorty" Marshall
Gene Monarchi
Pete Monarchi
Stanley Parkman
Edwin Roberts
Mrs. Jelp Robinson
Wayne Robinson
Bing Russell
John Tidwell
The Times-Georgian newspaper

A very special thanks to my wife, Virginia, for her support and patience during the writing of this book and all the rest of the time she has known me.

Most of all, I thank God for the many blessings He has given me.

About the Author

John Bell was born in Americus, Georgia in 1969 and lived there until 1995. He graduated from Americus High School in 1987 and earned a B.S. in Political Science with a minor in History from Georgia Southwestern State University in Americus in 1993.

John is a member of the Society of American Baseball Research (SABR) and affiliated with the Magnolia Chapter of Atlanta, Georgia of the organization.

In 2001, John published his first book entitled *Shoeless Summer: The summer of 1923 when Shoeless Joe Jackson played baseball in Americus, Georgia.* The book was nominated for SABR's Seymour Medal in 2002.

Having lived in Carrollton, Georgia since 1996, John is married to Virginia Bell. They have two sons, Jacob and Andrew.